Democratization and Authoritarian Party Survival

DEMOCRATIZATION AND AUTHORITARIAN PARTY SURVIVAL
Mexico's PRI

Joy K. Langston

OXFORD
UNIVERSITY PRESS

OXFORD
UNIVERSITY PRESS

Oxford University Press is a department of the University of Oxford. It furthers
the University's objective of excellence in research, scholarship, and education
by publishing worldwide. Oxford is a registered trade mark of Oxford University
Press in the UK and certain other countries.

Published in the United States of America by Oxford University Press
198 Madison Avenue, New York, NY 10016, United States of America.

Library of Congress Cataloging-in-Publication Data
Names: Langston, Joy (Joy Kathryn), author.
Title: Democratization and authoritarian party survival : Mexico's PRI / Joy K. Langston.
Description: New York, NY : Oxford University Press, [2017] |
Includes bibliographical references.
Identifiers: LCCN 2016041367| ISBN 9780190628512 (hardcover) |
ISBN 9780190628529 (pbk.) | ISBN 9780190628536 (updf) | ISBN 9780190628543 (epub)
Subjects: LCSH: Partido Revolucionario Institucional. | Democratization—Mexico. |
Mexico—Politics and government—1988-2000. | Mexico—Politics and government—2000–
Classification: LCC JL1298.R45 L36 2017 | DDC 324.272/083—dc23
LC record available at https://lccn.loc.gov/2016041367

This book is dedicated to all those who gave their time and energy to help me finish this project, especially my mother, Joann H. Langston.

CONTENTS

ACKNOWLEDGMENTS

This book began because of a conversation held over twenty years ago, in which a Mexican friend asked me and another political scientist who specialized in Mexican politics a very simple question: "What is the PRI?" Fifteen minutes later, we still had not answered the question to anybody's satisfaction, provoking great mockery on the part of the questioner. I thought: if two political scientists cannot provide a clear description or definition of Mexico's long-governing Institutional Revolutionary Party, it is because the party has been greatly understudied, so I decided to dedicate my next project to one of the world's longest-lived parties in power.

I would like to thank all those who have helped me with this work over the years, including my colleagues at CIDE, many of whom thought the study of the PRI required a historian, not a political scientist. The true base of the work consists of those whom I had the great pleasure of interviewing over the course of almost twenty years; I thank them for their generosity. Several people have read different chapters, including Rosario Aguilar, John Aldrich, Matt Cleary, Scott Desposato, Steve Levitsky, Gerardo Maldonado, Guillermo Rosas, Peter Smith, and Steve Wuhs. I have presented chapters at several institutions, including the ITAM, the Center for US-Mexican Studies at the University of California, San Diego, the University of California, Riverside, the University of Houston, the University of Notre Dame, and the Universidad Nacional Autónoma de México (UNAM). I had a great deal of help from research assistants over the years, including Paulina Gutiérrez, Rita Moch, Pedro Zapata, Bernardo Pérez, Carolina Torresblanca, and Melena Altamiranda, all of whom have been extremely patient and hardworking. I'd also like to thank Luisa Bejár, Roderic Camp, Alberto Díaz-Cayeros, Federico Estévez, Rogelio Hernández, and Jeffrey Weldon for their support. Several scholars who work on other nations helped me with the comparative section, including Tun-Jen Cheng, Eva Coffey, Petr Kopecky, Lukas Linek, Mikael Mattlin, and Alexander Tan. Finally, friends like Varun Sahni, Jorge Chabat, Mieke Beckhart, Bill Bernhard, Jim Granato, Allyson Benton, Javier Aparicio, Don Victor Alarcón, and Stephanie Jenson have all listened to their share of my grumping, for which I thank them.

GLOSSARY

CCP	Chinese Communist Party
CDE	State party branch of the PRI
CEN	National Executive Committee; national party headquarters
CFE	Federal Electoral Commission
CISEN	Center of Investigation and National Security
CNC	National Confederation of Peasants
CNOP	National Conference of Popular Organizations
COFIPE	Mexico's former federal electoral code
CONASUPO	National Company of Popular Subsistence Goods
CPN	National Political Council of the PRI
CPP	Permanent Political Commission of the CPN
CROC	Confederation of Revolutionary Workers and Peasants
CROM	Regional Workers' Confederation of Mexico
CTM	Confederation of Mexican Workers
FB	Facebook
FSTSE	Bureaucrats' Union
GATT	General Agreement on Tariffs and Trade
IFE	Federal Electoral Institute
IMSS	Mexican Institute of Social Security
INE	National Electoral Institute
ISI	import substitution industrialization
ISSSTE	Social Security Institute for Government Workers
JUCOPO	Joint Committee of Political Coordination, Chamber and Senate
KANU	Kenya African National Union
KMT	Kuomintang of Taiwan
LDP	Liberal Democratic Party of Japan
Los Pinos	Mexican presidential mansion
MMM	mixed-member majoritarian electoral system
NAFTA	North American Free Trade Agreement
PAN	National Action Party (created in 1939; its members are referred to as panistas)
PANAL	New Alliance Party
PARM	Party of the Authentic Mexican Revolution
PEMEX	Mexican Petroleum Company
PPS	Popular Socialist Party
PR	proportional representation

PRD	Party of the Democratic Revolution (created in 1989: its members are referred to as perredistas)
PRI	Institutional Revolutionary Party (created in 1946)
PRM	Party of the Mexican Revolution (created in 1938)
PNR	National Revolutionary Party (created in 1929; predecessor of the PRI)
PVEM	Green Party of Mexico
ROC	Republic of China on Taiwan
SMD	single-member district (also referred to as first-past-the-post and plurality election)
SNTE	National Teachers' Union
SNTV	single nontransferable vote electoral system
STPRM	Mexican Oil Workers' Union
TRIFE or TEPJF	Federal Electoral Tribunal

CHAPTER 1

The Dinosaur that Did Not Die

Mexico's PRI from 1982 to 2012

The PRI has never left; it has been here. The PRI has lost and it has won. The PRI under-stands very well the demands of democratic competition.[1]

I am more afraid of these Mexican dinosaurs than of those that existed millions of years ago.[2]

On July 2, 2000, the scene outside the national headquarters of the Institutional Revolutionary Party (PRI, Partido de la Revolución Institucional) was desolate: standing in the late-night drizzle were a few hun-dred party supporters, rendered silent by the greatest shock of their political lifetimes. The president of Mexico and informal leader of the party, Ernesto Zedillo (1994–2000), had just announced on television and radio the defeat of the PRI's presidential candidate at the hands of the National Action Party (PAN, Partido Acción Nacional). With this announcement, over seventy years of single-party rule came to an end.[3] Even before the PRI lost the presidency in 2000, many analysts and academics questioned whether the once-hegemonic party would fragment, as its politicians would leave the party and compete for more popular options or voters would simply reject the party's label and the candidates running under it (Crespo 1998; Manuel and Muñoz Patraca 2006).

---

1. Interview with Enrique Peña Nieto, *El Universal*, June 27, 2012, a week before the presidential election.
2. Guadalupe Loaeza, "El regreso de los dinosaurios," *Reforma*, July 5, 2011. After the electoral scare of 1988, hardliners within the PRI who did not want to open the politi-cal system to democratic competition were referred to as "dinosaurs."
3. The PRI's forebear, the National Revolutionary Party (PNR), was formed in 1929 by former president and strongman Plutarco Elias Calles; it was reformed and renamed by President Lázaro Cárdenas in 1938 to become the Party of the Mexican Revolution (PRM), before taking on its present name in 1946, at the end of the six-year term of President Manuel Ávila Camacho.

Without access to the federal government's resources to buy off members of the coalition and voters, and absent the leadership of the president to obligate its members to cooperate, it was not clear if the various internal party groups would be able to negotiate their differences over candidacies, money, and party leadership posts. The PRI had always relied on the financial resources of the Mexican state to prime the electoral pump, while it depended on its control of the national and state electoral agencies to steal votes or pad the totals. As vote totals fell, the party would be vulnerable to fragmentation as its politicians broke ranks to run under other party labels. It also remained an open question as to whether the party's candidates and leaders would be able to transform their campaign strategies to retain and win new voters without government subsidies or the support of the party's local leaders and mass-based corporatist sectors that had lost resources and members since the beginning of the 1980s.

During the long decades of hegemony, which lasted from 1929 to 2000,[4] each successive president of Mexico—and informal leader of the party—acted as a third-party enforcer, obligating the PRI's politicians to follow a cooperative strategy, so that they won more by staying in the party rather than leaving its confines to face certain defeat (Meyer 1986). Because the PRI won with large margins, the regime's ambitious politicians remained disciplined because they had no credible exit strategy (Langston 2003; Magaloni 2006).

But once a succession of economic crises crashed against Mexican shores—beginning in the 1970s and continuing into the 1980s—the incentives of almost all members of Mexico's society to place their faith in the PRI began to fall. These economic crises and the profound change in the development model from import substitution industrialization (ISI) to an open, market-based export model angered voters at the same time as it created critics within the regime. The transition away from PRI hegemony began in 1986–1987, when the PRI divided over the presidential succession. This split was led by the former president's son, Cuauhtémoc Cárdenas, who, together with Porfirio Múñoz Ledo, led a small number of supporters out of the PRI because they had little future within the new coalition that placed its future in pro-market economic policies.[5] The PRI then faced a cataclysmic electoral result in 1988, and resorted to using its control over the management of elections to bring

4. The PRI lost the presidency in 2000 and its simple majority in the lower house in 1997. One could argue that hegemony (and the transition to democracy) finally ended and democracy was successfully installed on the earlier date. The present work argues that, because of the enormous resource advantages of the federal government, full democracy began with the defeat of the PRI in 2000. See Geddes (1999) for more on this point.

5. Specifically, they demanded a fairer presidential nomination procedure and an end to the neoliberal economic opening. For more on the rupture, see Bruhn (1997), Garrido (1993), and Langston (2002).

down the (computer) system so it could win at least a majority of the popular vote. In the years that followed, the regime's leaders were forced to negotiate with the party opposition leaders over a host of electoral rules.[6]

Beginning in the late 1990s, several gubernatorial hopefuls left the PRI when denied the nomination, and then went on to defeat the PRI's candidate in the general elections. The problems of internal cohesion would become far more serious after the 2000 defeat. The growth of electoral competition, which had begun in the late 1980s and grown stronger throughout the 1990s, had shown ambitious PRI politicians in local, state, and federal elections that they no longer needed to obey the fundamental rule of the hegemonic era: remain loyal even when passed over for an important nomination or government post. Without the president of the republic acting as a third-party enforcer, the formal rules enshrined in the party statutes were weak because they lacked credible sanctions, so intraparty groups were often forced to cheat against others because there were no guarantees that the other side would cooperate and respect the statutes.

Yet the doomsday scenario did not come to pass: the PRI has not fragmented into several smaller parties after 2000,[7] it has not lost thousands of its best local politicians, and it has not been rejected by voters as a corrupt vestige of the past. To the contrary, the party retook the presidency in 2012 after two presidential terms out of office; it controls twice as many of the nation's thirty-one state governments and the Federal District as the opposition parties combined; and it holds a large number of major cities and a majority in the Chamber of Deputies and Senate in alliance with the Green Party (PVEM).

Today, the PRI is more decentralized than in its hegemonic heyday; it has modernized its campaigning skills, while still relying on localized electioneering and clientelist mobilization. Mexico's set of institutional rules had a large part to play both in the party's survival and in its transformation. Federalism combined with electoral competition strengthened the party's governors (Modoux 2006), who are informal party leaders with control over access to the party's ballot and resources to finance campaigns. Plurality elections in single-member districts (SMDs) have decentralized candidate recruitment because voters prefer local candidates with experience in area politics. The

---

6. Some argue that Mexico was democratizing as early as 1982 or 1985; yet, when one considers the party's methods of winning elections, it is clear this is not the case. See Lawson (2000, 276), where he writes that the PRI held onto power by: "shaving voter rolls . . . , padding the registry . . . , allowing PRI adherents to vote multiple times, and outright ballot box stuffing and intimidation." The PRI continued these activities well into the 1990s. See also, Alonso (1987).

7. One small party was created as the result of a division of both party leaders and members, called the New Alliance Party, or PANAL, which was formed in January 2005 using the organizational base of the National Teachers' Union (SNTE). The Citizens' Movement Party was formed by a former PRI politician, but did not include many PRI members. Both parties are small and PANAL often votes with the PRI in the Chamber.

proportional representation (PR) tier allows national party officials to remain powerful because they hold influence over who wins the highest slots in the nation's five closed multimember lists. Finally, the party did not fragment because the winners in the process of adjusting to competition were able to find ways to cooperate; as such, while the PRI has experienced a number of political exits, it has not split into dozens of disparate electoral options.

Mexico's transition to democracy, with all its problems, is a success in terms of political stability in large part because the PRI did not splinter into many smaller parties. Mexico's party system remained relatively stable from the early 1990s through 2012, retaining its triparty character (although the left has frayed since 2009).[8] The center-right PAN and the center-left Party of the Democratic Revolution (PRD, Partido de la Revolución Democrática), together with the PRI, still dominate the legislature and almost all state governments. Moreno (2009a) argues that as of 2006 Mexican voters could identify successfully the three major parties on a one dimensional ideological scale. Levels of voter identification with the party stayed relatively stable through 2012; and parties in both chambers of Congress vote in a disciplined fashion. The PRI's national party headquarters, named the National Executive Committee (CEN), has modernized national media appeals to sell the party label, while the candidates in SMDs—even in the face of a constitutional prohibition of consecutive reelection—responded quickly to new incentives and changed their form of campaigning.

This book does not pretend to be a history of the party, although chapter 3 has a section covering the history of the first decades of the PRI. Rather, it proposes an explanation for party change that begins with the faltering hegemonic party in the early 1980s, through the transitional years of the 1990s, before turning to its years out of executive office. The book begins with the elections in 1982 and ends with the return of the PRI in 2012.

The experience of Mexico's PRI can be used to gain a deeper understanding of both why certain parties survive (and others do not) and why they change as they do. First, it demonstrates how the institutional context strengthens certain internal factions over others as they strive to win control over resources, given the growing challenges of electoral competition. The present work argues that all authoritarian parties face strong pressures to split when facing rising electoral competition, and so one must ask how these tendencies to divide are resolved. This is a collective action dilemma: even if the players realize that it would be better to cooperate rather than destroy the party, it might not be possible. One solution is a takeover by a single party faction;

---

8. The number of parties in the Chamber went from four in 1976 (before the installation of a true PR system) to eight in 1985, to six in 1991, and rising to eight again in 2006. Despite these high numbers, until the 2015 elections, the big three parties consistently controlled around 90 percent of the seats.

another is that two (or more) internal groups find ways to cooperate because they enjoy autonomous and complementary resources. In other words, they need each other to survive, and have access to distinct sources of money and candidacies. Again, political institutions can affect the ability to cooperate.

In hegemonic party systems, other parties beside the hegemon exist, but cannot win enough elected posts to challenge government majorities and therefore cannot control the government or bureaucratic arenas (Sartori 1976).[9] Many regime politicians are skilled in internal negotiations, not vote winning; in palace intrigues, instead of campaigning. The internal relations of authority that kept the party intact under authoritarianism may not continue to work when the party is forced to compete for votes. As Roberts writes in the case of Communist and Socialist parties in Chile in the late 1980s and early 1990s, "The gradual shift . . . to electoral contestation placed a premium on new organizational features, political resources, and strategic orientations" (Roberts 1998, 127). An authoritarian party confronts unique challenges when facing rising electoral competition and fairer elections.

More generally, Anthony Downs (1957) placed electoral competition at the center of his explanation of party change; however, it became clear with different country studies that parties are not unitary actors that necessarily react rationally to a given external shock. Harmel and Janda (1994) focus on how some internal party groups[10] use external challenges—principally, losses at the ballot box—to compete more successfully against their internal party rivals. In a different line of argument are those scholars who argue that the "inheritable resources" of a former authoritarian party determine whether the authoritarian party will survive competition under new democratic rules, in particular Grzymala-Busse (2002), Loxton (2016), and Slater and Wong (2013). Gryzmala-Busse argues that elite skills and organizational capacity are the two basic resources that help former authoritarian parties survive into democracy. Those parties whose leaders had begun to reform their nation's economy before the transition began should be better equipped to reform their organizations to react successfully to the challenges of democratic competition. The present work contributes to this literature by focusing on the role of institutions and factional groups within the party in a nation outside

9. The PRI won all senate, governor, and presidential elections with huge percentage margins from its creation in 1929 until 1988, when it lost its first senate seats. Gandhi and Reuter (2007, 83) define hegemonic party regimes as "non-democratic systems in which one political party remains in office uninterruptedly while holding regular multiparty elections."

10. The present study defines internal party groups as a collection of individuals who share common interests, some of which can, at times, oppose those of the rest of the organization. The groups can be based on institutional position or ideology, for example, rank-and-file activists without great ideology or economic reformers lodged within the federal bureaucracy.

of Eastern Europe. Meeting the challenges of electoral competition is the central problem for authoritarian parties as they transition to democracy, and this competition is filtered through political institutions which help some party factions while harming others. All authoritarian parties face a strong incentive to divide when meeting the threat of rising electoral competition. This work problematizes the issue of internal unity to understand how actors resolved the collective action dilemma in a competitive world without a presidential Leviathan.

The literature on party organization is rife with works that outline the effects of how political institutions influence the organization and behavior of parties (Carey and Shugart 1995; Duverger 1954; Montero 2007; Riker 1964; Samuels and Shugart 2010). The most important political institutions that affect parties are: First, federal institutions that can create strong governors and/or state parties. Second, the two-tier electoral system, with both plurality races in SMDs and closed-list PR seats, strengthen local career paths for politicians and while also allowing the national party headquarters to retain control over some PR candidacies. Third, although very rare, single-term limits give much power to those groups that control candidate selection; and generous public funding for parties can be captured by either the party or candidates. Finally, presidential systems parties tend to have weaker influence over their executives than do parliamentary regimes (see chapter 2 for more on institutional effects).

From the nineteenth century onward, Mexico has been a federal, presidential regime, with a bicameral federal legislature (although the Senate was eliminated for several years in the nineteenth century). Since the 1930s, the president and state governors can serve only a single six-year term in office, and can never run for that same post again. Legislators and mayors can serve only one term (six years for senators, three years for local and federal deputies, as well as mayors), but can run for the same post again after one term out of office. After a constitutional reform, legislators will be able to run for reelection in 2021. Before 1964, Mexico's legislature was filled entirely through SMD plurality races. Between 1964 and 1979, extra deputies—known as party deputies—were awarded to those parties that had won a specific percentage of the national vote, with the upper limit eventually fixed at twenty-five extra deputies for each party.

The 1977 electoral reform instituted a mixed majoritarian electoral system for the Chamber of Deputies with a larger majoritarian tier, which is now made up of 300 SMD seats, and 200 PR seats elected in five regional districts in closed lists that contain forty names each. Voters are allowed only a single ballot for both tiers, and mark it for their preferred plurality (SMD) candidate. The votes from the 300 districts races are aggregated to one of the five regional multi-member districts in the federal Chamber. The Senate also has a mixed system, with each state electing two senators in a closed two-person list, while the second-place party in each state sends the first name on its two-person list to the Senate as well. Thirty-two more senators are elected through a national, closed PR list. Again, voters have only one ballot for both tiers.

Governors are elected in staggered calendar years, so that at any one time, the president serves with governors elected under the former president, and thanks to this electoral calendar, most governors do not ride the president's coattails to victory. Mayors are elected in a plurality vote, and the city council members enter on the mayor's plank. State assemblies follow the rough outlines of the federal electoral laws; each of the thirty-two state congresses has deputies elected in both SMDs and closed PR lists. Local parties (those without national registration) cannot compete in federal elections. Until 2015, independent candidates could not have their names printed on the ballots, and the process of winning party registration has always been long and difficult, even since the electoral reforms of 1996.

Many of these institutions were created long before the transition began in 1988, some during the nineteenth century (a federal, presidential form of government, with two houses of Congress), and others during the long hegemonic interlude (no consecutive reelection, no local parties in federal elections, and obligatory party registration of candidates). While new provisions were enacted in the 1990s to make elections fairer, these rules did not actually change the mixed majoritarian electoral system instituted in 1977 (except to introduce PR spots in the Senate).

During the electoral reforms of the 1990s[11] and into the 2000s (2008 and 2013) the PRI's leaders were able to negotiate with their PAN and PRD counterparts several modifications to the electoral code that enabled them to maintain control over ambitious office seekers. The 1996 electoral reform allocated campaign money not to the candidates but to the national party headquarters, which has great discretion in how it spends this money. A new electoral law passed in 2008 obligates radio and television stations to broadcast the parties' advertisements in "public service" time, making them free of charge, which, again, freed up an enormous amount of money to be spent in other activities (see chapter 8).

The effects of Mexico's federal government, a mixed electoral system at both the state and federal legislatures, and generous public funding for party activities help explain which party groups were empowered by the transition and which were decimated, and why these groups were then able to cooperate after the loss of the presidential Leviathan. The PRI's evolutionary adaption to electoral competition took more than a decade, which has allowed the present study to examine how the party changed over time while many other potential

11. See Becerra, Salazar, and Woldenberg (1997), Brinegar, Morgenstern, and Nielson (2006), and Eisenstadt (2004) for excellent discussions of the electoral reforms of the 1990s.

explanatory variables, such as political history and culture, most political institutions, and relations with the outside world, held constant.

The PRI's governors were collectively stronger than the national party leaders during the twelve-year interregnum because they controlled far more money, even though the CEN disposed of millions of pesos of public resources thanks to the 1996 electoral reforms. Governors won fiscal resources from the federal government and garnered greater control and influence over federal and local candidacies in their respective entities. The PRI governors gained more control over candidates because if they won many or most of their plurality districts for the Chamber, for example, the party would win more votes in the five multi-member PR districts, and thus, a larger number of PR seats, producing a stronger plurality in the Chamber and more financial resources.[12] If a PRI governor has a larger state delegation in the Chamber of Deputies, she is better able to extract fiscal gains during the yearly budget negotiations, so one sees governors' incentives strongly aligned with those of the CEN to win plurality districts. Furthermore, if the governors support the federal campaigns in concurrent elections, the presidential candidate will benefit from gubernatorial support as well. By supporting the presidential hopeful in his campaigning, the PRI governors set up a harmonious relationship should the PRI candidate defeat her rivals at the ballot box.

Finally, because state politics creates a large pool of candidacies and bureaucratic posts, governors often control important political resources as well. Generally speaking, plurality elections in SMDs and open-list PR systems with large district magnitude (the number of legislators elected from the district) promote stronger local career paths while the closed-list PR rules keep the national party leadership in control of some valuable candidacies, thereby giving it influence within the party.

During this period out of office, the party's two sets of leaders, the copartisan governors and the national party chief,[13] achieved a cooperative agreement that was based on independent control over candidacies and finances, mutual assistance, and the ability to sanction. Only when the president of the CEN also competed for the presidential nomination were there serious problems between the two groups. These two party groups (under different leaders) transformed the PRI into an electoral organization that was able to choose popular candidates, manage modern campaigns in national media outlets, and win fairer elections, so much so that the PRI retook the presidency in 2012 with a highly popular candidate and former governor, Enrique

12. In Mexico, unlike all other mixed SMD-PR systems, voters have only one ballot for the lower, first-past-the-post tier, which also determines the number of PR slots each party wins.

13. The PRI's CEN is largely controlled by its president, who enjoys wide-ranging authority over the rest of the party apparatus. For ease of argument, this work considers the CEN as a single actor unless otherwise specified.

Peña Nieto. Unlike the PRI's 2006 presidential candidate, Peña Nieto was able to unite the disparate party groups because he made credible commitments that he would not use his position as president (should he win) to undermine them, and he used his resources as governor to support copartisans in the Chamber of Deputies, as well as different gubernatorial candidacies, bringing new allies to his side even before the 2012 campaign began.

As important as the governors were for national party headquarters before 2012, the state executives also needed the national party office (CEN): first, the CEN of the PRI was the public face of the party out of the presidency, and it negotiated and battled with the president of Mexico (who was a member of the PAN) to shore up the party's interests, allowing the party's governors to negotiate with the president. The national leadership took care of managing and maintaining the discipline of the PRI's delegation in congress, another task that the individual governors found very costly, even with the collective efforts of the National Conference of Governors (CONAGO).[14] Finally, the CEN managed the national media appeals for the party, especially in the nonconsecutive midterm legislative elections. National party headquarters decided on a central message, hired the polling firms, and coordinated the efforts of the 300 SMD candidates. Finally, the CEN played a central role in choosing gubernatorial candidates in those states in which the PRI did not govern.

The PRI's transformative experience can be compared to those of other former authoritarian parties around the world. For example, the Kenya African National Union (KANU) is a former authoritarian party that collapsed after losing a single national election, while Taiwan's Kuomintang (KMT) survived its two terms out of executive office before retaking the executive. The KANU's former authoritarian leader devised a permissive electoral system during the transition years to divide the opposition forces, a strategy that was successful for roughly a decade. But once the party lost presidential elections, it essentially disappeared as its ambitious politicians left its ranks. Candidates in Kenya for parliamentary seats do not require strong party labels to win office because they can rely on ethnic cues, which reduce the value of the party's label. Once the KANU was defeated, however, these same rules caused devastation as the party's leaders left its ranks, formed their own short-lived organizations, or joined those that already existed.

Taiwan's KMT, on the other hand, retained its local voter mobilizers who were tied to the party, and while it suffered at least two divisions during the early democratization phase, it did not fragment and disappear, but held on to its majority in the Legislative Yuan, before winning the Executive Yuan after eight years out of office. Taiwan's KMT suffered a serious division during the transition period in the 1990s. Because of the nation's single nontransferable

14. For more on the governors' lobbying group, see its website, www.conago.org.mx.

vote (SNTV) rules (now changed), all parties required money both to pay off local vote brokers and to coordinate the number of candidates they would forward. As a result, the KMT splinter parties were not able to grow. One can see the powerful effects of institutions on the ability of politicians to leave the party, to reform the organization, or to cooperate within it. This comparison will be discussed in greater detail in the conclusions.

The question of why authoritarian parties survive once they are obligated to compete under democratic rules is important because, as Mainwaring and Scully have argued (1995, 1–2), it is difficult to maintain a democracy without a stable party system, and it is difficult to stabilize a party system without party organizations that are long-lasting, able to make credible policy commitments, rooted in their societies, and finally, in control of independent resources. Huntington (1968), Neumann (1956), Riker (1964) and Sartori (1976) among many others, agree that parties can integrate citizens into a new democracy as well as facilitate the reach of the central government to the states and localities. Parties can moderate conflict by reducing the number of options available to lawmakers. Most importantly, parties can create a stable base of support for the state and its policies (Levitsky and Way 2010; Mainwaring and Scully 1995; Stoner-Weiss 2002, 128). Other authors have shown what can occur when politicians in new democracies, such as Russia or Peru, do not need to use party vehicles to win elections: the party system becomes unstable, and democracy can suffer as a result (Hale 2006; Levitsky and Cameron 2003; March 2006; Smyth 2006).

The survival of the PRI after its exit from Los Pinos (the presidential mansion) in 2000 was by no means assured: several Latin American political parties that were in some ways similar to the PRI—populist, mass-based, and nationalist, such as Peru's American Popular Revolutionary Alliance (APRA), Venezuela's Democratic Action (AD), or Bolivia's National Revolutionary Movement (MNR)—were profoundly weakened or did not survive long periods out of power or the economic crises of the 1980s and 1990s (Coppedge 2001). In Africa, several former authoritarian parties have become has-beens and also-rans, incapable of winning elections or competing in the new party systems. On the other hand, many former Communist successor parties, such as in Poland, Hungary, and Romania, did surprisingly well in the years following the fall of their regimes (Golosov 1998; Grzymala-Busse 2002; Ishiyama 1999; March 2002).

Yet, for all the discussion of how the PRI returned to power in 2012, many analysts claim that the PRI was not transformed: that it continues to voice a vague, pragmatic view toward economic development and runs state and local governments with a cynical view toward personal reward at the expense of the public good.[15] In national politics, the party leadership

15. See Juan Luis Hernández, "El PRI no ha cambiado. ¿La sociedad sí?," 2012, http://

seemed bent on clashing publicly with the PAN executive (in the hands of the center-right party for two six-year terms, from 2000 to 2012) to win short-term political benefits while protecting its rent-seeking corporatist affiliates, such as the oil and electricity workers' unions. The party's governors are often involved in public corruption scandals.[16] Its national leaders refuse to take a public stand on abortion or same-sex marriage although it proclaims itself a social democratic, secular party, and it changed its position several times on fiscal reform since the 2000 defeat. On the ideological front, party leaders usually are highly vague as to what the PRI represents either on economic or social issues, which allows all ideological currents in the party to coexist.[17]

The PRI has been changed in important ways by the traumatic transition to democracy and by two sound drubbings by opposition presidential candidates; it is now a party that is both modern and traditional, based both on its successful governors and on a well-established central party office. It has not, however, been reformed into a programmatic organization that promotes internal democracy and fair dealing in government. Many of its politicians are corrupt (just as they are in the PRD and the PAN, and many of the minor parties) and overly pragmatic and more market-oriented on economic issues; but now, it is capable of both modern campaigning and old-fashioned clientelism. It never renounced its authoritarian past; instead it proudly proclaimed its successes in modernizing the nation after a decade-long revolution. In this sense, it is not like the former communist parties of Eastern Europe that had to reform and renounce to come back to power, most likely because the nature of the transition was not as profound in Mexico as it was in many Eastern Europe nations.

THE LAYOUT OF THE BOOK

This is the first monograph written on the PRI in English in thirty years, and because of this, it is necessary to understand the PRI's former hegemonic organization to capture how the party has survived and how it has changed.[18]

---

www.m-x.com.mx/xml/pdf/283/50.pdf, and Denise Dresser, "Va pa'tras," *Reforma*, May 17, 2010.

16. For example, a PRI governor was exposed using his public office to help persecute a social activist who uncovered a band of organized child pornographers, yet he was not repudiated by the national party leadership.

17. A columnist explains how the post-2000 PRI leadership confronted a thorny social issue: "The national president of the PRI, Beatriz Paredes, stated that abortion should be a woman's choice. What a shame that she did this a little late: after the local deputies of her party in 17 states had already voted to prohibit the right for a woman to voluntarily end a pregnancy"; Leo Zuckerman, "Juegos de Poder/Declaraciones a la mexicana," *Excelsiór*, March 9, 2010.

18. Two books on the PRI from the 1980s stand out: Garrido (1982), which is a detailed history of the first decades of the party, and Story (1986) on the PRI's

For this reason, background on the hegemonic party's relation with the president, its way of managing campaigns, its contribution to candidate selection, and the ability of its caucus leaders to manage the party representatives in the Chamber of Deputies and the Senate are all pertinent topics of study, so as to be able to compare them to how the party manages its basic tasks under democratic conditions.

The book is divided into two sections: the first part is made up of chapters 2 through 5. Chapter 2 contains a theoretical discussion; chapter 3 outlines how the PRI was organized under hegemony and, in doing so, offers a new interpretation of the relation between the hegemonic executive and the party. In chapter 4, the study turns to how the transition to democracy forced the PRI to adjust from 1988 through 2012. The following chapter continues after 2000 to demonstrate why the CEN and the governors found ways to cooperate and why the 2012 president candidate was able to unite the party when the 2006 presidential hopeful almost drove it apart. Chapter 6 presents a detailed picture of voting behavior in Mexico since the 1980s, employing both individual survey data and electoral results.

The second half of the work, made up of chapters 7 through 10, examines how party members and leaders carry out the most important tasks a party can undertake: choosing candidates, managing campaigns, and obliging its congressional delegations to vote cohesively, an approach that follows the work of Aldrich (1995), Crotty (1968, 250), Key (1958), Pomper (1990), and Schlesinger (1985, 1153). As Key (1958, 700) pointed out, the party machinery needed to designate candidates and win votes in a campaign is very different from that required to group representatives together in "a common cause under common leadership" in the legislature. By studying the substantive actions carried out by parties, these chapters help illustrate and test the arguments laid out in the theoretical chapter. These chapters examine how major party tasks changed over time, which party actor was responsible for them, and how different groups of leaders were able to cooperate.

Chapter 7 studies how candidate selection within the PRI changed from hegemony to democracy, and argues that the major objective of legislative and executive candidate selection before the 1990s was to include as many intraparty groups as possible in the distribution of selective goods, to keep regime politicians under control and cooperating. To do so, the chapter employs empirical data on the federal legislative and gubernatorial candidates to uncover the nature of the different groups within the PRI.

One would expect that as competition rose, internal PRI actors would fight to wrest control over nominations from the president, because with the growth of competition, popular candidates become more powerful within the party,

organization. Two others on elite recruitment, Camp (1980) and Smith (1979), were fundamental for understanding the PRI regime.

and those who could not win elections or manage campaigns would find their power reduced. Given federal institutions and SMDs, governors won control of nominations to most local elected posts in their respective states as well as candidacies for SMDs to the Chamber. The CEN took over responsibility for leading negotiations over federal PR list spots and federal SMD positions in those states not governed by a member of the PRI. Using the prior political trajectories of 300 randomly selected PRI candidates to the lower house from two plural congresses (2006–2009 and 2009–2012), one finds that legislative recruitment has changed as well: the corporatist leaders and federal bureaucrats who once won candidacies to the Chamber via plurality elections have been replaced by politicians whose careers are based in the municipal and state political arenas.

Chapter 8 compares how the PRI carried out congressional campaigning before and after democracy, and shows how quickly both district candidates and national party leaders adapted to growing pressures at the ballot box after 1988. Under hegemony, campaigning strengthened the links between local leaders and national PRI, which helped generate huge electoral margins. I present data to challenge the notion that the PRI's corporatist or territorial organization had a strong presence all over the nation; rather, the party's office seekers, with the support of mayors and governors, did much of the work of waging campaigns.

Since the late 1990s, national party headquarters won control over public campaign financing and professionalized national media appeals, giving them a central place in campaigning for federal posts. The district-level campaigns were "modernized" under the careful scrutiny of copartisan governors. The PRI governors have become even more important supporters of the congressional candidates in their states because they need the largest group of copartisan deputies possible and have the resources to promote copartisan campaigns. The deputy candidates continue to campaign using the time-honored method of brokering—providing access to local services in return for blocks of votes— and as a result, they rely heavily on paid local leaders who are able to mobilize voters. At the same time, they too have modernized their SMD campaign styles through videos, interviews, and door-to-door canvassing.

Chapter 9 illustrates how the PRI organized its legislative delegation before and after hegemony. Before the PRI lost its majority in the lower house in 1997, the executive searched out closely matched agents to help alleviate problems of mismatched incentives between the regime leadership (lodged in the executive) and the different PRI factions that made up the party's congressional delegation. Once the PRI lost its majority in Congress, the legislative branch became a fully functional part of the policy-making process. However, individual politicians continue to be weak vis-à-vis their party leaders thanks to the constitutional prohibition against consecutive reelection, so leaders still send trusted agents to lead the legislative committees. The findings in this chapter are based on comparing the political and professional backgrounds of over 1,000 PRI federal deputies from the hegemonic and democratic eras to examine which "type" of PRI politicians won committee presidencies.

The concluding chapter demonstrates how the findings for the PRI can be applied to other former authoritarian parties, using Kenya's KANU and Taiwan's KMT as cases. It also presents an overview of the book's argument and discusses how the PRI was able to win the 2012 presidential election after its abysmal showing in 2006, and it offers a short synopsis of how the party and its governors and national party leadership have adapted to a PRI president.

CHAPTER 2

Theorizing Authoritarian Party Survival

This chapter presents a theoretical discussion of why some former authoritarian parties survive the transition to democracy while others do not. The study of Mexico's PRI contributes to the literatures on authoritarian party survival—and party change more generally—by taking into account three central problems that have been underexplored. First, almost all authoritarian parties split or divide when faced with the pressures of electoral competition. By asking how party leaders manage to avoid the divisions that could destroy the organization or mitigate their effects, both before and after the party's exit from the executive, the present work acknowledges one of the highest risks to authoritarian party survival. Second, the work asks which inherited resources are the most important for party survival in a democracy, and how these resources are transmitted to the new party organization, while its authoritarian features are downplayed. Finally, it inquires about the identity of the factional groups that are best able to adjust to the challenges of the transition to democracy. To answer these questions, this chapter concentrates on the role played by political institutions in channeling electoral competition, in allowing party factions to cooperate, and in favoring one faction over another in the quest to control the resources—both old and new—of the former authoritarian party to use them in a democratic context.

This chapter places great stress on how vote-winning groups within the former authoritarian party were able to defeat their internal rivals and in doing so, transform the party so that it could survive. In fact, it will show that the economic reformers who took over the authoritarian regime in Mexico in the 1980s were not those who ended up controlling the party after 2000, in large part because they were not successful at the ballot box. For this reason, I refer to successful groups as vote-winners rather than reformers. The chapter will also demonstrate how vote-winning groups within the PRI managed to take over the party. This was not an easy or automatic process, as Downs (1957) would have it; rather, it took over ten years of the transition period (1988–2000) and ended when rival groups—in this case, economic reformers, party activists, and union leaders—were defeated by the party's governors and leaders of the national party office (CEN).

Party survival is defined as the ability to continue to field candidates and win elections, for either the legislature or the executive at any level of government (Ishiyama 1999). It does not necessarily imply the former authoritarian party's return to national executive power. Other authoritarian or predominant parties that adapted successfully to the rigors of electoral competition include: the Bulgarian communist successor party, Hungary's former Communist party, Ghana's former authoritarian party, and the Polish communist successor party.[1] In other cases, former authoritarian parties, such as Kenya's KANU, were devastated by internal divisions and subsequently disappeared when they had to compete under fair conditions.

There are differences between hegemonic, or authoritarian, party systems, as described by Sartori (1976), and dominant party systems, such as Japan's under the Liberal Democratic Party (LDP) or India's under the Congress Party (which fall within the realm of democratic politics). In hegemonic systems, other parties exist and may win a small number of races, but it is impossible for the authoritarian party to lose the national executive or the majority in either house of congress. This syncs well with Przeworski's 1986 definition of democracy, in which electoral outcomes must be uncertain. In dominant party systems, on the other hand, the ruling party can be defeated by its opposition rivals, as was India's Congress in the 1970s and the LDP in Japan in the 1990s. Authoritarian regimes and their parties can employ several different tools to garner overwhelming margins in almost all elections over the course of several decades, including: countercyclical spending, targeted subsidies, voter mobilization using state resources, electoral fraud and manipulation, and finally, solid economic growth (Cheng 1989; Greene 2007; Lust-Okar 2006; Magaloni 2006; Schedler 2006).[2] The problems for the authoritarian party begin when electoral competition rises, and opposition groups demand a level playing field so that citizens' votes are respected. These electoral pressures are often precipitated by severe economic downturns that alienate voters and reduce the regime's ability to buy off internal critics (Geddes 1999; Greene 2007).[3]

1. As these examples show, however, former authoritarian party success must be a concept bounded in time (Grzymała-Busse 2015; Loxton 2016), because while many of the former communist organizations survived and prospered during the first decade or so after the fall of the Berlin Wall, from 2000 to 2005, some have begun to decline significantly (the former Polish communist successor party), or the regime itself become more authoritarian (Hungary).

2. For a full list of authoritarian regimes that hold elections, see Levitsky and Way (2010).

3. This is not always the case, as demonstrated by the KMT's defeat in Taiwan.

An important set of explanations that focuses explicitly on authoritarian party survival rather than party change more generally argues that organizational history and the legacy of the party—the alliances, routines, and rules that were created in the party's formative years—have a weighty influence on whether and how the party can later transform itself (Duverger 1954; Grzymała-Busse 2002; Ishiyama 1995; Kitschelt et al., 1999; Panebianco 1982; Roberts 1998). According to these models, it is difficult to change entrenched practices within the party even after a cataclysmic electoral defeat because the party's organizational legacy retards change, and as a result, the party finds it more difficult to adjust to new electoral circumstances (Burgess and Levitsky 2003; Kitschelt 1989; Koelble 1992).

In terms of former authoritarian parties from Eastern Europe, Grzymała-Busse argues that these organizations hold "norms, patterns of political behavior, and organizational networks" (2002, 19) from the authoritarian era that continue to influence the party after the fall of the respective communist regimes. These inherited resources can either help or harm the successor party in its quest to survive the challenges of democratic competition.[4] If the authoritarian party's elite has experience in political recruitment outside the party, in policy adjustments, and in negotiating with the opposition, the party will most likely adjust and survive (Grzymała-Busse 2002, 59–69). With skilled elites, the inheritable resources that most former authoritarian parties enjoy, such as name recognition, the extension of the party's organization, and its recent history of negotiations with the opposition can be used successfully in the new, democratic context (Slater and Wong 2013).

Although the inherited resource argument is very suggestive for former authoritarian parties outside Eastern Europe, several issues arise when applying a theory that is designed to explain the behavior of former communist parties in closed, socialist economies to the behavior of former authoritarian parties in more open, capitalist economies. First, the preexisting patronage networks in authoritarian regimes can be at least partially maintained after the fall from power (unlike their communist party counterparts) if resources continue to be available from other sources. Second, the profound transformation of both the political and economic realms in a short period of time that characterized the experiences of Eastern Europe rarely exist outside of that region, with the exceptions of North Korea and Cuba. Even a change in the dominant development model, such as that found in Mexico, cannot compete with the (re)creation of a capitalist economy. As a result, many successful

---

4. In a different work, Grzymała-Busse (2001) discusses variation among communist party organizational coverage within society. If the former communist party in question had more extensive societal coverage in terms of party loyalty requirements, schooling, and the nomenklatura system, it would have greater difficulty adjusting to demands of free electoral competition.

former authoritarian parties do not need to renounce their pasts, especially if they presided over economic modernization.[5] In terms of the electoral environment, even if the former hegemonic party has been ousted, political parties will not necessarily be rejected wholesale by citizens. In those authoritarian party systems in which other parties were allowed to exist, voters had prior experience with opposition parties, and so the electorate often has some ideological moorings and uses partisan labels to ease problems of scarce information. As such, functioning party systems can either continue from the authoritarian period or be created quickly after the onset of democratization, and so charismatic personalities without party backing are less likely to win elections because party identity continues to influence the voting behavior of millions of citizens.

A second issue with the inherited resources and legacy arguments in authoritarian systems is identifying exactly which inherited skills and resources are most important during the transition period, and to uncover the mechanism of how these skills and resources are transferred to or maintained within the successor party, while antidemocratic traits and norms are shunted aside. The present book contributes to the work on inheritable resources by demonstrating that the elite skills that matter most to party survival outside of the Eastern European cases are not those related to negotiation, but rather to vote winning, such as running campaigns, managing mass media appeals, marketing the party, and mobilizing voters. These skills become far more central to the party's future than internal security and spying, economic policy battles, negotiating with rivals, and coalition maintenance.

There is no doubt that Mexico's PRI enjoyed several resources that it inherited from the authoritarian period. It governed the nation for seventy years and so its name was universally recognized (and its colors are the same as those of the Mexican flag). The party label maintained an average of 35–40 percent of voter identification from the early 1990s through 2010, more than its two opposition rivals, even as democratic institutions became stronger (see chapter 6). Its gubernatorial candidates continued to win elections in all regions of the nation with pragmatic, nonprogrammatic appeals. Furthermore, the economic shocks and the new economic development model had already been put in place beginning in the mid-1980s and continuing through the early 1990s, before the final defeat of the party in 2000, so that the new leaders of the PRI could simply blame the "neoliberal" economic model on the party's disgraced technocrats, while continuing to abide by the tenets of the export-driven economic program.

5. Slater and Wong (2013) argue that the authoritarian parties in successful developmental regimes in Asia use their past accomplishments to democratize while still in power.

At the same time, however, the PRI was dragging a long past of selective repression against dissidents; a twelve-year period (from 1982 through 1995) of constant economic missteps; a reputation for corruption that ran through every level and every branch of government; an inoperative judicial system; and decrepit union leadership. These too were party legacies that had to be discounted and downplayed for the party to continue to win democratic elections. Furthermore, there was no guarantee that the divisions produced among groups would be avoided, or that the surviving leaders would find a way to cooperate after losing the national executive.

Other scholars studying party change examine left and labor-based parties and find that, in addition to the party's legacy, the strength of the formal links between organized labor centrals and the party's organization often determines whether reformist leaders are able to take over the party, moderate its ideological appeals, and find new ways to reach voters (Koelble 1992). Roberts (1998) compares the Socialist and Communist Parties in Chile and finds that a more flexible organizational structure helped the Socialists adjust to new electoral demands, while the Communists were unable to do so. Levitsky's discussion of the case of the Peronists in Argentina during the 1980s and 1990s centers on two issues: the ability of the party's new leader to moderate the protectionist economic development model espoused by Peronism for decades, and the party's change from a labor-based party with union mobilization of voters to a clientelist party with clientelist mobilization. Levitsky (2003, 3) finds that less institutionalized parties are better able to delink from external organizations, such as unions, and allow new politicians to rise quickly within their ranks to replace nonreformers. This flexibility allows reformers facing a new and more challenging external environment to choose successful policies quickly and sell them to both party members and voters.

Levitsky (2003, 241–243) argues that Mexico's PRI is an intermediate case of party adaptation through the 1990s: the party's affiliated Workers' Sector had only partial rule-based control over candidate selection, and even these rules were often ignored by the president and the leader of the CEN (Bensusán 2004; Middlebrook 1985).[6] So when it came time to transform the party's economic development model in the 1980s at the cost of labor-sector privileges, the regime's leadership was flexible enough to do so. In the short term, however, the PRI found it difficult to stop the decline in its popularity in urban areas and as a result, saw its electoral returns continue to fall.

It is not clear, however, that the PRI's transformation from hegemony to democracy can be explained by the flexibility of its organization. A study of within-case variation demonstrates that vote-winning corporatist groups

6. According to Sirvent (1975, 17), by 1970 the Labor Congress, of which the CTM was by far the most important labor confederation, had thirty-three unions that grouped together about three million worker into the PRI's ranks.

within the PRI were able to survive the transition to democracy, while others were not, principally because of their inability to forward popular candidates, help in campaigns, or raise funds to mobilize voters. A few unions, such as the Oil Workers of the state's oil monopoly, STPRM (Mexican Petroleum Workers' Union), and the National Teachers' Union (SNTE), were (and are) large and extremely wealthy. They continue to use their financial resources to support the PRI at election time, and the SNTE was also able to use hundreds of thousands of teachers to support electoral campaigns. These unions affiliated with the PRI should have suffered the same fate as the Workers' Central if organizational flexibility were the main factor at play. The fact they did not makes us question this explanation.

One of the first explicit explanations of party transformation and survival is that of Downs (1957), who argued that parties facing electoral decline will automatically moderate their ideological appeals to capture more voters, much as a business firm responds to declining sales by offering more desirable merchandise at a better price. Downs placed electoral concerns and voters at the center of his explanation of party change, and ignored the mediating structures within the organization that might retard or even block successful party adaptation. But many parties have failed to respond correctly or quickly to electoral market signals, leading one to ask what internal structures, rules, or patterns of behavior affect a party's successful transformation (Kitschelt 1989; Levitsky 2003; Lowenthal 1983). Still, most explanations of party survival begin with the basic fact that the organization is facing new challenges at the ballot box (Ishiyama 1999).

Parties are not unitary actors: within each coexist different ideological tendencies, regional subgroups, generations, and types of members and leaders, such as campaign experts, party bureaucrats, and elected officials. These factions and groups act on their interests, whether the organization functions within an authoritarian or a democratic context (Belloni and Beller 1978; Camp 1980; Harmel and Janda 1994; Key 1958; Langston 2006; Panebianco 1982; Rigger 1999; Smith 1979). Factional dynamics play a large role in explaining whether and how parties change because some factions gain more than others when the basic conditions under which they compete for power are transformed. Harmel and Janda (1994, 274) define a party faction as an "intraparty combination whose members share a sense of common identity and purpose and are organized to act as a distinct bloc within the party to win goals."[7] This book focuses on the battles among factional leaders to take over the party after the onset of electoral competition and on how groups that emerge victorious from these battles manage to cooperate once they lose the authoritarian regime's third-party enforcer.

---

7. Within this group-based approach, we include the work begun by Schlesinger (1966) and continued by Kitschelt (1989) on office seekers versus ideologues within party organizations.

Harmel and Janda (1994) argue that if new groups take over the governing organs of the party, the organization will likely be transformed to reflect the preferences of the new leaders in the dominant coalition. In comparing the transformations of three former Leninist parties, Shafqat (1999, 40) finds what best explains the ability to transform the party given external electoral shocks is the dominance of the reform faction within the party. While it is difficult to argue against this proposition, one could ask why certain intraparty groups rather than others are able to win party leadership posts.

It is a fallacy to think that authoritarian governments do not hold elections: in fact, most of them do, although the results are never in doubt (Levistky and Wey 2010; Schedler 2006). Authoritarian governments use "democratic" institutions, such as campaigning and electoral management to strengthen their hold over their elite and opposition forces (Boix and Svolik 2013; Gandhi 2008; Lust-Okar 2006). Campaigns are run and elections are held to show the opposition and internal rivals the popularity of the ruling coalition within the authoritarian regime (Magaloni 2006); they help knit together the factions through the judicious distribution of selective benefits (Camp 1990); they help resolve conflicts among party factions and control the military (Geddes 2006).

The constant management of candidate selection, voter mobilization, and campaigning constitutes some of the most important aspects of the authoritarian party's responsibilities, allowing different wings of the party access to decision makers in the capital (Blaydes 2011; Lust-Okar 2006). Over time, vote-winning specialists in an authoritarian regime may lose some traction to the developmental bureaucracy and internal security forces, which was the case in both Mexico (Camp 1990; Centeno 1994; Teichman 1995) and Taiwan (Cheng 1989; Rigger 1999). But once the opposition begins to win elections, one can expect campaign experts and popular candidates to once again gain power within the party, as votes begin to determine the control of government. Therefore, the present work argues that the groups that are best able to retain or gain power when faced with rising electoral pressures are those that have prior experience in vote winning and mobilization, and are favored by the institutional structure.

In any authoritarian party, the leaders of different factions attempt to maintain their political interests and careers intact during the uncertain transition to democracy. The groups within the threatened party that are able to win fair and competitive elections are those that can best meet the demands of democracy. But which internal groups have these skills?

To pinpoint how skills and resources are transmitted or carried through from the authoritarian to the democratic periods, the present work underlines the role of political institutions. By examining which institutions pre-exist or are created during the transition period, one can better trace which party actors can take advantage of important resources that are inherited from the former authoritarian regime, such as name recognition and a large party base. Legacy arguments tend to ignore the importance of institutions for channeling resources to different groups within the authoritarian parties. Yet, institutions are crucial for determining which among all internal party groups are best able to grab resources that win votes and how these groups will be able to cooperate (Tavits 2012).

Institutions are sets of rules that constrain behavior and allow for mutual gains among actors because the preestablished standard operating procedures make it easier to predict the behavior of others (North 1990). By establishing rules, the uncertainty of everyday exchanges is reduced as actors involved in them understand how each should behave in a given situation. Several authors have demonstrated the importance of political institutions for the organization of parties and the behavior of politicians within them (Carey and Shugart 1995; Duverger 1954; Riker 1964; Schlesinger 1966).

Different institutions affect political parties: most important are whether the form of government is federalist or unitary, as well as presidentialist or parliamentary, and finally, the electoral rules. Federalist constitutions tend to form decentralized parties, while unitary governments usually have the opposite effect (van Biezen 2000; Montero 2007). Presidential systems often have weaker parties than their parliamentary counterparts (Samuels and Shugart 2010) because of the separate elections for the executive and legislature. Electoral systems such as plurality races in single-member districts (SMDs) tend to decentralize the parties and strengthen ambitious office-seekers over party leaders, while closed-list proportional representation rules normally create stronger party leaders who can control candidacies. Mixed systems, with both a PR and SMD element allow both strong local political careers and a powerful national party (Wattenberg and Shugart 2000). Further, the distinction between public party financing and self-financing matters as well: if it controls campaign financing, the national party headquarters remains a center of power within the party; but if candidates themselves must search out contributions from voters, businesses, or political action committees, then their loyalties will not be as centered on party HQ.[8]

Finally, electoral rules help determine whether citizens use party labels to orient their voting behavior, rather than other alternatives, such as ethnic or religious cues or tribal membership. If party labels affect turnout and the direction of the vote, then vote-winning groups have a higher chance of

8. The question remains how easily political institutions can be modified or completely changed during the transition period. A quick perusal of indicative cases reveals that outside Eastern Europe, in places such as Taiwan and several African nations, institutions were not much altered during the transition period. Russia, meanwhile, had to create new a new parliament based on the Russian nation and several of its regions became independent states; Czechoslovakia split into two nations; East Germany unified with West Germany, and so on.

prevailing over their internal party rivals, because their skills are central to the continued existence of the organization. If, on the other hand, ethnicity plays a larger role in orienting voters' behavior at the ballot box, and tribal leaders are responsible for mobilization, as in Kenya, then one can expect party organizations to be weak, fleeting, electoral vehicles that support a strong ethnic leader. It may also be the case that electoral rules are designed such that national, coherent parties are almost impossible to form or maintain (Levitsky and Cameron 2003; Mainwaring and Scully 1995).

How did the particular constellation of Mexican institutions affect the PRI's ability to survive and the direction of its transformation? First, the national party had always had an army of agents that traveled to the districts during campaign season to push the party's congressional candidates to campaign more actively and not to shirk these duties, which they had strong incentives to do knowing that they would win with high margins. During the hegemonic era, the PRI's national party office was one of the two sets of offices in charge of the collective outcome of convincing Mexican citizens to come to the voting stations on election days (see chapter 3). The other set of leaders were the governors (all of whom belonged to the PRI until 1989), who directed their mayors to support PRI candidates and pressed state bureaucrats into service, along with distributing campaign resources. The party's organization, defined as its territorial branches and affiliated mass sectors, was weaker than one might have expected given its seventy years in power, but it could afford to be because its leaders depended on elected officials and control over the bureaucracy of vote counting to produce such high vote margins (see chapter 8 for more on campaigning).

Further, the two winning groups within the PRI after 2000, the governors and leaders of the CEN, were able to cooperate because each required the other and each had autonomous and complementary resources, made up of money and candidacies. Governors were powerful because of federalism (combined with weak accounting rules, as will be shown in chapter 5). This allowed them to continue to spend on large infrastructural projects and clientelist goods, both of which are popular with pragmatic Mexican voters. The leaders of the national party headquarters depended on their powerful governors to deliver the votes once the PRI did not control the presidency. Yet, national headquarters and its leaders maintained their relevance because of generous public funding that was funneled to the party's coffers rather than the candidates, as well as their control over PR candidacies (although they had to negotiate top candidacies on the lists with their governors).

The counterfactual is revealing: if there had been no PR tier and all legislative candidates had been chosen in SMDs, then the CEN would not have had any candidacies under its control, which would have weakened its leaders because they could not have benefitted their allies with valuable candidacies. If the system had been pure closed-list PR, with the district consisting of a region (several states together), rather than the state, then the CEN would have not needed its ambitious governors as much. The particular combination of federalism, no consecutive reelection, and a two-tiered electoral system does much to explain why certain groups rather than others won out in the quest for resources, while it also explains why the strongest factions were able to cooperate without the presence of its former third-party enforcer—the president of Mexico.

Which groups were responsible for vote winning in the hegemonic PRI, and how did these groups respond to the challenges of electoral competition? The PRI's functional sectors (Worker, Peasant, and Popular) had a presence in roughly half of the nation's 300 federal electoral districts (see chapter 8), and they supported campaigns and vote mobilizing in those areas where their members or leaders won candidacies. However, the PRI governor of each state was still ultimately responsible for winning all of the state's elections, both local and federal, even in those in which a sector was active. And in the districts in which a sector was not present, the candidates, as well as the governors and mayors, were even more crucial to electoral outcomes.

When electoral competition began to grow in the late 1980s, the Workers' Sector had already been decimated by the economic crises that had exploded in the early part of the decade. Its candidates were unpopular, it was losing members at an accelerated pace because of neoliberal economic policies, and its unions did not have the resources to pay for campaigns. As a result, the labor-affiliated unions lost out in the race to adjust to competitive elections (with the exceptions of the SNTE and PEMEX unions). The regime's "technocrats," made up of US-educated, doctorate-wielding economists, were not able to win elections successfully, and they too lost out in the political accommodation after the party's exit from the presidency in 2000, in part because their economic promises had been dashed in the 1994–1995 economic crisis, and in part because the candidate who led this wing of the party lost Mexico's presidency for the first time in seventy years. Finally, local party activists who at one time had donated their labor to campaigning, attempted to win some influence over candidate selection in exchange for their aid and support in electioneering duties. This led to a decentralizing and democratizing move in the early 1990s to allow local activists some say over nominations. However, it became clear that their activities could be paid for by governors and the federal government and carried out by paid vote brokers, and so the party did not need to allow party members influence over who would represent voters at election time.

National party headquarters, meanwhile, took advantage of the constant electoral reforms of the 1990s to win autonomous, guaranteed resources from the Federal Electoral Institute (IFE) with which they could operate whether or not the president was from the PRI. During the first years after 1988, certain secretariats within the CEN modernized campaign techniques rapidly: learning about opinion survey research, marketing, and communication, studying voting patterns, and, most importantly, developing mass media appeals. Once the PRI lost the presidency in 2000, the CEN employed the generous public resources from the IFE, which it had negotiated with the opposition parties only a few years earlier. Therefore, party headquarters continued to play an important role in candidate selection (thanks to the five closed PR lists of forty persons each for the Chamber of Deputies and the thirty-two-person closed list for the Senate, as well as for those states that were not run by a PRI governor), as well as campaigning.

INTERNAL DIVISIONS AND PARTY FRAGMENTATION

One of the premises of authoritarian regimes is that a third-party enforcer, in this case, the authoritarian executive, is able to oblige members of the party and regime to remain loyal and disciplined, even when individual politicians within the regime face professional setbacks. All or most of the party's politicians are better off under such a system because cooperation allows the party to continue to dominate elections and government resources. If elite circulation is well handled, then most politicians will have an opportunity in the near future to maintain or improve their careers prospects. However, when electoral competition begins to rise, those who are denied a nomination now have an opportunity to leave the party and run for an opposition alternative (or form one of their own) with some possibility of victory.

Authoritarian party leaders face a dilemma when faced with growing electoral competition. They can devolve more decision-making capacity to local party members in an attempt to maintain their participation in other party activities, such as campaigning or attending rallies in support of the party. Furthermore, local party activists know which potential candidates have a better chance at winning the general election, and so by allowing them more candidate selection responsibilities, party leaders both energize the base and select candidates who can better compete in competitive elections. However, in devolving authority over candidacies, party leaders lose the ability to punish and benefit their local political elite because ambitious office seekers tend to place more emphasis on the demands of those who further their careers. Also, local party activists do not always select the candidates that party leaders need to balance the needs of the entire hegemonic regime. Thus, decentralizing candidate selection can cause as many problems as it solves. But if national leaders do not devolve candidate selection to the local level and continue to nominate unpopular candidates to satisfy the needs of the wider authoritarian coalition, popular politicians can leave the party and run against it.

Internal party splits in the face of electoral competition usually derive from three causes. First, office seekers leave the organization as electoral competition rises because it is possible to win under another party label. Second, ambitious politicians flee the party in large numbers because voters reject the label. Third, parties split because an entire group believes it has no future within the organization, so the costs of creating a new organization or joining another are worth paying.

Two solutions exist for the problem of internal divisions. First, if a strong leader takes over the organization after it has suffered a historic defeat, she can impose order. If the new leader is seen as a potentially winning presidential candidate, then she can stabilize expectations and forge a unified party. If, however, such a figure does not arise out of the party, and rival factions—whether they are electorally oriented or not—struggle to take over the organization, they must come to a cooperative agreement over resources and candidacies if the party is to avoid divisions. Cooperative agreements without a third-party enforcer are difficult to establish and maintain (Axelrod 1984; Hardin 1982). But if rival groups enjoy independent and autonomous resources, such as money and candidacies, the chances of cooperation rise, especially if each side requires the aid and assistance of the other and has the ability to sanction noncooperative behavior. The fact that both groups within the PRI survived and found ways to cooperate leads back to the discussion of the importance of institutions: formal federalism strengthened governors, as did plurality races in SMDs. The mixed-tier electoral system and plentiful public financing of campaigns allowed the CEN to remain a key player as it could place PR candidates and disburse much needed funds to candidates who were able to mobilize voters in many areas through clientelist exchanges.

In terms of internal ruptures, an ideological split within the PRI over the future of economic policy and the presidential succession helped initiate the transition to democracy. The 1986–1987 rupture of a small number of left-leaning political leaders (who fought against the neoliberal tide crashing on Mexico's shores in the 1980s) created a viable left electoral option for voters in the 1988 presidential elections, allowing disaffected citizens a way to show their anger with the PRI regime's abysmal economic performance. This internal party split and the 1988 elections that followed initiated a decade of electoral reforms that threatened the party's ability to win almost all of its races with huge margins. Individual exits by ambitious politicians—both those that were actually carried out and those that were only threatened—also changed the way the party selected its presidential and gubernatorial candidates during the late 1990s.[9] It became possible for disgruntled PRI precandidates in gubernatorial elections to leave the party, run against the official candidate,

---

9. Garrido (2014) reports that after 1988, only 748 PRI politicians left the party out of the thousands who were active; so clearly, the sheer number of exits was not an issue. However, many of these were popular state politicians who then ran against PRI candidates and won.

and win office under an opposition party banner—an outcome that would have been unthinkable from the 1950s through the early 1990s.[10]

Given these strong incentives to split, how did the PRI avoid debilitating divisions, either on a large scale or by individuals, especially after it lost the presidency in 2000? Chapters 4 and 5 will discuss this issue in greater detail, but before 2000, the party changed candidate selection processes several times to avoid the exit of powerful office seekers who could take their entire political network to another party and defeat the PRI in fair elections. After 2000, without the third-party enforcer in the form of the president of Mexico, groups within the PRI forged a cooperative bargain in which the party's governors were free to select their state's candidates for both subnational and federal posts with little interference from the national party office.

After the PRI's presidential defeat, national party headquarters had greater influence over those states without a PRI governor, it coordinated the PRI's legislative caucus, and managed federal campaign appeals via mass media appeals paid for with federal campaign funds (until a change in the electoral rules in 2008 which made these appeals free). The causes of this successful bargain were independent and complementary sources of resources and mutual benefits. The main source of governors' resources are the millions of pesos of tax revenue they receive from the federal government through rule-based mechanisms. The accounting rules set up to monitor how these funds are spent were and continue to be weak (Pardinas 2008), giving the state executives large quantities of tax revenue, a part of which they spend on campaigns and political networking in their respective states.[11] The CEN was far less wealthy than the PRI governors collectively, but received money every year from the IFE.[12] Both the governors and the national party headquarters had control over different candidacies thanks to the nation's two-tiered electoral system.

The PRI did suffer a division in 2003. The powerful head of the million-strong Teachers' Union was able to form a small party (PANAL) after the CEN leader and future presidential candidate blocked her alliances with the PAN presidency and policy changes in Congress. The Convergence Party (now Citizens' Movement) is also a splinter party that has managed to survive in coalition with larger parties. The PRI almost divided once again over the candidacy of Roberto Madrazo, who was leader of the CEN and a leading presidential hopeful for the 2006 elections. Madrazo used the office of the CEN to push his candidacy, angering other potential presidential nominees, but

10. See chapter 3 for a synopsis of the early ruptures made by PRI politicians in 1940, 1946, and 1952. Chapter 5 discusses the splits after 2000.
11. Reportedly, governors from large and wealthy PRI states often assist governors from smaller PRI states in their campaigning.
12. Interview subject 94 reported that the CEN allegedly received financial resources from its powerful governors. This information has not yet been corroborated.

was not so popular that he seemed like a shoe-in for the presidential office. It was possible to castigate him during the 2006 presidential campaign by not supporting his campaign, and in doing so, the PRI governors helped rid themselves of this noncooperative leader.

Once the PRI retook the presidency in 2012, the federal government's relation to its copartisan governors changed: the governors had to obey many more dictates from its president in Mexico City than they did in the twelve years the PAN controlled the presidency. The president and his allies were able to place more candidates in both the plurality and PR districts in the 2015 midterms. This issue will be discussed further in the conclusions, but it is clear the president cannot afford to alienate his copartisan governors to a large degree because the PRI's electoral results continue to depend on the organizing efforts and support of its governors. National party headquarters, on the other hand, has become a simple support mechanism for the presidency.

CHAPTER 3

The PRI under Hegemony

To understand why the PRI survived the pressures of electoral competition, one must begin with a clear picture of the hegemonic party organization under authoritarianism and how it was linked to the authoritarian regime. The background provided by this chapter is the starting point to understand the changes that the PRI underwent after 1988. Several specific issues stand out; first, the work that each president and his closest staff invested in keeping the ambitious PRI elite in check. A strong president acted as the ultimate arbitrator in conflicts among PRI groups, which meant that once the party lost this third-party enforcer after 2000, the party would have to find new ways of avoiding ruptures. Second, this chapter shows how central the governors were to vote winning during the hegemonic period. Thus, when competition began to rise, the directly elected state executives were uniquely situated to deal with this looming threat. Third, the party's organization, led by its National Executive Committee (CEN), was subordinate not only to each president of Mexico, but also to the powerful Secretary of Governance (*Gobernación* in Spanish). As this chapter will show, the hegemonic party did not itself have the resources to keep ambitious regime leaders cooperating, so that the struggle to rework the relations of cooperation among party factions after 2000 was even more difficult because of the party organization's inherent weakness. Further, while the PRI's territorial organization was far stronger than the opposition's, its party offices at the precinct, municipal, and state levels were inactive in many areas of the nation; and as a result, the candidates and agents of the CEN or the governors often had to invest in the local party branches so they could assist in campaign activities.[1]

---

1. Interview subject 54, a former senator and federal deputy active during the Echeverría and de la Madrid presidencies, April 11, 2000.

The PRI was an inclusive, mass-based, multiclass party that, following the orders of each president of Mexico, coordinated the overall electoral effort of the authoritarian political regime—one that allowed other parties to exist with the certainty they would never win the executive or control of the legislature (Brandenburg 1964; Hansen 1971; Molinar 1991; Sartori 1976; Scott 1964). Mexican and American academics had spirited discussions about the nature of the PRI and the regime in the 1950s and 1960s, but after roughly 1965, most agreed that Mexico was not a democratic nation; that the federal government controlled the PRI; that it was both judge and jury in all electoral matters because of its control over the government agencies that managed elections; and that it committed fraud and other illegal practices, all the while proclaiming its revolutionary goals of land reform, anti-imperialism, and prolabor practices (Adler Hellman 1978; Cornelius 1975; Eckstein 1977; González Casanova 1965; Hamilton 1982; Hansen 1971).

Despite Mexico's political institutions, especially federalism and plurality races in single-member districts (SMDs), the hegemonic regime was centralized because national political leaders held enormous sway over political and economic opportunities. The lack of electoral competition and the constitutional prohibition against consecutive reelection helped centralize political power, although governors remained important actors in their own right because of their ability to win votes and act as the first line of defense against social unrest.

The works of Gandhi (2006, 2008), among others, have highlighted the role of political institutions in helping autocratic regimes to survive because they incorporate and manage the opposition. I underline a different threat to regime survival: the constant attempts by factions, groups, and ambitious politicians within the regime to confront its leaders over candidacies and bureaucratic posts (Boix and Svolik 2013; Lust-Okar 2006; Magaloni 2008).[2] While leaders of all authoritarian parties focus attention on opposition movements outside of the governing coalition, they are perhaps even more concerned about how to limit powerful regime politicians (Brownlee 2007; Geddes 1999; Smith 2005). Many of the PRI's relations with the president and the relations of authority and delegation spelled out in this chapter were means of dealing with these internal pressures.

While the present work cannot provide a full history of the party from its formation in 1929 as the National Revolutionary Party (PNR), this chapter lays out various aspects of the party's formation and organization, as well as its relation to the executive, the governors, and the party-affiliated

2. Many authors writing on this topic refer to the dangers of military rebellions undertaken by rivals within the autocratic regime. However, this sort of threat is more likely in the early years of the regime or when the regime is based on a military junta, not in long-lived party-based authoritarian regimes.

corporatist associations under hegemony.[3] First, it discusses how and why the hegemonic party was created in 1929, helping to end almost twenty years of political and social violence that had been unleashed by the Mexican Revolution (1910–1917). The following section examines how political leaders centralized political authority during the 1930s and 1940s, away from the powerful state governors and army generals, toward the civilian presidency and federal bureaucracy. Then, it examines three consecutive "exit" attempts in 1940, 1946, and 1952, in which losing precandidates for the presidency left the party to challenge its official nominee in the general election, and the regime's responses to these internal challenges that effectively ended internal ruptures until 1987.

To illustrate the difficulties of elite management, the penultimate section of the chapter then examines the relation of delegation from the president to his hand-picked subordinates. Each president of Mexico played off his hand-picked Secretary of Governance against the leader of the national party headquarters to gather more information on his wide-flung political coalition and to potentially weaken the Secretary of Governance.[4] Finally, the chapter considers the different power holders within the Revolutionary Coalition, including the corporatist sectors, the governors, and the rural power-holders (called *caciques*), and how they interacted with the national party and the president.

The hegemonic regime was held together in part by distributing selective resources (bureaucratic posts, electoral nominations, economic licenses, etc.) to its wide-flung elite. But to know which group deserved which type of benefit (or sanction) the regime's leaders had to gather information on thousands of PRI politicians, monitoring their behavior in their posts, and sanctioning them when necessary. The general calculation of loyalty and discipline made by members and leaders of the PRI at all levels of government helped keep the authoritarian coalition united under each president from 1934 (when President Lázaro Cárdenas ejected the allies of his principal rival from their posts in the party and government) to the mid-1990s, with the exceptions of splits during the presidential elections of 1940, 1946, and 1952. Given the party's remarkably high electoral margins (the party often won elections with more than 70 percent of the vote), to remain within the confines of the party, even in the face of a personal defeat in a contest to win a nomination or a bureaucratic post, would always bring higher payoffs than challenging the regime from the ranks of the opposition. Regime leaders worked diligently from the 1930s through the 1950s to build up this discipline. As a result, the

---

3. For a recounting of the formation of the PRI, see Garrido (1982), Hamilton (1982), Hernández (2016); Huntington (1968), and Lajous (1979).

4. The Secretariat of Gobernación (which I translate as Governance) was responsible for managing domestic politics in general and the executive's relation with the rest of the branches of government in particular.

collective outcome of the individual decisions of PRI politicians to remain within the confines of the party was a stable authoritarian regime, in which it was in almost no politician's interest to exit, and the opposition had little to no chance of winning elections. The other fundamental basis of the successful regime was the continual work carried out by a host of regime and party officials to win votes, which is discussed in chapters 6 and 8.

THE CREATION OF THE HEGEMONIC PARTY

Former revolutionary general and later president of Mexico Plutarco Elías Calles (1924–1928) formed the PNR in 1929 to help end the period of great violence, uncertainty, and anarchy that had arisen from the roughly seven years of the Mexican Revolution (1910–1917) and the decade of political instability immediately following (1918–1929). At first, Calles designed a loose umbrella organization to incorporate local and regional political organizations under the banner of revolutionary ideals, but moved quickly to convert it into a national electoral machine that so closely overlapped with the government that it became known as the "official party," and remained the electoral coordinator of the authoritarian regime for over seventy years. The process of centralizing power to the federal government, rebuilding the economy, and taming the political ambitions of the revolutionary generals and regional strongmen (termed *caudillos*), took more than two decades after the end of the revolution. During the 1920s, army generals headed two rebellions to unseat the elected governments in Mexico City, while a wide-ranging social conflict that began in 1926, called the *Cristero* Revolt, sought to block efforts by the new northern leaders to reduce the power of the Catholic Church, embroiling large sections of the nation in violence and unrest for several years (Meyer 1973).

The national political parties that developed during the 1920s, before the creation of the PNR, were created in part by regional and local political leaders who were strong enough to place their allies into the Chamber of Deputies through their control over the voting behavior of local residents and electoral institutions. The national parties were active mostly *within* the national legislature, and were too weak to organize the local voters and so had to depend on these subnational leaders, who controlled blocks of voters, tax collection, and at times, the administration of justice (Garrido 1982; Lajous 1978; Meyer 1986). Scott (1964, 118) writes that many of the regional parties in the 1920s were simply civilian facades for military caudillos competing for political power, and elections often turned violent as armed gangs attempted to win elected office with bullets instead of ballots.[5]

5. Before the 1946 electoral law, mayors—95 percent of whom were members of the

After the assassination of president-elect Álvaro Obregón in 1928, former president Calles chose not to resume the presidency himself and announced he would form a single revolutionary party to assure that Mexico would be ruled by institutions, not strongmen. The party's ideology was vague, and included land reform, labor rights, and greater educational opportunities, as well as expanded political rights and fair elections. But Calles turned to the right ideologically, and many of these original promises were quietly dropped (Brandenburg 1964, 65).[6] The immediate goal of Calles and the PNR was to include all forces within the revolutionary coalition so that quarrels over who would win the presidency would not explode into military rebellions (Garrido 1982). The creation of the PNR forced those politicians who called themselves "revolutionary" to allow their party superiors to choose candidates for elected office; most importantly, to allow the Jefe Máximo Calles to choose the party's presidential nominee; and not to rise up in arms when they were denied the nomination (Garrido 1982; Meyer 1986). Calles stopped violent outbreaks against presidential authority; at the same time he allowed most of the new party's members to benefit from staying within the confines of the regime. In the first stage, local political leaders gave up very little, but over time, the erosion of local power (and corresponding national gains) made it more difficult for caudillos to challenge the national party regime. Because the revolutionary ideology was vague, almost all political figures could join the ranks of the PNR; and because Calles quickly gained the instruments with which he could punish defectors and benefit loyalists; it became rational to cooperate within the new structure.

After 1929, it gradually became more difficult for local potentates to impose their favorites as candidates for the PNR if they were unacceptable to the national leaders (Garrido 1982, 24), although the struggle between governors and federal government would not be resolved until the 1950s (Hernández Rodríguez 2008; Pansters 1996; Rodríguez Kuri 2008). Governors and caudillos had been able to place their political allies in the Chamber of Deputies to protect their interests against those of the national government, and it was this sort of regional power that would be attacked under the new PNR (Hernández Rodríguez 2008). Affiliation to the party's ranks before the creation and integration of the mass corporatist associations was on an individual basis, and thousands of state and federal bureaucrats were integrated into

PRI—were responsible for creating the voting list, installing the voting booths, and placing municipal electoral colleges (Medina Peña 1993, 162). The first three people to reach the polling station were its election authorities, which caused violence as each party tried to install its people.

6. The stated goals of the revolutionary generation were to rid the nation of clerical control over many aspects of social life, reduce foreign ownership over strategic areas of the economy, and subdivide large agricultural holdings (Brandenburg 1964, 66).

the party and forced to pay a part of their salaries to the party.[7] Even with these new members, the numerical base of the party was small because it had not incorporated large numbers of peasants or workers into its ranks (Garrido 1982, 89). During this early period, candidates were chosen in party primaries at the level of the election; however, these primaries were not regulated or fair, and local leaders found them easy to manipulate, allowing them to continue to be local powerbrokers within the party.

By forcing all to cooperate with the party through its growing ability to sanction, the party regime lowered the benefits of noncompliance, and brought down dramatically the discount rate of the future. However, it is costly to form a central authority that is capable of sanctioning those who might otherwise find it in their interests to cooperate if they could escape the prisoners' dilemma. Political entrepreneurs are often willing to pay the costs of formation as long as they are able to win the benefits of this investment (Aldrich 1995). The president of Mexico became a six-year Leviathan or third-party enforcer who was in effect "paid" so he would find it in his interests to punish defectors and allocate selective goods to those who cooperated.[8] Further, he could take advantage of those who did cooperate and little could be done to reduce his power during his single, nonrenewable six-year term in office. He was a term-limited Hobbesian figure: even if the Leviathan harmed the interests of some members of the coalition, all were better off than they would be in the state of nature—i.e., a nation in which regional power-holders found it in their interests to raise arms against the central government.

However, the creation of a central authority did not solve all problems of hegemonic cooperation, and Calles (and several presidents who followed) worked diligently to centralize power away from the states and localities as they strengthened the federal government by creating new ministries with expanded political and economic responsibilities. Two major changes in the early 1930s demonstrated the growing political power of Mexico City under Calles, who continued to rule behind the scenes after his term ended as the unofficial Jefe Máximo. First, in 1932 Calles changed the party from a confederation of regional and local parties to a hierarchical structure that was organized from the top down, and made up of municipal, state, and national PNR branches that would decide policy and select candidates (Scott 1964, 124). The protoparties, groups, workers, and peasants associations that had been incorporated in 1929 were now forced to renounce their names and separate memberships and affiliate their members with the PNR. In a parallel move

7. With the birth of the party in 1929, all public employees had to pay seven days a year in party dues (Scott 1964, 124); this practice was ended by Cárdenas in the late 1930s (Bertaccini 2009, 27).

8. A third-party enforcer does not imply a lack of conflicts, or that all automatically obeyed the party leader. It means the leader was able to enforce cooperation so that most were better off.

on the electoral front, in 1933, federal deputies from the PNR passed a constitutional prohibition against consecutive reelection (which had before that point existed only for the presidency) for *all* posts, including federal and local offices. In part, this radical move was taken to weaken the hold of the governors over local politicians' careers and strengthen the national regime leadership (Weldon 2006). All ambitious elected politicians now had to search out new posts every three or six years, and local politicians could no longer rely exclusively on their governors for their next jobs, as the presidents came to dominate candidate selection.

In 1933, Calles chose yet another former revolutionary general to run the country, with the expectation that Lázaro Cárdenas (1934–1940), would also submit to the authority of the Jefe Máximo, as had the previous three "minipresidents," each of whom had lasted only a few years in the presidential office instead of the mandated six. But Cárdenas used the growing power of the state to weaken the Jefe Máximo, firing twenty-two of the nation's governors who were allies of Calles, and placing his people in the Chamber of Deputies, at times using rigged elections (Anderson 1971, 51).

Cárdenas's most far-reaching move was to mobilize and integrate millions of Mexicans into mass associations formally tied to the party (Hamilton 1982). Starting with a very weak organizational base, the president created the state peasant leagues that were then integrated into a single National Confederation of Peasants (CNC). Urban workers had a long history of more autonomous organizations, but the state quickly enlarged these unions in the mid-1930s and then integrated them into the Confederation of Mexican Workers (CTM) or one of the smaller union federations (Collier and Collier 1991; Hamilton 1982). Luis Medina Peña (1993, 149) writes that despite being brought into the party, the CTM still expected to enjoy autonomy to promote the interests of its members. The Popular Sector (created in the 1940s) was far more amorphous, and the largest groups within it were the government bureaucrats and the owners of small private plots of agricultural land.[9]

As a result of this major organizational shift away from a territorial party toward a corporatist organization, the party changed its name, its internal organization, and candidate selection procedures in 1938, toward the end of Cárdenas's six-year term. The newly created Party of the Mexican Revolution (PRM) abandoned party primaries and replaced them with sectoral "quotas," a system under which each corporatist sector was allocated a certain number of candidacies for different elected posts at the municipal, state, and federal levels.[10] This period under Cárdenas was the high tide of corporatist influence

9. The peak-level association of the Popular Sector, the National Conference of Popular Organizations (CNOP), was organized in 1943, several years after the CTM and the CNC.

10. All candidacies, except for governors and the president, were distributed among the sectors according to their size. For each local district and municipality, the regional

over candidate selection and policy mandates (Paoli Bolio 1985). The governors continued to be powerful political figures, but were obligated with each passing year to obey more of the dictates of their national leaders, especially the president. President Cárdenas also eradicated the armed independent groups that had survived the revolutionary period. After the end of the Cárdenas administration, which had turned to the left by undertaking land reform, nationalizing the oil industry, and socializing aspects of the education system, subsequent presidents of Mexico shifted to the ideological center, while continuing to espouse revolutionary ideals (Camp 1999; Padgett 1966).

In the party's last name change, the PRI was created in 1946 to deal with the failure of the corporate party model in which sectors enjoyed great influence over candidate selection. Thanks to the growing economy, the Mexican middle classes grew larger and more differentiated, such that the sectors were unable to represent increasingly diverse societal interests. Further, many groups within the ruling coalition, particularly the governors, were unhappy with the powerful position held by the corporatist sectors (Basurto 1984, 90). The reform formally returned candidate selection to the activist base of the party in the form of closed party primaries, which would have decentralized authority to the rank and file, while also reducing the power of the sectors. In practice, however, this proved too radical a change.[11] After 1950, primaries were dropped and the sectoral quotas were restored, with the caveat that territorial interests, especially those of the governors, would be informally channeled through the Popular Sector, which eventually became the largest recipient of legislative quotas (Medina Peña 1993, 159; Scott 1964, 142).[12] After 1950, individuals who were not members of a union or an affiliated group could join the Popular Sector. In addition, in a subsequent electoral reform (1951), the regime's leaders prohibited *any* party from holding primaries by establishing that no party could choose an internal selection rule that was "similar to constitutional elections."

The strategic importance of candidate selection meant the president had ultimate veto power over all candidate nominations, although he allowed his subordinates (the Secretary of Governance and leader of the PRI) to take responsibility for choosing candidates for some posts, while deciding among

---

council of the party would decide which sector could place the candidate, and the candidate was chosen in a district assembly in which only that specific sector could participate. Candidates for governors and senators were chosen in a national assembly with delegates previously elected by each of the sectors (Medina Peña 1993, 151).

11. José Luis Reyna (1985, 103) lists the differences between the PRM and the new PRI: more centralized candidate selection, less decision making influence for the sectoral leaders, and a stronger CEN that coordinated and regulated electoral activities.

12. Medina Peña (1993, 164) writes that the primaries after 1946 were beset with factional struggles, which at times the federal government had to resolve. The sectoral leadership disliked primaries because their candidate hopefuls were often defeated.

those who were informally nominated by governors and corporatist sectors (this is explained in greater detail in chapter 7). In these reforms, the PRI as an organization lost a good portion of its ability to select candidates autonomously. Camacho Solís (1980, 99–100) argued that the basic relation between the executive and the party changed fundamentally during the administration of Manuel Ávila Camacho (1940–1946), because several former party responsibilities, such as capital-labor conciliation, social policy, and the general direction of economic development policy, were taken away from the party and placed in the hands of different government agencies, such as the secretaries of Governance, Treasury, and Labor. Moreover, politicians began to concentrate their careers in public administration, with only occasional ventures into electoral politics (Camp 1980). The party was left responsible for overseeing campaigning tasks and mid- to low-level political recruitment.

Much of the authority that the party lost shifted to the Secretary of Governance, with the president of Mexico, of course, overseeing operations. Both the leader of the CEN and the Secretary of Governance depended on the good will of the president to keep their respective positions, but by placing ultimate responsibility for political and electoral outcomes with a secretary of the executive bureaucracy, the president became the ultimate authority over party tasks, most importantly candidate selection. The PRI, which had never been a political party in the traditional sense, evolved into a "political or control secretariat" within the bureaucracy (Centeno 1994, 51) and an electoral agency responsible for managing and overseeing the overall strategy of voter mobilization (Garrido 1993). The bureaucracy controlled the party, not the reverse, as in China, the former Soviet Union, or Taiwan.

The party's role was now established as it would remain in subsequent decades: to receive and transmit executive decisions to the organized masses, to contain the possibilities of mass mobilization with the party, to organize popular participation in elections, and to give out limited benefits and favors to political supporters. On an institutional level, the next president, Adolfo Ruíz Cortines (1952–1958), continued to centralize political and policy authority under the executive branch rather than the party, thereby weakening the possibilities for ruptures within the coalition. Hansen (1971, 107) argued that the PRI controlled popular demands, it did not represent them.[13]

By the 1950s, branch offices of the party were created at both the state and municipal levels, although in practice, many were weak or even inoperative (Story 1986). The corporatist sectors had representatives in committees at all levels of party organization, as did the territorial affiliates. Each PRI governor could choose to ignore his party branches or strengthen them; the municipal

13. Former federal deputy, governor, and Undersecretary of Governance during late hegemony, interview subject 96, disputes this interpretation, arguing that the PRI was the mediator between society and the government, not an agent of the president.

affiliates were very weak outside of the state capitals and major cities. The CEN had control over the organization's branches, and could remove leaders of the state, municipal, or district affiliates (Basurto 1984, 108), although in practice, the governors usually controlled their state party branches by paying for their activities and placing their leaders. The actual strength of the national party leader depended on his personal relation with the president, who placed him in office and could remove him at will.

The hegemonic PRI won elections through the regime's control over the electoral institutions, targeted government spending, fraud, and its record of economic success (Eisenstadt 2004; Greene 2007; Haber et al. 2008; Lawson 2000; Magaloni 2006). Strangely, considering its hegemonic status, for the most part, its local and state organs were semi-abandoned between elections (Scott 1964, 151; Story 1986).[14] But the constant electoral cycle of municipal, state, and federal contests (an election was held almost every year in at least one state or municipality) kept the party and its bureaucracy alive, as money flowed through its organization, it leaders helped choose candidates, and its members campaigned to defeat the weak opposition with large margins. Campaigning, as will be discussed in greater detail in chapter 8, was a joint effort among the candidates, the mayors and governors who offered both organizational and material support, the national party, which acted to push the PRI candidates to campaign actively, and the Secretary of Governance, which controlled the Federal Electoral Commission (CFE).

Closing off Exit Options

As mentioned above, the threats to a hegemonic party regime are often greater within the coalition than they are from the opposition (Langston 2003; Magaloni 2006). To meet these threats, authoritarian regime leaders must devise institutional and informal rules to close exit options, drive up the costs of leaving the coalition, and thereby increase stability. From the creation of the PNR in 1929 until the 1988 presidential elections, the most serious challenges to the regime's survival came from internal party splits during the presidential successions in 1940, 1946, and 1952, not from opposition forces (Loyola Díaz 1990; Medina Peña 1993). In these internal splits within the governing coalition, losing PRI presidential hopefuls first attempted to win the nomination, and when they were denied, they left the regime, formed a personalist electoral vehicle, and ran against the "official" party's candidate, with all three challengers going on to lose the general election. The first

14. Interview subject 43 states, "(T)he territorial organization and the sectors were not well integrated, meaning that the sectional committees did not have people working in them."

paradigmatic exit from the governing coalition took place in 1939, when the sitting president, Lázaro Cárdenas, imposed the informal right of the president to single-handedly place his favored successor as the party's candidate. These challenges help us capture how dangerous the threat of internal dissention was to continued PRI survival and, in that way, underline the dangers faced by the party once it lost its unofficial leader in 2000.

General Juan Almazán's challenge to the regime (1939–1940) was emulated by Ezequiel Padilla in the presidential election of 1946 and Manuel Henríquez Guzmán in 1952. The outline of these internal ruptures is as follows: first, the regime challenger moved openly *within* the ranks of the party to promote his presidential bid several months *before* the sitting president chose his successor; and in doing so, the potential candidate was able to gauge his popularity and support within the regime. Almazán left the official party to form his own personal electoral vehicle and challenge the PRM (as the regime party was now called) at the ballot booth. Because the candidate of the official party enjoyed the resources at the disposal of the federal and many state governments, the electoral match was unequal in terms of spending, and because the PRM's local machines were able to gain control of the voting stations, the challenger was officially defeated, although election day was marred by violence and many questioned the official results.

After the first and most dangerous rupture in 1939–1940, the regime's leaders worked hard to find ways—both formal and informal—to raise barriers against this type of "exit option" on the part of ambitious presidential contenders within the party, dampening the probability of future succession struggles (Langston 2002). Formally, the regime changed the electoral law in 1946 to centralize the management of elections in the hands of the Secretary of Governance and take these responsibilities away from the municipalities, strengthening the national leaders' hold over elections (Molinar 1991). In this same electoral law, the CFE was created and given the right to register (or not) all parties that wished to compete in national elections.[15] New parties had to win registry a year before the election date, which made it next to impossible to form a new party quickly when an internal PRI challenger decided to leave the party and run against it. The requirements to register a new party were steep and grew more difficult over time. Regime leaders changed the constitution so that contenders for the presidency had to leave their posts with at least six months' anticipation, which did not leave them enough time to create a new party; again, lowering the risk of rupture.

15. The 1946 Electoral Law made the registration of new political parties by the Secretary of Governance a legal necessity for the first time (Molinar 1991). A new party had to have at least 30,000 adherents, with two-thirds of the states having party organizations of at least 1,000 members. These new rules made it difficult for elite breakaway factions to form parties to challenge their former colleagues (Paoli Bolio 1985, 146–147).

Regime leaders also modified *informal* practices to block internal splits. After the first exit from the ruling party, the universe of possible party presidential successors was informally restricted to the PRI politicians serving on the president's cabinet, entry to which was controlled by the executive, and so it excluded both sitting governors and former cabinet ministers—even if they were respected members of the party (Camp 1980; Smith 1979). Second, ambitious cabinet members were not permitted to openly admit their presidential aspirations, nor were they allowed to publicly criticize other potential rivals in the cabinet, or campaign outside the governing coalition. Openly mobilizing a group within the coalition to contest the presidential nomination was tantamount to betraying the president, and the battles to win the nomination had to be done discretely so as not to create momentum for a candidate not of the president's choosing. Once the nominee was chosen and announced, losing candidates and their supporters were expected to publicly display their support for the winner and declare their willingness to work for them (Cosío Villegas 1975).

The *dedazo* (finger tapping) was the informal right of the president to select his own successor as the PRI's presidential nominee, which meant in practice the next president of Mexico because of the lack of serious electoral competition. This was one of the main instruments of regime cohesion; leading members of the PRI had to remain loyal to the president because they depended on him for the chance to govern the nation in the next term. The personal right of the president to choose his successor developed during the 1939–1940 presidential selection controversy, and after 1940, an elaborate Kabuki theater grew up around the choice of party's presidential candidate, in which all knew that the president decided his successor and placed many of his cabinet secretaries with an eye toward allowing them to prove themselves (Castañeda 1999).

By the 1950s, the probability of defeating the PRI in a presidential contest was close to zero. The centralizing electoral reform of 1946 allowed the federal government—through the national electoral commission—to control the party registry, the voter list, and the management of elections, taking these powers away from the municipal governments. In the thirty-five years between Henríquez Guzmán's 1952 attempt and the rupture of 1986–1987, no other powerful losing presidential precandidate left the party to run against the PRI's official candidate (Langston 2002). As the risks rose and the chances of success declined, the negative incentives outweighed any possible future (and uncertain) payoff. With the constant circulation of elites and the opportunities for advancement, the potential gains from staying in the regime were high. Finally, the lack of an independent labor movement after the 1950s (see below) also reduced the ability to win an election against the party's official candidate, as they could not gain support from the loyal labor centrals (Garrido 1990).

INFORMATION AND DELEGATION: THE PRESIDENT, THE SECRETARY OF GOVERNANCE, AND THE PARTY

Some argue that authoritarian regimes with strong parties last longer because the autocrat can make credible commitments to delegate decisions over candidate selection to a separate organization, such as a party (Magaloni 2008; Reuter and Turovsky 2014). This section will help demonstrate that the Mexican hegemonic presidents depended more on its political agency, the Secretary of Governance, which limited the party's strength in these matters.

Weldon (1997, 22) states that the power of the Mexican presidency over the entire political system was based on four factors: constitutional provisions, the PRI's ability to win both houses of Congress with large margins, discipline within the ruling party, and presidential leadership over the party. Elite cohesion was based on the distribution of selective benefits on the part of the president and the lack of exit options due to these large margins of victory. But the president had to delegate some of his authority to his subordinates so they could gather information, select candidates, and sanction non-compliant behavior. The Secretary of Governance had the upper hand because this executive agency answered directly to the president.

A serious problem for authoritarian parties is the information asymmetries in which the subordinate has far more information about the job she is doing than the leader who is directing the work, allowing the subordinate to shirk her duties. While elections are often held in many authoritarian states (Levitsky and Way 2010; Schedler 2006), the number of votes won by the party's candidates does not provide much information to party leaders about the popularity of the regime's policies, the quality of its candidates, or the work done in campaigns, as it would in a competitive system(Langston and Morgenstern 2009). Party leaders must choose subordinates who are loyal and hardworking to assure that candidates are in fact mobilizing voters, which is known as agent matching. Paradoxically, the lack of reliable information provided by voters in unfair elections strengthens party subordinates, especially candidates for local posts and local political bosses, because they can prevaricate about their campaign effort.

Even though the costs of sanctioning disloyal or shirking subordinates was relatively low in the hegemonic PRI because of regime control over candidate selection and the prohibition against consecutive reelection, information on the thousands of coalition politicians remained crucial because of the incentives of party agents to shirk or overstate their popularity and importance. As a result, party and regime leaders invested heavily in information gathering and in agent selection mechanisms. In hegemonic Mexico, one found an elaborate system of delegation of authority from the ultimate leader, the president of Mexico, to his direct subordinates, the Secretary of Governance and the national party leaders. Among many other duties which will be set out in the chapters below, the president's direct subordinates provided critical information about the vast array of party politicians at all levels of government. This information included factional affiliation, friends and enemies, any acts of corruption, and, most importantly, the amount of support the politician or his group could muster.[16] The regime's leaders also invested heavily in the innumerable gamut of side payments to losing candidate hopefuls to reduce the need for sanctions or repression. While violence was used against many societal groups in Mexico under hegemony, especially at the local political arena (Gillingham and Smith 2014), it was less pronounced than in many other authoritarian regimes.[17]

The hegemonic presidents of Mexico delegated part of their authority over party affairs to their hand-selected agents for two reasons: first, because it was impossible from a practical standpoint to make the enormous number of decisions necessary to keep the government and the political class functioning smoothly.[18] The personality of each president dictated exactly how much control or authority he wielded, but the delegation of authority from the president to his hand-picked agents was broad in that it covered many areas of party activity, and deep in that state political bosses and even local caciques could make some decisions on candidacies. Second, the president also delegated authority to give his direct agents the instruments—authority over candidacies, campaigning, electoral results, and information over party politicians—with which they could carry out their jobs. If they had not had the power to protect, punish, and reward, they could not have been held responsible for political outcomes. The Secretary of Governance and national party headquarters in turn delegated some of this authority to governors and corporatist leaders.

One might ask why the presidents of Mexico required *two* agents to undertake this array of political and party tasks, many of which overlapped. In other words, why not simply allow the party to carry out candidate selection, campaign monitoring, and legislative management (Magaloni 2008)? Why was it necessary for the Secretary of Governance—an executive cabinet post—to be involved in these party responsibilities? Hegemonic PRI presidents were

16. Interview subject 4. Agents from both the Dirección General de Investigación Políticas y Sociales and the Dirección Federal de Seguridad were responsible for domestic information gathering.

17. The authoritarian PRI regime used mass repression against labor strikes in the 1950s and early 1960s, as well as the student movements of 1968 and 1971, and more selective violence against the guerrilla movements in the 1970s. According to the Mexico Project data, 436 people were "disappeared" between 1968 and 1988. This report, known as "The White Book," was never endorsed by the Mexican government. The Mexico Project of the National Security Archive at George Washington University, http://nsarchive.gwu.edu/mexico/.

18. This book focuses on the political authority of the president; however, each executive also had great prerogatives over economic policies as well.

willing to pay the costs of maintaining two agents because of the importance of the information they provided and the worry that one agent would work for his own interests and not those of the president. In particular, the dual-agent structure provided insurance against the powerful Secretary of Governance at the same time it allowed more centralization over political or party decisions in the executive branch. Had the Secretary of Governance been the sole agent of the president, he might have been able to coordinate the hopes and ambitions of a section of the political class and in doing so, become a danger to the president.[19] By dividing this responsibility and placing the two agents at odds, the president was strengthened.[20] Each president in turn did not delegate full control over the electoral fate of the regime to the party because that would have placed too many resources outside the direct control of the president. The uncertain nature of the relation between the CEN and the head of Governance allowed the president to be the final arbiter of the disputes between them.[21] The unwieldy delegation model in hegemonic Mexico also provided the executive with more information in an information-poor environment in which electoral returns did not provide reliable clues as to the government's efficacy or the popularity of opposition groups.

The Secretary of Governance was a more powerful actor than the head of the CEN, in large part because he was a leading member of the president's cabinet and because he was almost always a potential presidential candidate (while the leader of the CEN was not). Because the Secretary of Governance was charged formally with the political peace of the nation,[22] he had influence over various party tasks so he could do his job: without the ability to benefit his allies and those who were loyal and disciplined, the problem of elite unity would have been magnified.[23] But at the same time, the official party would not have been useful without at least some ability to distribute selective political goods.

The Secretary's regulatory guidelines assigned it with managing the internal politics of the nation in any matters that the constitution allotted to

19. Other scholars have recognized that Governance's control over federal elections was a major quiver in its bow (Molinar 1991), but few analyzed its ability to decide candidates, monitor campaigns, and force the deputies to vote as a unit in the legislature. One important exception is Bailey (1987).

20. If the Secretary of the Governance were a potential candidate for president, he might try to replace the leader of the CEN with an ally to help him with the succession (interview subject 1).

21. Interview subject 18 stated, "The system caused the fights between these two forces, which were the executors of the president's will."

22. Interviews with former leaders of the CEN, Subjects 11, 66, 5, and 8. Interview subjects 5 and 8 are two former high-ranking Governance bureaucrats.

23. When asked why the Secretary of Governance was allowed such influence over candidate selection, interview subject 11 answered, "Go read the *Ley Orgánica* of the Ministry. The Ministry's job is to maintain the political peace of the nation."

the executive:[24] "to manage . . . the relations of the executive with the other branches of government, and with the governments of the states and municipalities." The Secretary of Governance was also formally responsible for managing the work of the legislative branch, as well as the relations between the nation's political parties and the executive, not to mention civic associations and religious organizations. If there were electoral problems in the states, that is, if the opposition either threatened to win an election or actually had won an election, the Secretary of Governance resolved them with the help of the PRI. It monitored the nation's radio, television, and print media. Finally, the Secretary of Governance operated a system of information retrieval, called the Center of Investigation and National Security (CISEN).[25]

This powerful Secretary was ultimately in charge of the governors because it was the link between the federal government and the political groups at both the state and federal levels. According to a former Deputy Under-Secretary of Governance in the Zedillo administration, the uber-ministry had informal jurisdiction over the local congresses, the states' attorney general offices, and the local justice system.[26] Agents of the Secretariat went to the states to help certain governors, while threatening others.[27] If the governors wanted to survive in office, they had to obey the mandates of the Secretary of Governance, because the secretary could recommend the replacement of a governor to the president, regardless of the constitutional term. If the president decided to remove a governor, a high-ranking bureaucrat of the Governance went to the states to manage and carry out the departure of the governor, which was costly because it meant reworking all the current political alliances in the state, especially with members of the state assembly, who had been placed by the disgraced governor.

The relationship between the president of the CEN and the Secretary of Governance was always problematic, because "they were two brides fighting for the same man (the president)."[28] At times, the interests of CEN and the Secretary of Governance were in conflict because each actor wanted more political influence. The president placed the Secretary of Governance in the cabinet at the beginning or middle of the six-year term and automatically at the top of the list of potential presidential candidates. The same was not

24. Castelazo (1985) explains the regulatory mandate of the Secretariat: to present initiatives to Congress; and most importantly, "to conduct business of the executive with other powers of the Union," including the state governments, Congress, and the judicial branch.

25. The Mexican political intelligence archives were opened in 2002. Some fascinating historical works have come from these files, such as Navarro (2010). See Torres (2009) for a contemporary view.

26. Interview subject 5.

27. Interview subject 8, a former deputy and Undersecretary of the Interior.

28. Interview subject 11.

true of the leader of the CEN. According to a former Secretary of Governance during the late hegemony, the secretary gave the leader of the CEN room to maneuver, choose candidates, and negotiate, avoid conflicts, but usually, the best future post a CEN leader could hope for was a cabinet position—not the presidency.[29] Still, the power and influence of any CEN leader were dependent on his personal relation with the president of Mexico. The president was much more willing to choose CEN leaders who were not members of his closest group within the party or bureaucracy, and so at times, party presidents did not enjoy the president's fullest confidence, which made them "weak" leaders.[30] As one writer stated, the PRI was a "bureaucratic organism that in some administrations was at the level of a cabinet secretary and in other, bad periods, was a kind of undersecretary of the Secretariat of Governance."[31]

The hegemonic presidents of Mexico did not determine their agents' *input* in terms of strategies or effort: judicial threats against angry PRI politicians were acceptable, as were a range of financial and bureaucratic side payments. Rather, all understood the general rules on *output*: stability and obedience. As long as the Secretary of Governance and the national party managed to avoid internal party ruptures or public embarrassment, the president did not normally dictate exactly how these ends were achieved.

At the second stage of delegation, both the Secretary of Governance and the leader of the CEN channeled some of their authority to the governors and the leaders of the mass corporatist sectors. State governors were responsible for most municipal and state level nominations to elected posts and could place all their state functionaries with the exception of their own successors in office, a prohibition that gradually came into force during the 1940s and 1950s to avoid state political dynasties that had flourished after the revolution (Brandenburg 1964; Camp 2010; Scott 1964).[32] The PRI state executives were also charged with supporting campaign efforts in their states, and with negotiating with all groups both within and outside the PRI regime that circulated within the geographical regions. Again, the governors conducted electoral affairs in their respective states under the watchful eyes of the Secretary of Governance and the CEN.

The authority of the president was based on his six-year ownership of political and bureaucratic assets. The president chose his own successor although he had to prepare him to be accepted by the leading members of the governing coalition (Castañeda 1999). This informal right to impose the next principal in

29. Interview subject 88.
30. Interviews with former leaders of the PRI, interview subjects 2 and 66.
31. See Vicente Oría Razo, "La muerte del viejo PRI," *Notimex*, May 25, 1999.
32. Gillingham (2014) has found that local PRI groups and the national PRI corresponded copiously over different options for PRI mayoral candidates in the 1960s. While the CEN could veto bad choices, it was the governors who had to work with these elected officials and could normally decide most of them.

the following round was crucial for understanding the stability of the organization across time periods: even though the individuals who were the principals and agents changed, the structure of the organization did not. The leaders of the CEN left their posts in somewhat predictable cycles that never lasted longer than the president's term.

The Federal Bureaucracy and the Party Organization

The PRI and the federal government were often confused with one another, because it was not clear where the resources of the government left off and those of the party began (although most observers believe that the Treasury was responsible for paying for part of the PRI's activities; the governors supported their state branches) nor who actually made important decisions in the name of the party or exactly what the party leaders and militants did, as compared to the tasks of government bureaucrats (Rodríguez and Ward 1994).

As discussed above, although the PNR and the PRM were important ideological players in the first decades of the hegemonic regime, the ability of the party to determine the ideological direction of the administration waned thereafter (Camacho Solís 1980; Stevens 1977). The government took over many party responsibilities over union matters, such as conciliation between capital and labor, as well as social policy (Camacho Solís 1980, 99; Camp 1990; Dion 2010). Camp (1990) argues that from the 1940s onward, the revolutionary generation was slowly phased out as university-trained bureaucrats took over the federal government, creating intraregime groups, or *camarillas*, that were centered on bureaucratic experience.

The political leaders within the administration began to use the PRI to manage candidates and campaigns, and gave it legal and financial advantages to carry out these tasks, although the party was never the official party of the regime, nor was it ever the only party competing in elections. Outside of campaigning, however, the national party was no longer in charge of either high-level political recruitment or ideology. Almost all authors agree that the PRI was beholden to the federal bureaucracy, and the bureaucracy did not follow the dictates of the party (Brandenberg 1964; Hansen 1971; Rodríguez and Ward 1994). Reveles Vázquez (2003c, 21–22) states that under hegemony, the PRI recruited leaders; subordinated workers' demands; socialized citizens; integrated dissidents; and promoted the government's program. We argue here that while the *government* undertook many of these activities, the party was responsible for only a few.

Rodríguez and Ward (1994, 169) write that while the PRI enjoyed the advantages of the conflation of party and the regime in the minds of citizens and voters, they were different entities, with different responsibilities, so that the party had "little to do with the structure of government, forming policy, or disbursing resources."[33] Rather, the different secretariats of the federal government were responsible for most social spending (see Grindle's 1977 discussion of CONASUPO, a major social program in the 1960s and 1970s). Hansen (1971) writes that the PRI was the electoral arm of the authoritarian government. However, for Rodríguez and Ward (1994, 170), the party's responsibilities did not end there: government officials saw the PRI as an agency that kept social unrest under control by diverting demands for social goods that the government either could not or would not deliver to lower-income Mexicans. The PRI dispensed few material goods to its supporters; rather, the bulk came though the government agencies and their programs.[34] The lowest levels of PRI officials were expected to provide some sort of clientelistic exchange and access to government programs in return for support in marches, rallies, and voting to lessen and divert the demands made on the government. However, access to social programs did not depend fully on party leaders, but rather on bureaucrats and elected officials who controlled the resources of the federal government. This distinction between party and government would be crucial once the party lost access to the federal government.

After the 1950s, as political power moved to the federal bureaucracy and away from the party structure, it became increasingly difficult for party leaders to force "their" government officials who had access to resources to respond to certain issues, especially those of the poor, a problem that became more serious during economic downturns.[35] By the 1980s, there were calls to promote "permanent action" on the part of the party, not just during campaigns.[36] This tells us that the party's branches were not active serving the needs of the population in many areas of the nation.

A central instrument of political recruitment and selection within the hegemonic regime was the small, cooperative teams of PRI politicians called *camarillas* in Spanish (Camp 1990; Grindle 1977). These intraregime teams were only loosely based on shared ideological interests; rather, they were groups of regime politicians who relied on a more successful PRI leader who herself

33. Rodríguez and Ward argue forcefully: "The PRI does not have the resources to exercise ongoing or extensive patronage with which to win friends and influence people" (1994, 171).

34. For example, in 1984, when federal spending on social programs fell, the PRI promoted a new program in which 100 CONASUPO centers (that provided subsidized food basics, like milk and tortillas), were set up in the poor neighborhoods. "Son ya cien centros Conasupo administrados por la comunidad"; *El Nacional*, November 16, 1984, 1. But these subsidies and social spending projects came from the federal government, not the party.

35. The leader of the PRI in Mexico City complained that public functionaries in Mexico City did not attend to the party's needs; Enrique Ramírez, "Como mayoría, los priistas debemos ser atendidos por los funcionarios," *Día*, November 28, 1985, 3M.

36. Alejandro Ortiz Reza, "Acción permanente, no sólo en elecciones, pide aguirre al PRI," *Excelsiór*, March 6, 1983, 1.

enjoyed access to posts because of her membership in a more powerful, larger camarilla. Camarillas protected both the interests of their leaders by providing them a group of loyal (and hopefully, competent) workers they could place in posts, as well as the interests of their members, who could depend on a higher-up to help them find jobs in the ever-circulating universe of Mexican politics. This was a crucial issue in a political environment without a civil service or the comforts of incumbency in elected posts (Camp 1990; Grindle 1977; Smith 1979). The camarilla system allowed group leaders to lower their costs of monitoring their subordinates' performance because the superiors knew the person's background and capabilities; and the subordinate's future payoffs depended on the success of their bosses, closely aligning their interests.

Some camarillas were based in the financial sector of the federal bureaucracy,[37] and for many decades until the 1970s, these well-educated and specialized members of the authoritarian regime were isolated from the rough and tumble of electoral politics, but could not rise to the presidency. Other camarillas consisted of politicians who managed electoral politics and held elected positions (Camp 1990; Centeno 1994). With the growing importance of the development state that began with President Luis Echeverría (1970–1976), the financial wing of the bureaucracy became more important in internal regime dynamics, pushing its camarilla members to the highest reaches of the government (Centeno 1994; Rousseau 1998). This change would have an important impact in the late 1980s when financial-sector camarillas were poised to take over the presidency a second time and a small group of more protectionist PRI politicians rebelled.

The Political Role of the Governors

Institutions help create powerful political actors. Yet, many of the classic works on Mexican politics and federalism argued that the governors (all of whom were members of the PRI until 1989) were little more than paid administrators of the federal government's will (Anderson 1971; Riker 1964).[38] Although the constitution of 1917 explicitly recognizes a formally federal polity (Article 40), the extreme centralization of the authoritarian regime, the argument goes, overawed the state governments. Graham (1971) called Mexican governors "elected prefects" and argued they were "local representatives of federal power" whose political role was minimal because the important political decisions, such as health care, educational policy, and national

---

37. For a fascinating view of the Secretary of Planning and Budget in the 1980s, see Rousseau (1998).
38. For an important reconsideration of the governors under hegemony, see Hernández Rodríguez (2008).

economic planning, were made by the federal government, not in the states (Brandenburg 1964; González Oropeza 1987; Pérez Correa 2003). Anderson's classic study (1971) of Mexican governors in the 1960s describes the state executives as "appointed administrators" of the president's policy programs, with no independent goals of their own. Before the early 1950s, the governors held great power both within their states and within the national hegemonic coalition. But as Hernández Rodríguez (2008) argues, the state executives overstepped their bounds when they continued to play succession politics in the 1950s, by which point the federal government was strong enough to weaken them substantially. As the power of the presidency grew, the power of the governors diminished (Martínez Assad and Arreola Ayala 1987, 109).

The hegemonic presidents of Mexico had three instruments to control their state executives. First, the national executive could informally name the PRI's gubernatorial candidates (Amezcua and Pardinas 1997; Martinez Assad and Arreola Ayala 1987). In effect, the president of Mexico appointed his governors, and was not overly limited by electoral popularity because of the high probability that even a very unpopular candidate would win an election (Graham 1971). Second, presidents could control the behavior of their state executives through the particular fiscal arrangement that had developed after the 1940s. Between the 1930s and the 1970s, governors gradually relinquished their right to collect income or consumption taxes and delegated this power to the federal government, which then doled out resources to the states in a discretionary fashion (Díaz-Cayeros 2006). Because the governors depended on the federal government for almost all of their budgets, they were unable to defy the president or the Secretary of the Treasury. The federal government also had the ability to invest public resources in different states as it saw fit, and often did so for political rather than developmental reasons (Díaz-Cayeros 2006; Mizrahi 2003, 197; Ward, Rodríguez, and Cabrero 1999).

Finally, PRI presidents of Mexico had the informal prerogative to dismiss governors who did not perform well and replace them with more obedient interim executives (Amezcua and Pardinas 1997; Beer 2003; Drijanski 1997; González Oropeza 1987; Hernández Rodríguez 2008). Between 1940 and 1995, just over 13 percent of all elected governors were removed for political failings, while slightly more than 6 percent of sitting governors won political promotions to the executive bureaucracy (Drijanski 1997).[39] In the words of former governor of Baja California Xincoténcatl Levya, who was removed from his post by President Salinas in 1989, "In certain cases, governors were 'invited to leave their constitutionally elected posts;' and in my case, I was

39. Due to the profound political struggle with Calles, Cárdenas removed seventeen governors, Miguel Alemán, nine; and Adolfo Ruiz Cortines only five. Under Echeverría, only six fell; under López Portillo, two; and four during De la Madrid's term (Martínez Assad and Arreola Ayala 1987, 109).

invited to ask for a leave of absence to take a post abroad. I must admit, it turns out it is very difficult for any politician to say no to a President of the Republic."[40]

Despite gubernatorial weakness during later PRI hegemony (the 1970s onward), the state executives played extremely important political roles that would assure their political survival and growing strength once electoral pressures began to climb in the 1990s. Political hegemony was not generated exclusively in Mexico City or by the corporatist sectors; rather, under the watchful eye of national leaders, the governors controlled their states politically, often with more repression than national leaders (Hernández Rodríguez 2008).

It would have been extremely costly and inefficient had the Secretary of Governance been forced to negotiate with union leaders, business groups, peasants, and neighborhood leaders in every state of the union.[41] The president of Mexico and the head of Governance had to delegate some of their enormous power to the state executives. For the governors to control their states politically, they had to be able to control resources, such as candidacies, money, access to business opportunities and government jobs. These relations of power and authority were usually very clear, even if largely informal.

The research done on public policy making and implementation in Mexico from the 1970s onward shows that while the governors could not decide government policy, they actively negotiated, subverted, and modified federal policy in many issue areas, including food policy, agricultural programs, and electoral reforms (Fox 1994a, Grindle 1977; Middlebrook 1985; Rubin 1990; Sanderson 1986). Grindle (1977, 127) has convincingly shown that the relationship between federal bureaucrats and governors was not one of submission, but rather, "mutual attempts at manipulation and accommodation." Fox (1994a) examined federal subsidy programs for rural producers and found that local power brokers and governors were able to appropriate many of the funds and impose political control over the rural networks that were supposed to administer them. These gains often went directly against the wishes and plans of those federal bureaucrats who were responsible for the projects.

On the political front, the governors were able to slow or modify party and political reforms that harmed their interests. When the national party president attempted to democratize the PRI's candidate selection process for municipal offices in the 1960s, the governors blocked the measure and brought down the CEN president (Hernández Rodríguez 1998). Middlebrook (1985) notes that when the federal government decided to reform the electoral system in the late 1970s, the PRI governors slowed its implementation in the states. Governors were also able to reverse the informal political agreement

40. Interview with Xicoténcatl Leyva, Felizardo Bojórquez, "Lunes Político," in *Panorama de Baja California*, July 24, 2011.
41. I thank Alberto Diaz-Cayeros for this point.

that president Miguel de la Madrid (1982–1988) held with the PAN in the mid-1980s to respect municipal and state electoral victories.

The literature on the ability of the state executives to use federal monies, resources, and programs to their advantage while blocking or slowing political reforms was not linked well to the more politically oriented studies of federalism under hegemony. It is difficult to argue that the hegemonic governors were little more than paid administrators and that federalism had been stifled while acknowledging that state executives were capable of subverting or modifying many national programs for their benefit. To understand this relation better, one must capture the nature of delegation from the national principals to the governors.

The state governors had two central tasks: to maintain the social peace and to win elections—local and federal—in their respective states. The governors were given both formal and informal instruments to achieve these goals, and the president did not tell each governor exactly how to operate politically (Loret de Mola 1978, 64; Meyer 1986; Rodríguez Prats 1990, 53). The president did not have enough information or the instruments with which to *directly* punish or reward local politicians, so power was delegated to the governors so they could be held accountable for political outcomes in their respective states.

The governors were directly responsible for the task of managing and winning elections in over 2,400 municipalities and in thirty-one states, and the federal electoral districts for the entire period of PRI political domination.[42] Political autonomy was tied to results: as long as the elections were won and organized groups did not take over the streets, the governors were free to organize state politics within wide limits. In effect, governors ran and controlled the party in their respective states (although this was always done under the watchful eye of the Secretariat of Governance and the leader of the PRI). They were in charge of the corporatist associations in their states (with some exceptions, as seen below) and they managed relations with the local producer groups. They ran state government with little oversight from their local congresses and could place and remove state judges and prosecutors (Alvarado 1996).[43]

To accomplish these political goals, the governors had to manage the dense network of political groups that preexisted their tenure in the state (and would continue after their single six-year term ended); rural caciques, antagonistic party factions, and regional business people.[44] Governors placed the leaders

---

42. When they did not achieve these goals, they were openly criticized by party leaders. See Francisco Arroyo, "Gobernadores miopes originaron los reveses del PRI," *El Heraldo*, July 24, 1983, 1.

43. See Hernández Rodríguez (2008) and Ward and Rodríguez (1999).

44. Interview subjects 4 and 18.

of the state party affiliates and could remove them; they brought in different factional leaders to state government, and placed others in elected positions (Hernández Rodríguez 2008).

Even though governors normally controlled the nominations for local posts, they could not simply impose their close friends and family members as candidates and were obligated to compromise and negotiate the municipal candidacies.[45] As one former governor explains, "every municipality has at least two families that have controlled the town for decades.[46] In most states, different elected posts would be divided up among the relevant families, the governor's close allies, and the important sectors.[47]

The PRI's sectoral organizations (Worker, Peasant, and Popular) were active in all states and usually the Workers' Sector was the most autonomous, while the Peasant and Popular groups tended to depend on the governor, who could place and remove their state leaders.[48] Not all corporatist sectors mobilized their members into national peak-level associations that answered only to their national leadership and the president. Rather, many unions belonging to the Peasant and Popular organizations were politically beholden to the governors as well as their national leaders, and had to negotiate with the state executives to win local posts (Mackinlay 2002).[49]

In addition to selecting candidates and assuring their victory, the governors were of course responsible for running state government, which they did with almost absolute impunity, as long as corruption scandals did not get out of hand. Alvarado (1996) lays out the constitutional prerogatives of the hegemonic PRI governors. The governor could veto laws from the local congress, initiate and guide laws through the local assembly regarding the municipalities, and legislate in urban zoning and rural development (Alvarado 1996, 51). Each state assembly had the right to monitor how the state budget was spent,

45. Interviews subjects 9 and 40. A former leader of the PRI's state party (Comité Directivo Estatal, or CDE) in Jalisco (subject 13) states that all governors who had national careers had to make agreements with local groups to be able to govern their states. Subject 45, a former president of the CDE of Guanajuato, agrees, as does subject 29, a former local and federal deputy in Chihuahua.

46. As one former governor explained, a governor's job was to decide between the local families based on how strong they seemed and which had held important posts in the past few terms. It was dangerous not to take these negotiations seriously (interview subject 26).

47. Subject 30, a former president of the CDE in Baja California, complained bitterly about the corporatist candidacies. See Hurtado (1993) for more on the control certain sectors had over candidacies for specific locations in Jalisco.

48. Bertaccini (2009) writes that the governors controlled the state CNOP organizations. So did interview subject 20A, who was a former member of the CDE in Jalisco, and with subject 7, a former representative of Baja California Sur to the federal government.

49. Subject 38, a former leader of the CNC in Baja California, stated that governors could replace the state Peasant Sector leaders if they chose.

but local legislators had little incentive to do so because the governor helped place them in office and would promote them after their single term in office ended (the no consecutive reelection clause also applied to local deputies). In terms of the judicial branch, the governor was charged with executing the rulings of the courts (Alvarado 1996, 57). The governors could name and remove judges and public prosecutors, effectively erasing any judicial independence. The governors had power over the mayors because they had the informal right of nominating candidates for mayoral office, and because they had the right to ask the local congress to impeach municipal governments, removing mayor and city councils. Furthermore, the municipalities were cash poor and depended on the governors for their budgets.

There was (and is) no civil service at the state level, making public jobs the temporary private property of the governors to distribute as they saw fit. The governors could name all of their government workers without the ratification of the local congress, including the attorney general of the state, and they could remove all bureaucrats from their posts. A former member of the state party in Jalisco,[50] remembers that state officials could do as they pleased as long as they had the consent of the governor, allowing for a great deal of corruption, which kept the party factions and their allies content. One former leader of the PRI in Baja California[51] stated that it became difficult for the PRI to compete in Baja California by the late 1980s because "the members of the PRI were always searching out jobs, public works projects, and licenses; it was the selling off of power."

The Political Role of the Corporatist Sectors

If the governors were in charge of the territorial base of the party, the corporatist sectors were the functional base of the organization. To understand the fate of the party after 2000, one has to capture both the problems and the advantages created by the corporatist sectors before the transition to democracy.

President Cárdenas began to organize and integrate the sectors into the party in the late 1930s (at first, the military had its own sector, which disappeared in 1946), so that organized workers, peasants, public bureaucrats, and teachers formed the mass pillars of the PRI regime. In return for certain clientelist and policy benefits, the leaders of the sectors promoted labor peace, restricted demands from their base, and publicly supported government policies (Adler Hellman 1978; Collier and Collier 1991; Hamilton 1982;

50. Interview subject 16.
51. Interview subject 32.

Middlebrook 1991).[52] Thus, the regime held political control at least in part through the mass organizations of peasants, workers, and middle class groups (Reyna and Weinert 1977).

The PRI-affiliated Workers' Sector was dominated by the CTM, which grouped hundreds of small local and state-level industrial, transportation, and construction firms into the national peak-level association.[53] The peasant central was based on the CNC, among many other smaller peasant organizations, while the unions of bureaucrats (FSTSE) and of teachers were integrated into the Popular Sector, or National Conference of Popular Organizations (CNOP). The three sectors received a certain number of candidacies in each three-year federal and local electoral cycle, and in return for this political representation in the Chamber and many other sector-specific benefits, corporatist leaders were expected to keep the demands of their rank-and-file members under control, publicly support government policies, and assure that their members voted in elections.

Campuzano Montoya (1990), Collier and Collier (1991), and Zapata (1995, 27) make a very strong case for the political importance of Mexican labor unions in the PRI regime, arguing that the CTM had direct access to government decision makers and resources. According to Zapata, labor leaders won political electoral representation and other concessions from the government, in return for restricting members' demands.[54] Formal sector workers were able to strike, and labor arbitration boards and minimum-wage commissions "link(ed) labor to the administrative structure of the state" (Middlebrook 1991, 8). However, the number of formal sector workers in Mexico was in the millions, but never was much more than 16 percent of the economically active population.[55]

The Peasant Sector, led by the CNC, also enjoyed a close, ongoing relationship with the government that was predicated on exchange: economic concessions from the government in return for political support (Mackinlay 2002, 168). Land reform and government-led distribution of private and

52. Samstad and Collier (1995, 11–12) list the mechanisms the federal government used during hegemony to keep the CTM labor unions under control, including distributing selective benefits, such as contracts, registration, and financial support. The government, at both the federal and state levels, could influence selection for union leadership posts. The PRI regime financed labor organizations and could declare strikes legal or "nonexistent."

53. For a history of the CTM, see Camacho Solis (1980). The Secretary of Labor provides a list of the CTM's affiliated unions. See http://www.stps.gob.mx/02_sub_trabajo/03_dgra/cent_ctm.htm

54. Campuzano Montoya (1990, 161) states that the CTM was able to win political space on labor conciliation boards and in the state and federal legislatures in return for its support of governmental decisions in difficult economic moments.

55. In 1950, 9.8 percent of the economically active population belonged to the Workers' Central, a figure that climbed to about 16.3 percent by 1978 (Zazueta and de la Peña 1984).

state lands into collective peasant holdings, known as *ejidos*, with all their myriad problems, allowed many Mexicans a form of collective land ownership. While president in the 1930s, Cárdenas distributed 18.4 million hectares of land, a figure that later fell to 7.2 million hectares distributed under President Ávila Camacho (1940–1946), and remained low until President Gustavo Díaz Ordaz's term (1964–1970), at which point it jumped to almost 25 million. The problem with these later numbers was that the lands distributed were of very low quality and the time that was required to legalize land rights was measured in decades, not months or years (Hardy 1984). At the same time, many of the newly formed collective holdings fell under the control of local caciques, a process that was encouraged by the government and the party (Gutiérrez 1975; Mackinlay 2002). The CNC's role in the political system was to link millions of peasants to the regime using state resources. It was a "massive, collective, and often involuntary incorporation into the party in power" (Paré 1985, 89).

Finally, the Popular Sector, the CNOP, was by far the most heterogeneous sector, and was made up of unions that represented state and federal bureaucrats, teachers, professionals (such as architects and economists), small vendors, and representatives from poor neighborhoods (Bertaccini 2009; Craske 1994, 13). The federal bureaucrats and teachers were grouped into the FSTSE-affiliated unions (Sirvant Gutiérrez 1975, 12). Teachers were brought together under the National Teachers' Union (SNTE), which is today one of the largest unions in Latin America. The FSTSE groups together bureaucrats, who enjoy with great privileges, such as benefits through ISSSTE and the Social Security Institute (Dion 2010).[56] The Popular Sector was also able to act as a broker between the government and affiliated groups to petition services, licenses, or other benefits (Bertaccini 2009, 344).

Purcell (1977) and Rubin (1990) were among the few authors to challenge the view of the strong corporatist state in Mexico. The PRI regime did integrate mass organizations into to the party to restrict demands and mobilize voters, but the corporatist sectors were only one of several ways the regime accomplished these goals, and this incorporation was uneven across the national territory (Rubin 1990, 249). As we have seen, the governors were a crucial element of this local control and, as discussed below, rural bosses were another factor. As chapter 6 shows, sectoral candidates were well represented in elected posts, but had to share these "quotas" with politicians tied to governors and state party factions, as well as those connected to the federal

---

56. The Social Security Institute for Government Workers (ISSSTE) was created in 1959 as a decentralized organism that regulated the social benefits the government gave to federal workers, such as health and accident insurance, housing credits, and retirement benefits (Sirvent Gutiérrez 1975, 15). Dion (2010) argues that the PRI regime used a two-sided approach to organized labor: first repressing its demands and then creating a social agency to serve its needs.

government. Once the economy fell into an enduring crisis in the early 1980s, several of the unions that formed the sectors found it difficult to continue to provide services in the 1980s, which weakened them politically as they could not deliver goods to their members.

The Political Role of the Caciques in Rural and Urban Areas

The PRI's municipal branches were weak in that most did not have their own resources, did not meet often, had little influence over candidate selection, and in most cases, did little party work between elections.[57] In poorer, more rural areas, the municipal PRI was often captured by caciques. *Cacique* is an indigenous term that entered the Spanish language during the Conquest, and simply signifies a local leader. In Mexico, the modern caciques emerged after the revolution, and their authority was first based on the ability to battle or negotiate the restitution of village lands (Friedrich 1965). Over time, the role of local caciques changed as the revolutionary generation died off and its successors made connections with the party, most importantly, the governors. The governors allowed the rural bosses to operate with a certain level of impunity and channeled resources to them so they could reward their followers. The incorporation of local caciques into the postrevolutionary party benefited national party leaders, because through them, the national party consolidated its control over rural areas.[58]

By the 1920s, the role of the cacique had acquired a negative tone. Ugalde (1973, 124) defines a postrevolutionary cacique as a local leader who "has total or near total political, economic, and social control of a geographic area." He ruled by threatening to or using violence against his opponents and by disbursing goods and favors to his supporters (Friedrich 1968). The cacique has also been described as a rural political broker who bridges the gap between peasant villages and the national political system, and as an economic middleman linking a capitalist national market with noncapitalist forms of agricultural production (Bartra 1993; Paré 1975).[59] Some were strong enough to protest candidate choices made by governors in municipal contests.[60] The

---

57. See Juan Manuel Magaña, "El PRI debe trabajar más en épocas no electorales," *El Día*, July 22, 1983, 6.

58. The caciques also had close relationships with the agents sent down by the PRI to the area (Bertaccini 2009, 141).

59. According to a case study of a cacique group in a poor, rural area in the 1970s, the dominant group in a village designated judges, placed the ejido leaders, decided the party representatives of the polling stations and the sectional committees of the PRI (Gutiérrez 1975, 76).

60. Luis Gutiérrez, "El PRI ante su lucha más difícil . . . ," *Uno más uno*, September 22, 1987, 1.

cacique was especially important in areas in which poverty and a lack of economic opportunities reined.

Because of this relation with the governors and party agents, local power
holders were often able to place their favored candidates in local elected office
and keep others from doing so.[61] Caciques controlled a certain level of violence, but their crimes were not usually prosecuted because of the reluctance
of state or federal officials to become involved in local matters. The governors
needed these local leaders in many of the smaller towns and villages, so it was
often not in their interests to protect the weak.

An academic dispute grew up over the role of these rural political leaders,
with political scientists for many years arguing that the corporatist sectors
of the party had taken over the role of the once-powerful caudillos (state
or regional leaders) and caciques (local, village leaders). According to many
authors not only did the sectors allow the president to dominate other political groups and parties, they eventually strengthened the federal government
against the local power holders. As Scott wrote (1964, 135), "The corporative
nature of the PRM had the effect of sounding a death-knell for the political
machines of the once all-powerful local caudillos." With the creation of the
sectors, the destruction of the smaller parties within the umbrella of the party,
and the growing ability of the federal government to distribute money, the age
of the caudillos drew to a close, and the era of what Scott calls "corporate centralism" began. Reyna and Weinert (1977) wrote that the regime had achieved
social and political control through the state-sponsored mass organizations
(the sectors). Historians, on the other hand, have recently done interesting
work on candidate selection for municipal presidencies during hegemony and
have found that in many cases, the candidate selection process within the PRI
did take into account the wishes of different groups within the municipality
other than just those of the strongest sector (Gillingham 2014). Other authors
did not believe the institutionalization of the three mass sectors spelled the
end of the local power holders, in large part because the national party used
local political bosses, especially in rural areas, to deliver the rural vote (Haber
et al. 2008; Loyola Díaz 1990, 42; Medina Peña 1993, 152).

Not only did rural caciques survive, once urbanization began in the 1940s
through the 1970s, urban caciques began to emerge. Thanks to large-scale
migration to Mexico's cities, enormous settlements grew up around the
major urban hubs from the 1950s onward. These new population centers did
not have established legal rights to the land, as many had invaded privately
owned or communal farm land. As a result, it was difficult to obtain property
rights, paved streets, water, light, and other urban services. Urban caciques
found a unique niche in this environment because they formed links between

61. "Un Cacique Pretende Seguir Imponiendo Alcaldes en Su Feudo de Hidalgo,"
Excelsiór, September 20, 1990, 30.

nonpolitical urban squatters and local government, controlled by the PRI. In return for negotiating local public services, the urban caciques mobilized large numbers of residents under their control to attend PRI meetings and rallies and to vote (Cornelius 1975, 159). The urban caciques' position depended on their ability to gain access to services, for which they were personally rewarded; they were not externally imposed by PRI leaders in the areas and the followers could oust them for failing to channel goods to the community.

One might ask why the local PRI branches did not play the role of broker, to which Cornelius responds (1975, 183), "the caciques act as ward heelers for the PRI." The local PRI branches did not play this role because by and large, they were too weak organizationally: it would have been far more costly for the government and the national party to maintain thousands of local branches with both staff and access to government resources between elections.

Once electoral competition rose in the 1980s and 1990s, caciques in rural areas were obstacles to opposition victories. San Pedro Pochutla, Oaxaca is a good example: when a local member of the PRI did not win the party's mayoral nomination, he left the party, ran for the Party of the Authentic Mexican Revolution (the PARM, a PRI-sponsored party), and won the election. At this point, the cacique and his supporters stepped in and threatened to murder him if he took office, and then blocked the highway; they then held rallies against the new elected mayor, and closed streets and businesses.[62]

During the period of political opening and electoral reform at the federal level, the local political scene was far less regulated, and national PRI leaders often had a difficult time controlling their local allies, who refused to turn over political office to non-PRI candidates (for more on the difficulties of local democratization, see Cornelius, Eisenstadt, and Hindley 1999).[63] With growing electoral competition and party reforms to open and decentralize local candidate selection, these caciques felt pressured both by rivals within the PRI and by opposition candidates.[64] PRI leaders had often voiced concern about its dependence on local caciques (and their violence), but did little about them because they helped win votes for the official party.[65]

After 2000, reports of rural bosses managing elections continued to come to light, especially in the fight to retain the rural vote.[66] Most of

62. "Caciques recurrirán a la violencia para evitar que asuma el parmista Cortés Gaspar," *Uno más uno*, September 9, 1989, 4.

63. Héctor Pérez Delgado, "Huejutla: el temor al caciquismo vs. la limpidez," *El Día*, November 15, 1990, 4.

64. Hugo Jiménez, "Acusa Valdés Rodríguez a los Caciques Resentidos del Sabotaje en el Proceso de Selección Interna del PRI," *El Sol de México*, September 27, 1990, 10.

65. Enrique Proa, "CNC, CTM y CNOP, sólo membretes del PRI, afirma la Corriente Crítica," *El Universal*, June 2, 1990, 4P.

66. For an interesting description of the role of caciques and elections in Oaxaca, see Ernesto Núñez, "Priva en Istmo coacción a voto," *Reforma*, October 4, 2004.

the rural caciques remained with the PRI, according to newspaper reports, although one finds traditional rural bosses who are willing to change parties.[67] The local bosses continue to be strongest in rural areas and with citizens who are dependent both economically and politically on a strongman. As one report states, "there is no law in the area except that of the cacique." Because of the poverty and isolation that reigns in many areas of rural Mexico, it is still possible to find these rural strongmen. But, with the rise of narco-violence, little is known of the relation between rural bosses and the drug-running operations, especially in states such as Veracruz, Guerrero, and Michoacán, where illegal drug operations have been prevalent for years.

Hegemonic Elections and the PRI

It is not known exactly how many members belonged to the PRI in large part because sectoral officials and other party leaders had strong incentives to inflate their membership numbers to win more candidacies to elected posts (Garrido 1987). The official numbers ranged from 15.9 million in the mid-1980s to under 8.5 million by 1990, after the reality of the 1988 elections forced party and regime leaders to face the weakening of the party.[68] Membership in the PRI did not automatically connote special privileges, such as bureaucratic jobs, elected posts, or public goods. Unlike the case in many communist parties, one did not have to be a card-carrying member of the party to win a government post, although one could not be a member of the opposition to be a high-ranking bureaucrat. Needy peasants who had won a small plot of land were automatically enrolled in the party's ranks, as were many workers in smaller industrial or craft unions—often without their knowledge—and these types of rank and file could be induced by their leaders to attend a rally occasionally, as well as vote on election day.

67. A former PAN mayor, Fabiola Vázquez Suet, was the daughter of Cirilo Vázquez Lagunes, who was known as one of the most prominent caciques in Veracruz. She admitted she won her race thanks to the work of her father, rather than the party label. Her father had fought with the PRI governor, which sent him to the arms of the PAN; see Carlos Marí, "Mantiene AN cacicazgo de Cirilo," *Reforma*, September 10, 2004.

68. Ada Hernández, "El Padrón Electoral del PRI contará con 15,900,000 afiliados," *Heraldo*, March 2, 1985, 1, and Manuel Ponce, "8.5 millones de priístas en todo el país," *El Universal*, October 22, 1990, 1. Of this total, the PRI reported that 3,086,000 belonged to the Popular Sector, 2,068,000 to the Peasant Sector, and fewer than 777,000 to the Workers' Sector.

The PRI was never the only party in the political system, nor was it an official party (as was the Communist Party of the Soviet Union). Rather, the hegemonic regime used the federal government and its control over the legislative branch to write electoral rules and regulations in its favor. The PRI also allowed and fomented the creation of what were called "satellite parties," the PARM and the Popular Socialist Party (PPS), whose leaders were paid by the party to offer a noncompetitive alternative to the PRI. These opposition parties existed and competed in unfair elections, with the almost complete certainty that they would not win at the polls, in any type of election (legislative or executive) at any level of government—municipal, state, or federal. As we have seen, the 1946 electoral reform created the CFE, which centralized electoral management from the municipalities to the federal government. The CFE was an agency of the Secretariat of Governance until the electoral reform of 1989–1990, so the authoritarian government was both judge and interested party in all electoral matters, such as the voter registry, party registration, and the counting of votes. The CFE and Governance thereby decided which opposition parties would have the right to compete against the PRI, and high registration barriers dropped the number of parties from hundreds in the 1930s to roughly four, the PRI, the PAN, and the other two "satellite" parties.

The Secretariat of Governance kept two co-opted opposition parties alive by channeling resources to their leaders and falsifying electoral returns (or simply ignoring their own electoral laws, as they did in the 1964 elections).[69] Before the introduction of proportional representation in 1977, the regime leaders maintained the leftist party alternatives so the center-right PAN (an authentic electoral option) would not be the only opposition party. When voters moved against the PRI, they split the opposition vote between the left and right, allowing the PRI to continue to win elections, albeit with fewer votes.[70]

The center-right National Action Party (PAN) was created in 1939 as a protest against many of then president Cárdenas's more leftist social and economic policies. For many years, few within the party hoped to win elections; rather, they wanted to educate the population in the virtues of

69. The smaller satellite parties did not meet the 2.5 percentage minimum of the national vote to win "party deputies" as they were termed, so the Secretariat of Governance simply gave them seats.

70. The Secretariat of Governance helped create the PARM. The PPS, another satellite party, always supported the PRI presidential candidate (Medina Peña 1993, 165). In the three federal legislative elections between 1955 and 1964, the opposition captured a total of twenty SMD seats, but after the 1963 electoral reform, opposition parties were allowed to seat up to twenty-five party deputies in each congress.

liberal democracy (Loaeza 1999; Mizrahi 2003). The party was concentrated in several states such as Guanajuato and Jalisco, and competed in many municipal races, but did not have a strong national party organization (although it had vibrant leadership from the 1940s to the 1960s; Shirk 2005). Constant competition and defeats at the ballot box eventually drove the PAN leaders to demand fairer conditions under which they could compete (von Sauer 1974), and the PRI answered with reforms to the electoral code in 1963 and 1977. Despite more representative electoral rules, the PRI allowed as few victories as possible to PAN candidates for local and national posts.

The center-left Party of the Democratic Revolution (PRD) was formed in 1989 from a constellation of former PRI leaders, small left parties that had grown up after the 1977 PR reforms, and Mexico City–based social organizations. Its leader, Cuauhtémoc Cárdenas, had come close to defeating the PRI's 1988 presidential candidate, and he believed he could win the next election in 1994, but to do so, he would have to unify the political left under a single banner. Due to its rejection of the PRI's hierarchical impositions, the PRD had internally democratic rules to choose candidates and party leaders. However, because of the different elements of its first members, it also allowed the free creation and representation of different wings or tribes, as they are called. Two of its three constituent bases were from Mexico City, while Cárdenas had a strong base in his home state of Michoacán. The unified left party found it difficult to expand outside the poor southern ring of states and its bastions such as Michoacán, especially since it was attacked by President Salinas in its early years (Bruhn 1999).

CONCLUSIONS

The PRI and its predecessors were a party that supported and obeyed the dictates of each term-limited president of Mexico from 1930 to 2000. After the 1950s, the party did not produce independent ideological platforms, or control access to all government programs. The PRI did not control candidate selection but, together with the Secretary of Governance, it gathered information on local and federal PRI candidates to elected offices and negotiated with other powerful members of the regime. The party did have an extensive network of municipal and state branches, but the municipal affiliates especially were weak and undermanned, while the state organizations depended almost completely on the good will of their governors to decide the scope of their activities.

The governors were crucial players in the hegemonic regime: they supported copartisan campaigns, maintained social peace, negotiated with the federal government over federal programs, and offered economic opportunities to local business interests. The Secretariat of Governance was the executive agency (together with Treasury) with the capacity to sanction and delimit the actions of the state executives.

Political institutions, such as federalism, the mixed PR and SMD electoral system (after 1977), and single-term limits played different roles in maintaining the stability and longevity of the authoritarian regime. But once electoral competition began to rise, these institutions would help determine winners and losers in the competitive PRI.

CHAPTER 4

The Transition to Democracy and the Struggles to Take Over the Party

The chapter provides an analytic narrative of the process of party change from 1988 to 2000 to examine how the first of the explanatory factors presented in chapter 2—the role of political institutions in creating or strengthening vote-winning groups—helped the PRI survive. I divide this chapter into the Salinas years (1988–1994), characterized by a strong president and the Zedillo term (1994–2000), in which the traditional power of the president of Mexico was muted by an economic crisis and rising electoral competition. The next chapter will examine the party after 2000, and will concentrate more on how the winning groups within the PRI were able to cooperate after the loss of their Leviathan.

The PRI was able to adapt successfully to the rigors of electoral competition because vote-winning groups within its ranks took over the party and defeated their internal rivals who were less able to respond to the challenges of the ballot box. Political institutions, such as federalism and the two-tiered electoral system helped define winners and losers within the party. First, the party's governors expanded their power significantly because of rising electoral competition and were able to win control over guaranteed resources from the federal government thanks to new rules for revenue sharing and transfers. Because the state executives won votes and elections in their respective states, they gained control over a larger number of federal and local candidacies, even before the party's 2000 defeat.

National party leaders also grew more powerful as competition grew because the proportional representation tier of the Chamber of Deputies and the Senate allowed them control over these candidacies. The public monies that leaders of the CEN helped negotiate in 1996 were allocated to the national party headquarters, not the candidates, so it was able to modernize national media-based campaigning and support the party in states that did not have a PRI governor. Thus, when the party lost the presidency, it continued to continue to function with these funds and candidacies for the PR lists. In fact, the PRI's leadership grew stronger than it had been under hegemony thanks to these resources and the loss of both the PRI executive and the Secretary of Governance.

If this argument is correct, then those PRI groups that *could not* post good candidates, manage media campaigns, or help finance district plurality races, should have lost their prerogatives as electoral competition began to climb and electoral rules were reformed to favor fair elections. The Workers' Sector and its affiliates were unable to place popular candidates, while large unions, such as the National Teachers' Union (SNTE) and the Mexican Oil Workers' Union (STPRM), were able to maintain their prerogatives within the party because they disbursed large quantities of money for campaigns and used their members to mobilize voters. The inability of several unions to promote popular candidates will be further discussed in chapter 5.

Finally, rank-and-file PRI activists were not able to win much influence over candidate selection because their volunteer campaign help turned out to be unnecessary. The governors and the national party office were able to pay for vote brokers and campaign workers, in part because of the lax auditing rules for federal transfers (the governors) and in part because of generous public campaign funding (national party leaders).

THE ECONOMIC CRISES OF THE 1980S AND 1990S AND THE TRANSITION TO DEMOCRACY

The PRI's transformation—from an electoral organization tied to an authoritarian state to a political party that competes in fair elections—began with the 1988 electoral scare in which former PRI politician Cuauhtémoc Cárdenas left the party, ran under an electoral coalition's label, and almost defeated the PRI's presidential candidate. This electoral disaster had three political consequences for the regime: first, it obligated regime leaders to negotiate a series of electoral reforms with the center-right PAN and later the center-left PRD that would ultimately make elections far more fair and transparent. Second, the new president, Carlos Salinas de Gortari, and his closest allies, attempted to formally restructure the party's organization against the interests of many of its internal factions to meet the growing electoral challenges. Finally, the Salinas administration overspent in the 1994 presidential campaigns to defeat a serious electoral challenge from the PAN, which was one of the causes of the economic meltdown of 1994–1995. This economic crisis led to more electoral reforms and a fiscal decentralization law, which strengthened the PRI governors at the same time it primed voters to reject the PRI in 1997 midterm legislative races and the 2000 presidential contest.

The PRI's share of the presidential elections fell from 74 percent in 1982 to just over 50 percent in 1988. This followed several years of catastrophic economic crises, downturns, and humiliations due to a drastic current account imbalance in the early 1980s (Lustig 1998) and, more generally, the end of a closed, protectionist economic development model (Tello and Cordera 1981). Since the 1930s, the Mexican state had been deeply involved in strategic economic planning, in investing in both heavy and light industry, in imposing import licensing agreements, and in establishing tariff barriers against imported goods (Solís 1970). Upon entering office, Miguel de la Madrid's new government (1982–1988) confronted a toxic mix of high external debt, rising international interest rates, and the inability to pay back the nation's foreign loans as the price of petroleum dropped. The de la Madrid government attempted a short-term fix to correct the current account deficit in its first few years with policies such as dramatic cuts in public spending, especially in social policies and subsidies, as well as increases in consumer prices for basics such as tortilla, bread, milk, and gasoline. The government did not allow wages to rise as inflation surged and also restricted union strike actions (Murillo 2002).

But these short-term budget fixes did not work, and after the economy failed to grow by 1984, a more profound and long-term solution was promoted by a group of young economists closely tied to the Secretary of Planning and Budget (SPP), Carlos Salinas. Middlebrook (1989, 195–198) reports that between 1982 and 1987, minimum wages fell in real terms by almost 42 percent, while inflation averaged more than 95 percent a year in the same period, and then shot up to 177 percent in early 1988, an election year. As businesses began to lay off workers and state-owned enterprises were closed or sold off, wages and employment fell as inflation increased (Bensusán 1995; Lustig 1998, 31; Murillo 2002, 4–5).[1] Market-oriented economists within the federal bureaucracy promoted a structural transformation of the Mexican economy: from one that was protected and guided by the state to one that was based on growth through competitive exports (Newell and Rubio 1984). This proved to be a painful process that caused the electoral backlash in 1988.

Party ruptures are both cause and consequence of authoritarian regime downfalls. The lack of serious electoral competition from the traditional opposition parties and the formal and informal set of rules surrounding the presidential succession had resolved the problem of party ruptures for several decades

1. The de la Madrid administration fought back on two policy fronts: first, a change in monetary policy, so that Mexican products could compete in foreign markets to earn foreign exchange dollars; and second, a liberalization of its trade policy that began with its entry into the General Agreement on Tariffs and Trade (GATT) in 1986, a move that had been considered under the former administration, but eventually rejected (Lustig 1998).

(1958–1987). But the economic crises of the 1980s and the administration's draconian policy response ended this period of successful successions from one PRI president of Mexico to his hand-chosen successor. The near disaster of 1988 was preceded by what seemed at the time to be a "minor" rupture led by former PRI governor Cuauhtémoc Cárdenas and Porfirio Muñoz Ledo, a former cabinet secretary, in 1987.

One of the central reasons a group of left-leaning party leaders and bureaucrats left the party in 1987 is that they would have had almost no political future if economic neoliberal Salinas won the 1987 presidential nomination.[2] The "technocratic" neoliberal wing of the PRI regime had become its most powerful faction in the 1980s (Camp 1990; Centeno 1994; Rousseau 1998), and its members excluded the more economically protectionist PRI politicians so they could deepen their promarket reforms. Opposing party leaders within the PRI used the closed presidential nomination process to criticize the lack of political democracy within the party and to attempt to block President de la Madrid's nomination of Salinas.

De la Madrid had no intention of allowing an open nomination process despite the new method of announcing several precandidates (Bruhn 1997; Garrido 1990). A more traditional candidate such as Manuel Bartlett (the Secretary of Governance) had no chance of winning the nomination. Thus, the discount rate of the future had become almost total for this group of protectionist politicians, and the once unassailable calculation of the PRI politician— remaining loyal to the party is always better than leaving its ranks—was no longer valid. The small, elite split within the PRI detonated the transition to democracy because it showed that the PRI could be defeated at the ballot box at the same time it helped created a viable, united left electoral option.

Some have questioned whether one should define the 1980s as a hegemonic period in Mexico. The Chamber votes shown in Figure 4.1 help put that argument to rest. Although the economy crashed between 1982 and 1984, in the 1985 legislative midterm elections, the PRI governors and sectors refused to allow more than a few opposition victories. Furthermore, as Lawson (2000) argues, the hegemonic regime practiced electoral manipulation, fraud, and vote stealing, all of which continued apace in the 1980s and well into the 1990s.

The wave of voter anger in the 1988 elections proved too great for the PRI regime leaders to block. This near defeat in the presidential election and the drubbing suffered by many PRI Chamber candidates was caused by a combination of factors, including six years of economic decline, the inadequate response of the government to the suffering after the 1985 earthquake that devastated parts of Mexico City, and the split within the PRI in 1986–1987.

2. Teichman (1995) writes that entire areas of the federal bureaucracy that once housed left-leaning economists disappeared.

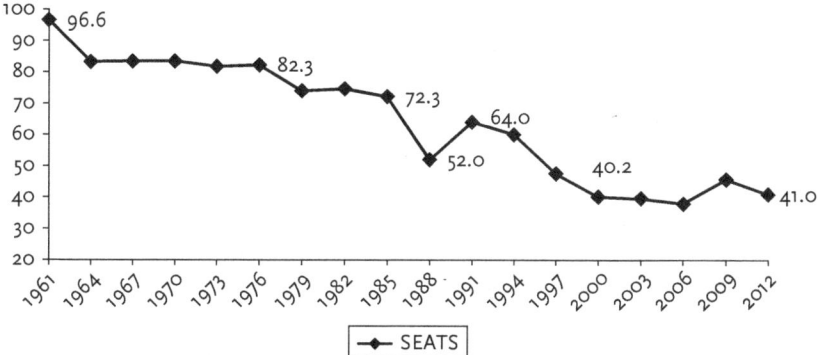

Figure 4.1 PRI seats in the Chamber of Deputies, 1961–2012, in percentages.
Source: Sistema de Información Legislativa, http://sil.gobernacion.gob.mx/Numeralia/Legisladores/
NumeraliaLegisladores.php?SID=.

PRI leaders at the time insisted that very few PRI leaders left the regime's confines in 1987.[3] While this is correct, the rupture forced Cárdenas out of the party, at which point he unified a group of smaller left parties in an electoral coalition (National Democratic Front) that gave voters a way to protest the devastating economic downturn.

Thanks to the regime's control over electoral institutions in the 1988 presidential elections, the PRI candidate was announced as the victor after the computer belonging to the CFE (an agency of the Secretary of Governance) "went down." Protests against the alleged fraud cropped up around the nation and the PAN's defeated presidential candidate (Manuel Clothier) joined Cárdenas to question the legitimacy of the new president.[4] Carlos Salinas then reached an agreement with the PAN's leaders by offering them a new electoral reform to alleviate some of the egregious institutional advantages held by the PRI in exchange for the PAN's support of his economic and social reforms in Congress. The PAN won on two fronts from this negotiation: for decades, one of its central ideological planks had been to remove the overbearing state from the economy, while it also pushed for fairer electoral laws.[5] The newly formed PRD, on the other hand, refused to accept Salinas's election as president, and would pay the price during the Salinas term, especially at the

3. Interview subject 3, and José Comas, "El presidente del PRI pide a los disidentes que cesen en sus críticas o se vayan," *El País*, March 6, 1987.
4. Clothier, a popular businessman from Sinaloa, was killed in a car accident in 1989.
5. Eisenstadt (2006, 724) writes that they had to continue negotiating IFE reforms with the PAN, or depend on their regional machines to defeat the more antagonistic PRD. For more on PAN strategies, see Wuhs (2007).

local level, as over 400 PRD activists were assassinated during the 1988–1994 years, according to the PRD and Amnesty International.[6]

President Salinas faced a dual liberalizing task: to continue to open the protected economy as well as to reform the electoral laws to allow fairer and freer elections. This was a difficult two-step dance because opening the economy required more short-term pain as many Mexican businesses were simply not ready to compete internationally, the financial and banking sectors were weak, and the public education system was a dramatic underperformer. These economic problems translated into greater voter discontent. Party leaders knew that if the PAN and the PRD were able to compete under fairer conditions, the PRI might face dire outcomes at the ballot box (Eisenstadt 2004). But President Salinas pushed forward with both reforms, in part because he created a large social spending program, called Solidarity, to mitigate the worst pain of the economic adjustment, and in part because he could obligate PRI leaders to adapt to electoral competition while they still enjoyed the advantages of belonging to the regime's party.

During his first Congress (1988–1991), President Salinas faced a Chamber of Deputies in which the PRI did not hold the supermajority required to change the constitution or certify his election. Because the new president had planned several liberalizing reforms that required a two-thirds majority in the Chamber, he sought the support of the PAN caucus.[7] As noted above, payoff for the PAN during the Salinas administration (and into the Zedillo term) was a series of electoral reforms (passed in 1990, 1993, 1994, and 1996) in which the last two hegemonic PRI presidents and their political teams negotiated a transition to democracy on the basis of fair and equitable elections, at times at the expense of their own party.

The combined changes to the constitution and the electoral code (COFIPE) from 1989 to 1996 included almost every conceivable aspect of electoral organization: a new voters' list; a new, autonomous electoral agency; a refashioned voter card; the creation of reasonable campaign spending limits; and finally, generous public funding and access to mass media for all parties, not just the PRI.[8] The changes to the constitution and COFIPE helped pave the way for the PRI's loss of its absolute majority in the Chamber of Deputies in 1997 and the presidency in 2000. These changes to electoral rules also influenced the present form of the PRI's internal structure because as electoral competition grew, it became more difficult to steal elections, which weakened those party groups that placed unpopular candidates or did not have a comparative advantage

---

6. Gerardo Mejía, "Mueren 108 del PRD en periodo de Zedillo," *Reforma*, December 28, 1995, 4.

7. The PRI controlled a supermajority in the Senate.

8. For more on the battles over electoral reform and electoral fraud, see Becerra, Salazar, and Woldenberg (1997), Cornelius, Craig, and Fox (1994), and Eisenstadt (2004).

in campaigning. The two-tiered electoral system and the single-term limits remained in place, strengthening the national party headquarters and the governors.

One of the results of the 1989–1990 reforms was to form a new electoral agency—the IFE—that was no longer part of the Secretary of Governance, although the secretary of this agency still had the deciding vote on the council until the 1996 reforms.[9] In the 1994 reforms, party representatives lost their vote on the council (they still have voice), and were replaced with "citizen councilors" who were supposed to be independent experts without overt party preferences (Estévez, Magar, and Rosas 2008). The IFE's bureaucracy and responsibilities grew dramatically compared to those of the old CFE. The IFE (today called the National Electoral Institute, or INE) is responsible for the voters' registry,[10] it places the voting booths in federal elections, it prints election material, and it trains the thousands of volunteers who work the polling stations on election day. The Institute also places public service announcements.

Campaign spending limits were included in the COFIPE regulations for the first time in 1989, but as late as the presidential elections of 1994, the limit was set so high that in practice, the PRI continued to enjoy enormous advantages because it alone reportedly received government funds for its campaigns (a charge that was denied by party leaders). This problem was finally dealt with in 1996 reforms, when more reasonable spending limits were placed on campaigns and public financing took precedence over private sources. Audits of campaign and regular party spending were also instituted, although they were and continue to be difficult to carry out.

SALINAS'S FAILED PARTY REFORM, 1989–1990

In addition to negotiating electoral reforms with the opposition, President Salinas strove to meet the challenges to the hegemonic regime on both the economic and party fronts. On the economic side, the president deepened the changes in the market-oriented, export-based development model. Once in power, Salinas controlled the specter of rampant inflation with orthodox policies that included eliminating the nation's fiscal deficit, continuing to open markets, and putting in place a restrictive monetary policy (Ramírez de la O 1996, 12). This also meant a drop both in the number of state-owned

9. Jorge Carpizo as head of Governance declined to use his vote on most issues in the 1994 presidential elections (Córdova Vianello 2008, 665).

10. A new voters' registry was formed from scratch in the 1989–1990 reforms, replacing the old list. Voters' identification cards with photographs followed in the next reform round (1993) and are considered so reliable they are still used as official identification in Mexico, rather than drivers' licenses.

enterprises and union density.[11] The president continued a restrictive labor policy that lowered strike actions, which the government controlled through the Federal Labor Law (Zapata 1995, 71).[12] The Salinas government also began the process of decentralizing certain large-scale government services, such as education and health provision to the states, but did not devolve tax responsibilities to state governments. The administration negotiated a wide-ranging free-trade agreement with Canada and the United States, although exports were climbing even before Mexico's entry into the North American Free Trade Agreement (NAFTA). The president also undertook a radical restructuring of the rural property regime when he changed the constitution to end agrarian reform, and allowed the privatization of communal lands.[13]

The new president quickly took advantage of the combination of electoral demands and the economic weakness of organized labor (due to economic restructuring) to reduce the power of the Workers' Sector within the party and strengthen what is known as the territorial base of the party.[14] The territorial base is made up of precinct and district committees, as well as the municipal and state party committees (which include sectoral representation, but are in geographic areas that coincide with political demarcations).[15] Salinas decided to reduce the workers' power over candidacies because of the low quality of their candidates and because they could no longer mobilize millions of voters (Pacheco 1990). The traditional exchange relation between the mass-based sectors—especially the workers' unions—and the government broke down after the economic crises and restructuring, and the electoral

11. Alcalde Justiniano reports (2006, 116) that membership in the CTM alone dropped from roughly five million (self-reported) members of its unions to about one million in the early 2000s. For the OECD numbers on union density, see https://stats.oecd.org/Index.aspx?DataSetCode=UN_DEN.

12. Unions must be registered by the government, which has the right to declare strikes illegal. Collective bargaining agreements and closed shop rules gave union bosses great control over workers on the shop floor; see Bensusán (2004) and Middlebrook (1995).

13. The 1992 reform of collective land holdings meant: first, the government no longer had to distribute land to those who demanded it (land redistribution ended); second, private owners who invested in their property could not have their lands expropriated; third, the ejido population could obtain titles to their plots. Those who went through the legal process could then rent, sell, and present their land as a guarantee for loans. The vote to sell lands had to be approved by two-thirds of the members of the ejido in its general assembly (De Ita 2003, 12).

14. Party leaders under de la Madrid again attempted to decentralize candidate selection for municipal posts and once again failed. Jazmín Rodríguez, "Myrna Hoyos, contra el dedazo . . . ," El Universal, November 26, 1986, 22.

15. Even before the 1988 disaster, Salinas warned the sectoral leaders that they would come under fire if they did not work arduously to win votes; see Miguel Angel Rivera, "La reforma del PRI, vital para la democracia," Jornada, April 27, 1988, 32, and Francisco Cárdenas Cruz, "Pulso Político," Universal, February 15, 1988, 1. After the questioned victory, the drumbeat of reform became louder; Yuri Serbolov, "Caciques y Feudos, Trabas a la Democratización del PRI," Financiero, December 26, 1988, 53.

disaster of 1988.[16] Because of the recurrent economic crises, the unions could no longer demand government subsidies, generous social policies, and other goods from the government at the same time as their importance to vote winning declined.

It is also important to note that Mexico's first truly unified left party, the PRD, was born in 1989, creating an electoral option to the left of the PRI which could potentially rob many of the party's typical voters who were disaffected by almost ten years of economic crises (Bruhn 1997). The result was a growing interest within the PRI in capturing the urban masses that had not been incorporated into the party's corporatist structures because they were not part of the formal economy (Craske 1994; Foweraker and Craig 1990). Craske (1994, 1–2) writes that Salinas had serious plans for democratizing, decentralizing, and desectorizing the PRI. Salinas' hand-picked choice to head the PRI, Luis Donaldo Colosio, attempted to open the party to new members to increase the party's support with voters, and both leaders were willing to do so at the expense of the unpopular labor representatives.[17] Some experts consider this a political manifestation of a struggle present in the party since the 1980s between economic modernizers and traditionalists (Hernández Rodríguez 1998), but one can also see it as an early warning that those groups that could not win votes would see their prerogatives reduced.[18] It is worth remarking that Colosio's criticism of the party before the 14th National Assembly of the PRI also included the governors and their powers over candidate selection and political action more generally. Once it became clearer that the governors were crucial for vote winning (and all the governors who had not won their states for Salinas in 1988 were removed) the criticisms against the party's state executives disappeared.

It was widely acknowledged by members of the PRI at all levels of government that many of the Workers' and Popular Sector candidates were corrupt, incompetent, and unqualified for office.[19] But attacks on sector privileges were only one aspect of the overall party reform experiment of Salinas. Gómez and Bailey (1990, 71) write that Salinas wanted to modernize the party: strengthen

16. Teresa Losada, "Nada cambió en el PRI, al fin que ni falta le hace," *Uno más uno*, March 5, 1987, 8. Middlebrook (1989, 201) writes that in the 1988 federal deputy elections, of sixty-six CTM candidates who ran in SMDs, eighteen lost their elections: by far its worst showing ever.

17. Elías Chávez, "La CNOP convertida en fantasma política," *Proceso*, October 17, 1988, 27, and Sara Lovera, "Sólo 3 cetemistas de cada mil votaron para el PRI," *La Jornada*, February 25, 1986, 5.

18. For more on the PRI's attempts to reform itself after 1988, see Arnaut (1997), Dresser (1994), Garrido (1994), Hernández Rodríguez (1991 and 1998), and Bailey and Solís (1990).

19. As one former leader of a state PRI committee stated, "The sectors will not be able to place the leaders' drivers (as candidates) anymore. They are going to have to place people with capacity" (interview subject 14, a former leader of the PRI in Jalisco).

its bases, choose better candidates, compensate the militants of the party, and make the party more attractive to a complex society that could no longer simply be placed into one of the three sectors.

The presidential attack on the corporatist prerogatives was directly related to the push to decentralize candidate selection to the rank and file (who were mostly members of the territorial base, not the sectors). Under this scheme, the workers' centrals (CTM, CROC, and CROM) would win fewer candidacies. The workers' leaders were against introducing primaries because they were aware that their potential candidates were unpopular with both territorially based activists and voters.[20] The government's leaders also ended automatic corporatist membership and once again allowed individuals to become members without joining a sector. Corporatist and territorial groups would be equally represented in party affiliates at all levels of the party (Hernández Rodríguez 1998).

Modernizing regime leaders who worked under President Salinas believed it was necessary to give rank-and-file activists some space to decide candidacies, in exchange for their volunteer work in campaigns, which would cost less and could mark the difference between winning and losing (Langston 2001). The territorial activists would win what the corporatist sectors had lost. The regime leaders would weaken labor's influence in internal party matters, allowing the party to become much more electorally oriented in a shorter period of time, because the party could nominate better candidates and receive the free campaign labor of its millions of activists in return for allowing them influence over candidate selection.

But the party's rank and file took Salinas's democratizing message too far, and in the 14th National Party Assembly, held in September of 1990, the energized activists present at the assembly rebelled against their national leadership, and devolved candidate selection for subnational posts to party members in primaries against the wishes of the CEN's leader and the president of Mexico, who wanted less radical change. It quickly became apparent that the activists might refuse to choose the "proper" candidates (those the leadership desired) which would have weakened the president's authority and his ability to control the coalition.[21] As a result, Salinas ended the party

20. Middlebrook (1985) relates that in the 1977 electoral reforms, the workers' unions had not wanted PR representation in the lower house because they feared if the legislative branch were more important, their ability to negotiate with the president would be weakened.

21. Two problematic gubernatorial candidate selection processes (Nuevo León and Colima) sealed the reform's fate; see Arturo Zárate, "Todo candidato priísta a gobernador será "de unidad," *Universal*, January 3, 1992, 1. The rules for the 1991 deputy selection process allowed for the possibility of "unity candidates" to avoid internal ruptures; Antonio Garza Morales, "Selección de Candidatos, por Consulta Directa a la Base: PRI," *Excelsiór*, May 7, 1991, 1. Morris (1993) reports that in 1991 midterm elections, 90 percent of the 300 SMD candidates were imposed by party leaders.

reform experiment in 1992 and changed the statutes to allow candidates to be chosen in conventions of "democratically elected delegates," who were almost always given only a single option from which to choose.[22] The president also realized that he did not have to openly antagonize the sectors to weaken them, and allowed many of the formal attributes of the sectors back into the party statutes, while not reestablishing the informal quotas of candidacies they had once enjoyed.[23]

By 1990, the president had developed a targeted social spending program—the National Solidarity Program—that could solve many of his electoral problems by targeting federal spending to poor areas and/or those areas with rising electoral competition, so President Salinas felt less pressured to decentralize candidate selection to the rank and file. Solidarity was an umbrella organization, controlled from the federal bureaucracy, that funded targeted social spending programs at the local level, and whose resources did not pass through the party (Cornelius, Craig, and Fox 1994). During the Salinas years, especially after the troubled 14th National Assembly, the Popular Sector saw many of its resources and tasks taken over by Solidarity (Craske 1994; Morris 1993).

The party's stupendous showing in the 1991 midterm elections (see Figure 4.1), which had been spearheaded by modernizers within the CEN, seemed to confirm that neither candidates chosen by activists nor the volunteer labor of party rank and file in campaigning were needed to win votes. Rather, a popular president who promoted economic growth, low inflation, and judicious social spending would afford the party several more years of dominance over electoral outcomes, even as elections became fairer. These two facts are crucial to understanding the new shape of the party after 2000: those groups that could not win elections or manage campaigns fared poorly in the new party's structure, while those who could, transformed the party to suit their needs.

During the period between 1988 and 1991, the different secretaries within the CEN began to modernize congressional campaigning from the national level, not in the districts (more on this in chapter 7).[24] Before the midterm

22. PRI leaders in the early 1980s had made an attempt to restructure the precinct committees, but failed; Francisco Pérez, "Reestructura el PRI sus comités seccionales," *El Universal*, July 28, 1983, 18, and Ubaldo Díaz and Roberto Santiago, "Se restructuran todos los cuadros directivos estatales del PRI," *Uno más uno*, October 16, 1984, 4.

23. The new president of the CEN, upon taking power in April 1992, stated that the sectors were fundamental pillars of the party and that they should be conserved; see Néstor Martínez, "Las reformas priístas no incluyen la desaparición de sectores: Borrego," *Jornada*, April 14, 1992, 3, and José Ureña, "No pretende el PRI desaparecer a los sectores," *Jornada*, March 12, 1992, 3.

24. Interview with a former leader of the PRI (interview subject 68), who stated that in the 1991 elections, the party undertook a national strategy that concentrated on difficult electoral precincts, but it did not have a mass media strategy.

1991 elections, the CEN organized a voter registration drive to fill the new voter registry that was mandated in the 1990 electoral reform. The CEN, with electoral experts now in positions of power, produced a new electoral mobilization strategy that was expensive and run by party leaders in competitive districts, in addition to the campaign work done by candidates.[25] This was costly but effective work, and because the party restored much of its former electoral might in the 1991 midterm legislative elections, the volunteer labor of the party's rank and file was not needed, so there was no need to devolve candidate selection to them.

A lesser-known transformation occurred during the Salinas term that had an important influence on the party's transformation: the Uber-Ministry of Governance was decidedly weakened by the president. Many have pointed out that Manuel Bartlett was the last head of the Governance Secretariat who lasted the entire term (of de la Madrid, 1982–1988); Salinas named three different secretaries to the post, and Zedillo, four. But more importantly, several important responsibilities were transferred from Governance to other agencies of the government, such as the mass media's coverage of the government, alliances with other parties at the national level, and some decisions about politics at the state level. The management of elections was moved successfully to the IFE, and while the secretary had a vote on the executive council, the electoral agency was nominally autonomous. The Office of the Presidency took over informal negotiations with many opposition actors. This continued through the Zedillo administration, which allowed the governors to become more powerful faster than might have been the case with a fully functioning Secretariat.[26] Salinas changed the dominant delegation model in the federal government and the party, and claimed more authority over political outcomes.

At the end of the Salinas term in late 1993, the administration was celebrating the signing of NAFTA and what appeared to be a successful announcement of the next PRI presidential candidate, Luis Donaldo Colosio, for the1994 elections. However, 1994 and 1995 would turn out to be two extremely difficult years that helped end the seventy-year rule of the PRI. The presidential election year began in January 1994 with an armed indigenous rebellion in the southern state of Chiapas, followed by the assassination of the PRI's

25. Interview with subject 57, a public opinion survey expert who was in charge of opinion polls for the PRI during this period; and Bruhn (1997).

26. A former Secretary of Governance publicly blamed the weak leadership of the Secretariat during Zedillo's administration for a surge in organized crime; see Sergio Cortés Eslava, "Inestabilidad en Segob, causa de inseguridad," *El Financiero*, October 27, 1999. The head of the CEN at the time stated that because the Secretary of Governance needed the support of his copartisan governors to win the presidential primary, he did not keep the governors in line (interview subject 66).

presidential candidate in March. Still, President Salinas was able to impose a second technocratic ally, Ernesto Zedillo, on the party and government notables.[27]

Even though the PAN's presidential candidate, Diego Fernández de Cevallos, began to rise in the polls after the first televised debate in Mexico's history, Ernest Zedillo won the 1994 presidential election with little difficulty; a victory that the PAN accepted, but the PRD did not. Cárdenas and the PRD followed a national, presidential strategy during the 1990s to win power away from the PRI: meaning that the only way to remove the hegemonic PRI was to defeat it in presidential elections. The PAN was willing to run a federal strategy and start winning important municipalities, then state governments, before attempting a serious run at the presidency (Lujambio 1995).

Salinas left the presidency in December 1994 having negotiated a series of electoral rules that made Mexican elections fairer, but not more equitable in terms of spending (this reform would have to wait until 1996). The president attempted a profound party reform that would have decentralized and democratized the party's candidate selection process, but soon realized that the costs outweighed the benefits and reversed the initiative. The president negotiated electoral defeats (*concertacesión*) of his own party's candidates in several states after the state election[28]—against the wishes of the party's state political class—to maintain power at the federal level and kept a firm hold over his governors, state politics, and his own succession. Despite these political successes, his last year in office defined his presidency and he unwittingly gave the transition to democracy an enormous push.

President Zedillo and the PRI's Transformation

The Salinas government overspent during the 1994 electoral year, which allowed the PRI to win with a comfortable margin, but helped set off a string of events that quickly led to the catastrophic economic crisis of late 1994–1995. After the Zapatista uprising in January of 1994 and the assassination of the PRI's presidential candidate in March of that same year, Salinas and his team negotiated an emergency electoral reform before the elections with an eye toward keeping the peace before a difficult contest. The 1994 reform was crucial because it took the IFE out of the hands of the Governance Secretariat by creating citizen councilors, and then took away the votes of the parties

27. Fernando Ortiz Arana, then leader of the CEN, was the pick of the more traditional wing of the party to replace the assassinated Colosio.

28. In the Salinas years, the opposition had used marches and demonstrations to topple several PRI governors elected under questionable electoral conditions, such as in Aguascalientes and Guanajuato in 1991, Michoacán in 1992, and Chiapas in 1995.

on the General Council where the PRI had held a majority. The next electoral reform of 1996 was influenced by the 1995 economic crisis, as well as the 1995 Zapatista uprising, and was negotiated against the interests of many of the more conservative members of the regime.[29]

Facing an economic catastrophe a month after taking office, the Zedillo administration formally decentralized government tax revenue, and informally devolved much political authority to his copartisan governors. The president did not impose his own successor in the Presidency as his predecessors had done, and organized an open primary to select his party's presidential nominee to avoid an internal rupture (although he reportedly used government funds to support his favorite).[30]

After Zedillo took office in December of 1994, foreign investment began to flee Mexico because many investors did not believe the administration's promises of continued currency stability. The economic disaster that began in December of 1994 was caused in part because the Zedillo government could not control the movement against the peso, which fell dramatically against the US dollar. In a few short months following December 1994, the Mexican peso lost half its value and the annual rate of growth of the economy plummeted from 3 percent to negative numbers.[31] Interest rates soared and because of the easy credit policy of the Salinas years, millions of Mexicans suddenly owed thousands of pesos more a month in interest on their credit cards, car payments, and mortgages than they had the month before (Lustig 1998, 196). The banks could not collect on these loans, the economy stalled, and thousands lost their jobs. Inflation surged, rising from less than one percentage point in the month of November 1994 to more than eight points for April 1995 (Lustig 1998, 198). Even though the nation quickly exported its way out of this calamity, the fall from economic grace helped cause the loss of the PRI's majority in the Chamber in the 1997 elections and the presidency in 2000.

29. The political reform was negotiated in the Secretariat of Governance in January 1995, not in the Chamber, so that liberal regime leaders could obligate party leaders and their congressional representatives to accept the terms of the 1996 reform (Hernández Rodríguez 1998, 89).

30. According to a PRI representative before the IFE's General Council, Zedillo wanted to end the practice of the presidential dedazo before the economic crisis of 1994. So, in fact, he was not obligated to do this by Madrazo's pressure to split from the party (interview subject 97).

31. The term "Error of December" was coined by Salinas when he criticized Zedillo's handling of the currency devaluation. Hufbauer and Schott (2005) write that in the last year of the *sexenio*, the Salinas administration spent heavily to support its electoral campaigns, which increased the current account deficit, which was running at 7 percent of GDP. The government issued a new debt instrument indexed to dollars, but Mexico lacked sufficient foreign reserves to maintain the fixed exchange rate and was running out of dollars at the end of 1994. The new Zedillo administration failed to calm investors and had to devalue the peso after publicly promising it would not, thereby causing dollar investments to flee the country.

President Zedillo had promised as part of his 1994 electoral campaign (before the onset of the economic crisis) that he would allow PRI leaders more autonomy in internal matters, especially candidate selection. And in fact, during the gubernatorial selection processes of 1995, the president told the leader of the CEN that she should write the rules in the most democratic fashion possible.[32] Yet, during the six-year term, Zedillo replaced one leader of the CEN with another, a statement about the true autonomy the president allowed his party.[33] Still, the very idea that a president who had been elected under the banner of the PRI would then seem to forsake his party by not guaranteeing election results created confusion and conflict. For example, when Zedillo needed to raise the value added tax in March of 1995 because of the economic disaster, he turned to his party leadership in congress to force the PRI's deputies and senators to support the harsh measure. The PRI resented his style of first denying his party and then using it to pass unpopular policies.[34]

The Electoral Reform of 1996

In this difficult context, characterized by an economic crisis, the continuation of the problems in Chiapas, and growing electoral pressures in the states, in 1996 the Zedillo administration negotiated a wide-reaching electoral reform to keep the opposition parties cooperating with the regime, while not angering his own party leaders too greatly. Many PRI leaders were already furious over the mistakes of the promarket economists and Salinas' grandiose claims that his market-oriented reforms would bring Mexico into the first world; yet Zedillo still needed these leaders to win elections and important votes in the legislature.

The electoral reform of 1996 was profound in breadth and scope: the IFE became fully autonomous from the Governance Secretariat, which no longer had a vote on the council. The councilors were now selected by members of the Chamber of Deputies, making IFE autonomous from the executive (but not from the parties in congress, which still controlled the selection of councilors, the IFE's budget, and the ability to reform the nation's electoral law). Regime and party leaders negotiated the rules to funnel public money to the national party offices. Because of the enormous advantages the PRI enjoyed in campaigning, the new COFIPE had to provide generous public financing, but these funds are disbursed by the national party headquarters—not directly to

32. Interview subject 9, one of the presidents of the CEN during Zedillo's term.
33. They were: Ignacio Pichardo, María de los Ángeles Moreno, Santiago Oñate, Humberto Roque Villanueva, Mariano Palacios Alcocer, José Antonio González Fernández, and Dulce María Sauri.
34. Interview subject 66, a former leader of the CEN during this period.

the candidates.[35] And while all parties enjoy access to mass media, as of 2008, candidates are prohibited from buying advertising spots. Candidates had to be registered by a party to appear on the ballot until 2015, and no elected official can run for the same post in the next period until 2021.

Money had always been an extremely important issue in Mexican hegemonic elections because the PRI alone benefitted from government resources while the opposition parties had worked under severe resource scarcity (Castañeda 1991; Eisenstadt 2004). Under hegemony, the resource-poor opposition faced PRI candidates who collectively received millions of pesos to run campaigns, mobilize voters, and deliver selective goods during campaign season (as will be discussed further in chapter 8 on campaigns). Two related problems had to be solved: first, reasonable spending limits with credible sanctions had to be established; and second, all parties—not just the PRI—had to receive public funds for campaigns.

The internal party groups that could support both local and federal campaigns became stronger as a consequence of the new electoral rules passed in 1996. The electoral reforms negotiated by the president and the national party leaders of all the major parties converted the leader of the CEN of the PRI into a far stronger actor *after* 2000 because the laws provided parties with millions of dollars' worth of public financing yearly that was not dependent on the Secretary of the Treasury. The public money meant that low-level party activist volunteer labor was not needed as the party could pay for vote mobilizers, because it allowed the party to modernize its campaigns, and because it gave the CEN the ability to operate even when the PRI did not hold the presidency.

President Zedillo pursued these reforms because he was playing a two sided game: one with the opposition party leaders and the other with his own party's hardliners, some who were able to win or organize elections, and others who had little hope of competing successfully (Brinegar, Morgenstern, and Nielson 2006). The president calculated he could convince some of his party's hardliners to accept further electoral reforms if they benefitted, which they did in terms of campaign finance, continued control over office seekers, and candidacies for the PR lists. During the last hegemonic PRI presidential term, the groups within the PRI that could manage, support, or pay for campaigns and place popular candidates won more power within the party and more resources. Once the term had ended, and the PRI lost the presidential contest in 2000, these groups took over the party.

35. One of the reasons for this is that the parties in the constitution are political entities, and only they, not the candidates, can be held legally responsible for violations of the COFIPE. I thank Leonardo Valdéz for pointing this out to me (personal communication, October 22, 2012).

The Rise of the Governors

This period of crisis after 1995 and the administration's response to it marked the true rise of the governors onto the national political stage, where they had not been permitted to shine since the 1950s (Rodríguez Kuri 2008; Scott 1964). The 1994–1995 economic disaster and growing electoral pressures allowed the governors to challenge the hierarchical structure of the PRI regime. As discussed above, one of the informal prerogatives of the hegemonic presidents of Mexico was to remove governors at will. President Zedillo would not have this same power because the governors were at the front lines of electoral competition and were able to win battles against the president and his Secretary of Governance that their predecessors had lost as late as the Salinas term. This growing gubernatorial power helped the party survive once it lost the presidency.[36]

Because of the staggered electoral calendar, some states hold their gubernatorial elections before the current president takes office and others after the beginning of the presidential term. Those hegemonic governors who took office under the former president operated politically under a new president, which often created friction. For example, a Salinas ally had won the PRI's gubernatorial nomination in the oil-rich state of Tabasco in mid-1994 while Salinas was still in power, but ran for office when Zedillo was about to assume the presidency. Tabasco was the home state of a charismatic local politician, Andrés Manuel López Obrador, who had left the PRI in the late 1980s and now posed a serious risk as a candidate for the PRD in the 1994 governor's race, against the PRI's candidate, Roberto Madrazo.

With growing electoral competition, the interests of local PRI leaders and the national regime bosses began to diverge: the national leaders, beginning with Salinas, were willing to "sacrifice" some states and large municipalities to the opposition to keep the presidency and the majorities in both houses of congress in the hands of the PRI. However, local members of the PRI were far more interested in the political fate of their home state, and would lose everything in the event of a gubernatorial defeat or the downfall of the PRI governor through negotiations between national regime leaders and the opposition.

36. For example, the governor of Quintana Roo allegedly had ties to drug cartels. The administration knew this, and it came out in a *New York Times* article while he was still in office; yet, Zedillo did not remove him. The weakness of the president against his copartisan governors should not be exaggerated, however. Zedillo eventually removed the governors of Chiapas, Guerrero, and Morelos because of mass murders in Acteal and Aguas Blancas and because of charges of involvement in criminal activities. None of the governors were criminally prosecuted except Mario Villanueva of Quintana Roo; the others asked for a leave of absence from their posts.

When it appeared that the new governor of Tabasco, Roberto Madrazo, would soon be sacrificed by the new president because of mounting evidence of gross electoral fraud, local forces tied to the PRI both in Tabasco and in the State of Mexico were able to push back against Zedillo by gathering a group of business and political leaders to block the president's attempt to bring down the newly elected governor. Instead of Madrazo losing his post, the Secretary of Governance was sacked, a shocking reversal of forty years of PRI centralism and weak federalism.[37]

A second element of growing subnational power was Zedillo's decision to decentralize and formalize both shared tax revenue and earmarked government transfers. The 1994–1995 economic crisis helped spur a fiscal decentralization of federal transfers to state governments, increasing the electoral strength of the governors, who now had more resources to spend in their states both on infrastructural projects and on copartisan campaigns. To understand the importance of Zedillo's fiscal reforms in 1998, one has to grasp the extremely centralized nature of Mexico's fiscal regime up to that date. Díaz-Cayeros (2006) relates that the tax coordination system between the states and the federation had grown up around a series of political agreements dating from the 1920s that were finalized in the late 1970s. Over several decades, PRI governors had, one by one, delegated their state's financial authority to the federal government in return for economic development support.

The states gave up their right to collect taxes and, in return, received unconditional transfers (*participaciones*) out of the collection of revenue from exclusive federal excises. State budgets were filled mostly through these revenue-sharing agreements because after 1980, state governments generated almost none of their own revenue (Díaz-Cayeros 2006; Flamand 2006). But the states had to negotiate yearly with the agencies of the federal government, which distributed funds as it saw fit, making long-term planning difficult because there was no legal certainty that the states would receive the same resources in subsequent years (Ortega 2004, 12).

Before the fiscal decentralization under Zedillo, PRI governors could not win control over political assets in part because of their budget vulnerability. Governors would not challenge the president on most of his policies or candidate choices since they did not raise their own funds. Flamand (2006, 353) argues that opposition governors (those from the PAN and the PRD), as well as PRI governors from competitive states, were on the frontlines of pressuring the federal government for greater rule-bound allocation of annual transfers of federal resources to the states.[38] Another specialist states that

---

37. See Eisenstadt (1999) for a complete recounting of this episode.
38. Governors have a great deal of discretion over how they allocate federal funds. Local congresses do not play much of an oversight role and there is little punishment for noncompliance with federal mandates (Pardinas 2008).

President Zedillo was worried about the debt load of states in the aftermath of the 1995 economic crisis (Hernández and Jarillo 2008). Regardless of the reasons for the fiscal decentralization, the PRI governors quickly took advantage and became even more important political actors.

The power enjoyed by PRI governors is greater than their PAN and PRD counterparts because the PAN state executives had to respond to their president between 2000 and 2012, while the PRD has more independent factions than those of the PRI.[39] Even in those states with a PRD governor, the party's state factions do not always align with their governor. Finally, the PRI has far more governors than either of the other two parties, and so they are proportionally a much larger political force within their party than those in the PAN or PRD.

Today, state governments spend millions of pesos of federal money with little accounting oversight. First, the governors receive revenue-sharing monies (Ramo 28) that are state taxes collected by the federal government and are accountable only to their state legislatures. Because the governors normally control party majorities in their state assemblies, state legislators exercise little effective oversight over budgets. Second, earmarked transfers (Ramo 33) are sent to the states, roughly 65 percent of which is channeled directly to pay teachers' and doctors' salaries (Ortega 2004). In practice, the federal government finds it difficult to audit how the rest of these funds are spent (Pardinas 2008). Third, governors rely on the resources that the various ministries of the federal government spend in their states, with highways, credit programs, and public health programs being of central importance (Hernández and Jarillo 2008). Finally, during several years covered in this study (2000–2012), oil prices rose steadily and the governors won a fair-sized share of the windfall profits from the state-owned oil monopoly, Mexican Petroleum Company known as PEMEX; (Pardinas 2008).

This is a governor's perfect world—what Diaz-Cayeros (2006) has called perverse federalism. As a result of enormous outlays of both revenue sharing and conditional transfers, the state executives are rich; as a result of weak accounting institutions, they can mostly spend as they chose, and many choose to spend on visible infrastructural projects and local clientelist exchange, activities that win votes.

Because the PRI governs so many states, the party can perform badly in a presidential election and continue to do well in local and federal races because of the governors' support. Gubernatorial popularity helps copartisans win votes in both local and federal elections (Magar 2012). As will be shown in the campaign chapter, governors are active supporters of their copartisan Chamber candidates. And because public campaign finance money is allocated

---

39. Interview subject 86, who had been a powerful member of the PRI but later joined the PRD because of a candidacy dispute.

to parties based on their showing in the last federal Chamber races, the governors (of all parties) play a central role in helping their parties win more resources by supporting their copartisan federal deputy candidates.

A Party Reform (1996) that Could Not Be Reversed

With growing electoral pressures, the internal balance of power between the president of Mexico and the CEN, as well as between the national party and its state affiliates, began to change. Federal institutions, combined with competitive plurality elections, reworked the existing relations among these actors. The PRI's governors avidly sought more control over candidate selection for all elected posts, at the same time they fought to be considered for their party's presidential nominations.

Since Lázaro Cárdenas selected Manuel Ávila Camacho to succeed him in 1939, the PRI's presidential candidate had been chosen informally from among members of the presidential cabinet, *not* from a wider pool of politicians within the PRI coalition, such as the governors and senators. This allowed the autocrat greater control over his powerful governing elite because the president single-handedly controlled who won and kept a cabinet post, while many different regime actors were involved in choosing candidates for elected posts. The president selected his secretaries based not only on their competence in office, but also on their loyalty to him and their expected role in the presidential succession (Castañeda 1999; Langston 2006). Once the choice had been made public (*el destape*, or unveiling) in the fall of the fifth year of the six-year term, all *priístas*—including the losing precandidates—rushed to support the president's choice (*la cargada*) or risked the wrath of the new president.[40]

At the end of the Zedillo presidential term, the ambitious PRI politicians who were not on the president's cabinet had to revoke the informal rule that limited the universe of potential candidates to cabinet secretaries if they hoped to compete for the 2000 presidential nomination. With the reforms of the 17th National Assembly of the PRI, held in 1996, two of the party's governors positioned themselves to compete for the presidential nomination against the president's interests. The 17th National Assembly can be seen as a gubernatorial-party leader rebellion against the more technocratic wing of the regime (Langston 2001, 508). Both governors and the party's professional electoral managers had by this point realized that their skills at the ballot box

40. See Castañeda's excellent 1999 book on the topic, which explains how each president protected and promoted his choice of successor against other leaders within the coalition.

were increasingly valuable in the age of rising electoral competition, which elevated their status as potential presidential candidates, even though they were *not* holding cabinet posts. During the 1996 party assembly, the formal statutory rules were rewritten to reverse decades of informal presidential control over the succession, and unlike President Salinas, President Zedillo was not strong enough to eliminate the statutory changes. As a result, the informal prerogative was taken from the president to decide his successor.[41]

After the calamitous downturn in the economy in 1995, the 1997 legislative midterms presented a grave challenge. Added to the fury and disappointment of Mexican voters, the regime's leaders had to deal with the consequences of the 1996 party assembly and electoral reform negotiated and passed the same year. Zedillo still had many legislative projects he wanted to see enacted in the second half of the term and would need at least a simple majority to do so. This laid the foundation for another change in PRI practice: knowing the difficulties presented by the economic situation, the president of Mexico allowed the national party leadership to give sitting PRI governors more authority over the 1997 midterm plurality candidacies for the lower house in their respective states—far more than had been the case during traditionally.[42] The effects of the gradualist electoral reforms (passed in 1990, 1993, 1994, and 1996) made it difficult for the PRI to steal votes or pad the results, forcing the party to choose more locally based and popular candidates—not simply representatives of different groups within the party. Thus, the governors were able to trade off their electoral responsibilities for greater influence over federal plurality candidacies, even before the party's defeat in 2000. This gave them greater power within the party even before 2000.[43]

The second step for the PRI governors was to win control over placing their preferred successors in the governor's mansion. As electoral competition grew and the possibility of winning the general election under the banner of an opposition party rose, strong PRI politicians in the states began to leave the party

41. Two PRI governors, Roberto Madrazo and Manuel Bartlett, each sent an ally to the podium to protest the current wording of the requisites to be a PRI presidential candidate. The president's allies sent a changed version of the statutes in which hopefuls had to have been *either* leaders of the party, *or* have held elected office, *or* have been a member for twenty years. During the tumultuous meeting, the wording was changed to, "have been a member, *and* have been a party leader, *and* have held elected office."

42. Interview subject 23, who worked with the leader of the SNTE during the 1997 selection process; and with a former leader of the CEN, who stated that the sectors' participation in candidate selection for the Chamber was reduced (subject 66). Another former leader of the CEN (subject 68), states that governors and sectors were both involved in the selection process.

43. Before the final defeat of the PRI in 2000, some leaders warned that if the president of Mexico pulled away from party affairs, one could expect the return of "caudillos, governors, mayors, or regional caciques"; see David Carrizales, "Riesgo de que caudillos, gobernadores, y alcaldes tomen el control del PRI," *La Jornada*, October 31, 1998.

when they were passed over in the nomination. The CEN and the Governance Secretariat turned to open primaries to select the gubernatorial standard-bearer in several states. However, sitting PRI governors began to use these primaries to impose their favored ally as the party's candidate (this point is explored in more detail in chapter 5).

Party factions began to prepare their strategies going into the 1999 presidential nomination for the 2000 elections. In early 1999, the head of the CEN announced that the party would change the PRI's formal selection procedure: instead of the traditional delegate convention method (in which the president's choice was simply ratified by standing ovation), the party would hold an open primary of all registered voters. The president of Mexico was willing to allow an open primary in 1999 in part to avoid another devastating rupture within the PRI and in part because he believed the party and its eventual candidate would win more support if it could show that it was independent from the regime.[44] Zedillo reportedly spent federal government resources to sway his copartisan governors to support his choice, former Secretary of Governance, Francisco Labastida, who then won the party primary with a convincing margin.[45] Former governor of Tabasco, Roberto Madrazo, recognized his defeat in the primary,[46] although there were rumors that Madrazo's operatives in the southeast region of the nation did not support Labastida's general electoral campaign the following year. By not leaving the party, Madrazo paved the way toward becoming the PRI's presidential candidate in the 2006 elections.

Neoliberal Economists against the Traditional PRI Politicians

Many authors writing on the change in the PRI during the 1990s concentrate on the ideological battle between the technocrats within the economic or

44. Interview subject 97 recalls that when Zedillo was still president-elect, he argued that a primary should be considered for the next succession round. See also "Favorece Zedillo primarias en el PRI," *Reforma*, June 10, 1998, 1.

45. Several governors reportedly supported Labastida, including those of Chiapas, Coahuila, Durango, Hidalgo, Mexico, Michoacán, Puebla, Quintana Roo, San Luis Potosí, Sonora, Tamaulipas, Veracruz, and Yucatán. See Enrique Méndez, "Madrazo Pintado y Roque Villanueva Exigen Se Aplique Sanciones . . . ," *La Jornada*, October 30, 1999; "Establece Madrazo condiciones para aceptar la derrota," *El Economista*, November 2, 1999; and "Preparan Fraude Para Favorecer A Labastida," *El Diario de Chihuahua*, November 1, 1999. Zedillo issued a warning to governors to stop favoring one candidate over others.

46. The total number of votes in the 1999 primary was a healthy 9,722,576, of which Labastida won 5,337,545 and Madrazo, 2,766,866, with the remaining two candidates sharing the rest. Many believed this figure is inflated, but use it as a base-line of strong party identifiers.

financial wing of the executive bureaucracy and the more traditional politicians who were active in the electoral side of PRI duties as well as the "control" apparatus of the federal government (Governance, Labor, Agriculture, among others).[47] According to this line of argument, because the neoliberal economists took control of the government during the de la Madrid administration (1982–1988) and during the following two six-year terms, traditional political abilities such as campaigning, mobilizing voters, and negotiating were undervalued. Many leaders within the PRI—especially governors from the poorer states—criticized the regime's neoliberal policies because they hurt workers and the poor, the traditional bases of the party's vote. Opening the economy to foreign investment harmed domestic industry and drove up unemployment, while reduced social spending weakened the social bases of support for the government and created tensions among the government and its corporatist sectors (Reyes García 2005, 64). Many traditional PRI politicians believed the technocrats simply did not understand the electoral consequences of their neoliberal reforms.[48]

As we have seen, Presidents Salinas and Zedillo took advantage of formal sector labor groups' economic weakness to reduce their importance within the PRI, as measured by candidacy allocation. The cleavage between neoliberal economic reformers (who were not necessarily prodemocratic) and economic traditionalists helps explain the rupture of 1987 and the reforms to the party in the early 1990s, but by the end of the decade, the internal party battles had become more political than economic. Conflicts over electoral reform, negotiated electoral outcomes, campaign strategies, and of course, candidacies all became more important than whether to continue the export-oriented development model, which many saw as irreversible by 1999. The technocrats may have won the economic battle, but they would lose the political war, in large part because they were not good candidates for legislative posts, mayors, or governors, as can be seen in the recruitment figures presented in chapter 7. The end of the technocrats' control of the PRI came when Zedillo's choice to succeed him—another more technocratic PRI politician—lost the 2000 presidential election. In this dual economic-political transition, economic reformers worked within the hegemonic party, but lost control over the political transition to those more electorally oriented elements who managed campaigns and won elections.

47. For more on this debate, see Camp (1990), Centeno (1994), Espinoza Toledo (2004), Hernández Rodríguez (1998), Reyes García (2005), and Rousseau (2010).
48. According to one source, the governor of one of the nation's poorest states went to speak to an Undersecretary of the Treasury in the mid-1990s, and reprimanded the undersecretary for not understanding the potential for popular unrest if his state did not receive more money from the federal government (interview subject 98).

TESTABLE IMPLICATIONS OF THE 1990S NARRATIVE

Before turning to how the PRI changed after 2000, this section will reexamine the observable implications of the argument presented in chapters 1 and 2. While some party factions grew stronger thanks to the demands of electoral competition, others were unable to adjust. In the years between the near electoral disaster of 1988 and defeat of 2000, the PRI governors became more powerful because of their ability to support elections, which allowed them to win greater influence over candidate selection from the president and his two agents, the Governance Ministry, and the CEN. The state executives from all parties also won guaranteed fiscal resources from the federal government, which then further strengthened their electoral power.

Political institutions played an important role because they determined how votes would be won, and therefore, which party actor was best able to take advantage of competition. National party leaders were able to negotiate electoral reforms with the opposition that gave them resources to allow them to survive the party's 2000 defeat. These reforms also reiterated the power of the party leaders over legislative office seekers in the requirement for party registry of all candidates for elected office, the continuance of no consecutive reelection, and centralized public campaign finance. Because of control over resources and the mixed majoritarian electoral system, the national party office took over the candidates of the PR closed list, although it negotiated these with its governors.

The party's rank-and-file activists were briefly strengthened in the *early* 1990s because of President Salinas's belief that their voluntary labor was necessary to mobilize voters and support campaigns, which would allow him to weaken the sectors and the governors. In return for their work in campaigns, they would receive more influence over candidate selection. However, the democratizing reform within the party was short-lived because it gave activists power over the future careers of party politicians, marginalizing the regime's leaders. Furthermore, it became apparent that the party did not need volunteer activist labor as long as it had the funds to mobilize voters. Despite many claims to the contrary, rank-and-file activists remained weak. Even though open primaries were again used in the late 1990s to select both gubernatorial and presidential candidates, in these cases the governors played a crucial role in the mobilization of vote brokers.

The corporatist sectors, especially the unions incorporated into the Workers' Central, did badly in both the economic and the party reforms. The CTM leadership saw its legislative candidacies fall as the decade wore on. Competition at the district level was not kind to the Workers' Sector as its candidates tended to be unpopular. Other unions, such as the National Teacher's Union and the PEMEX Union, remained politically relevant because of their large, captive membership and the resources they controlled, both of which were useful for vote winning. These leaders continue to win posts in the Chamber and the Senate via the closed PR lists.

CHAPTER 5

The Challenges of (Authoritarian) Party Survival after Democratization

This chapter focuses on why the PRI was able to survive its exit from the executive after its defeat in the 2000 presidential race. Many former authoritarian parties are at risk when they lose state resources and the ability to manipulate electoral institutions and outcomes, principally from the ever-present threat of internal ruptures or because voters reject the party label. Ambitious politicians might find it easier to leave the party and run for another electoral option if they are denied a nomination. While an exit might be an individually rational option, the collective outcome is an exodus from the party label and its possible collapse. Without control over the national bureaucracy, the party leadership loses its ability to promote clientelist vote buying with national government funds and other methods of electoral manipulation.

However, former authoritarian parties also enjoy many advantages even after the transition to democracy. First, parties that once supported the authoritarian regime are often the strongest electoral option in their respective party systems, while opposition parties either do not exist at the beginning of the transition or are relatively unknown because they have never governed (Magaloni 2006). This fact has two consequences: first, many former authoritarian parties continue to enjoy high levels of party identification, especially those that have governed relatively successfully (i.e., taken their nation through the process of modernization, such as Indonesia and Taiwan) or at least have not chosen to employ high levels of repression (Grzymała-Busse 2002; Rizova 2008; Slater and Wong 2013; Tan 2001).

Second, former authoritarian parties usually enter democracy with a stronger party organization—based on their clientelist networks or territorial affiliates. Taiwan's KMT is a clear example of the power of local clientelist networks that survive transitions (Cheng 2008). As a result, some former authoritarian parties continue to win subnational and legislative elections, even if they were defeated in the national executive contest. The Communist Party of the Czech Republic, for example, won substantial percentages in both subnational and parliamentary elections, although it never moderated its socialist nature and no other party would enter with it in a formal governing coalition (Rizova 2008). Finally, if the outgoing authoritarian regime and party leaders were able to participate in the creation of new electoral rules, they can negotiate new electoral codes that benefit their interests or those of all party organizations (Grzymała-Busse 2008; Riedl 2014).

Slater and Wong (2013) also examine how authoritarian parties can modernize and transform the economy, and, in doing so, "regenerate" while allowing the democratization of the regime. In the same work, the authors argue that a wide-ranging structure of territorial party affiliates and experienced candidates for elected office are two other resources that former authoritarian parties possess that their weaker opposition rivals do not. Finally, Loxton (2016) highlights voters' knowledge of the former authoritarian party, its clientelist network and sources of financing, all of which surpass those of rival opposition forces.

As noted in chapter 1, the present work on the PRI contributes to this literature on authoritarian party survival under democracy; first, by clarifying how the resources that help win elections are transmitted through time within the now former authoritarian party. Authoritarian parties have both positive and negative legacies, and it is not clear how the positives survive while those that promoted authoritarian relations, impositions, fraud, press manipulation, corrupt unions, extrajudicial actions, among many others, simply fade away (if they in fact do disappear). The case of the PRI demonstrates that the groups that were able to carry the vote-winning resources into the competitive age were those that had been directly involved in campaign management and support during the hegemonic era: the governors and the leaders of the national party office. Those groups that did not have the capacity to win votes, on the other hand, lost power within the party to determine candidacies and posts, which allowed the party to continue to win elections and, in doing so, survive the transition to democracy.

Second, almost all authoritarian parties are faced with divisions in the difficult years of the transition as ambitious politicians leave their ranks; but some party organizations are able to maintain value for voters and politicians and remain united. This chapter shows why Mexico's authoritarian party resisted the tendency to fragment when it was forced to meet the challenges of the ballot box without its Leviathan. So, even though the PRI experienced a split during the early years after its 2000 defeat, it was able to minimize the damage because most politicians and voters continued to use the label to win office and choose representatives and executives.

Noam Lupu (2014) argues that since the beginning of the third wave of democratization in the 1980s, several established Latin American parties dissolved because of a process he calls "brand dilution," in which party leaders retracted decades-old economic policies and formed coalitions with traditional rivals in an effort to win votes. But in doing so, the parties lost their connections to their traditional voting base, leaving them more vulnerable to short-term economic setbacks. Because parties cannot depend on voters to support their brand when the economy turns sour, electoral volatility grows and some parties disappear. Mexico's PRI was spared this fate because it began the profound and painful process of economic restructuring in the early 1980s, before it had to compete in fair elections (which began in 1997, with the passage of the 1996 electoral reform). Furthermore, the PRI brand was not just based on a protectionist development model, but also clientelist mobilization. Once the governors were able to control federal resources, they were able to maintain a good deal of these more traditional instruments as well as devise and implement new ones.

Political institutions play a critical role in explaining which former authoritarian parties survive the difficult transition to democracy and which fragment beyond repair. Federalism promotes strong state-level political arenas because of resources and political opportunities. Mexico's unique set of electoral rules also played an important role in helping the PRI survive. The most important of these rules were the mixed electoral system, generous public funding for parties, and single-term limits. The two-tiered mix of 300 SMDs and 200 proportional seats in the 500-member Chamber of Deputies allowed the national party to reserve some of these candidacies for its allies, while also giving it the ability to negotiate with leaders of the party's different groups. The SMD seats gave the governors a great deal of power over candidacies for their states' politicians, keeping them loyal to the state executive. The public funds disbursed by the national electoral authority (IFE, now INE) were sent to national party headquarters, not directly to the candidates; the majority of this money was then spent on national media appeals before 2008, leaving the candidates dependent on their governors and, if they did not have a copartisan boss, on the party itself.

In the aftermath of the 2000 defeat, the party was in disarray, as its factions fought over who was to blame for the defeat and who would lead the party in the absence of a PRI president.[1] But in the mid- to long term, PRI

---

1. For more on the worries over divisions within the PRI after the 2000 defeat, see: "Consecuencias de la derrota del PRI," *Diario de Yucatan*, July 31, 2001; "La división en el PRI: Campesinos abandonados por 'líderes' priístas," *Diario de Yucatan*, August 6, 2001; Virtudes públicas, *La Crónica de Hoy*, August 14, 2001; Editorial Galaxia, "El PRI

leaders did not change its name;[2] and they resisted apologizing for its authoritarian excesses, all the while insisting that the PRI had done great things for Mexico. They modernized their campaign strategies using electoral studies and mass media appeals, but did not eschew their traditional clientelist mobilization tactics. The party's governors were able to support the campaigns of their copartisan candidates for federal legislative posts such that the party's caucuses were always large enough to force the governing PAN to negotiate all important legislation with the centrist PRI. And as a result, during the period 2000–2012, the PRI was able to weaken or block almost every important structural reform pushed by the PAN administrations. This helped the PRI to return to power, and once it did, the new president of Mexico and his party's caucus leaders helped form a wide legislative coalition to pass new versions of these very same second-generation promarket reforms.

Unlike the former communist parties in Eastern Europe, the PRI had to moderate its policy stance very little after 2000, in large part because its former leaders had already liberalized the economy beginning in the mid-1980s. More painful economic adjustments were undertaken by President Zedillo's administration.[3] Until 2000, the PRI was seen by voters as conservative because of its stance on democratization, not on the economy (Domínguez and McCann 1996). Once the party gave up power in 2000, the regime dimension disappeared, and a left-right economic dimension took its place. The PRI became perceived as a centrist party on the now dominant economic dimension (Moreno 2009a).

The resources that were inherited from the authoritarian period can be categorized as name recognition, organization, and experience in government (and a lack of experience on the part of the opposition) (Grzymała-Busse 2002; Loxton 2016; Slater and Wong 2013). The negatives were a reputation for corruption, almost twenty years of recurring economic mismanagement and crises, and selective repression against both electoral and social opposition. Still, constant elections at all levels of government allowed and obliged party politicians to demonstrate their capacity to win votes under conditions that became more equitable with every electoral reform passed (federal reforms are required to be followed at the state level). After the loss of the presidency,

corre riesgo de fractura con la elección de su presidente," *ACCIÓN*, February 20, 2002; "Autoflagelación del PRI," *Excélsior*, July 20, 2001, 6.

2. One of the few important PRI leaders who argued for a name change was Genaro Borrego, head of Mexican Institute of Social Security (IMSS) under President Zedillo and a former governor.

3. A second round of structural reforms had to wait until the Peña Nieto term because the PRI refused to negotiate structural changes with the PAN administrations, such as opening the petroleum monopoly to private investment, strengthening the antimonopoly agency, opening the television industry to new actors, among many others.

the capacity to bring in the vote without the resources or the manipulation of the rules became even more critical, and not all internal factions reacted successfully.

The former opposition party that takes over the executive branch normally has little experience in government and may find it very difficult to make good on the promises they have made and correct what they criticized so long from the sidelines. This turned out to be the case for the center-right PAN in its twelve years in office. Once known as a promarket, anticorruption party, it failed to take on public and private monopolies that would have helped unleash economic growth and found itself embroiled in several scandals involving the use of public office for private gain.[4] The center-left PRD was characterized by internal factions and had serious problems expanding its base to the north and central regions. This meant in practice that the PRI maintained its capacity to win in all regions of the nation.

The PRI was able to return to power when Enrique Peña Nieto, the governor of the largest and wealthiest state in the nation (the State of Mexico) became a focal point for the hopes and ambitions of the PRI as his electoral fortunes rose during his six-year gubernatorial term (from 2005 to 2011). His ability to unite the PRI as compared to Madrazo's divisive tendencies in 2005 and 2006 provides us with a within case comparison to understand posttransition survival and transformation.

PARTY UNITY AND THE DRIVE TO DIVIDE

To better understand the nature of divisions within a struggling former authoritarian party in the years after losing the executive, I study three different types of divisions in the PRI from 2002 to 2012: one that was successfully averted; one that ended in a split and the creation of a small party; and one that did not involve the exit of any politicians, but rather, imposed sanctions by one group against the leader of another. By examining types of divisions, we appreciate better the different ways that they can weaken the former authoritarian party and how their effects can be ameliorated.

The loss of the party's third-party enforcer in the guise of the president of Mexico created even stronger incentives for the PRI politicians to leave the party after the 2000 presidential defeat. A rupture appeared imminent several times in the first years of the new millennium: the first directly after the loss

---

4. The main criticisms of the two PAN administrations are that President Fox did not take advantage of the transition moment to make a more dramatic break with the authoritarian past by putting more members of the PRI in jail on corruption charges, breaking the power of large public unions, and limiting the power of the private-sector monopolies. For President Calderón, the most serious criticisms center on the war against organized crime, especially drug cartels.

of the presidency in 2000, again during the 2001 national party assembly, and a few months later when the rivals accused each other of vote stealing and vote buying in the February 2002 election to select a new president of the party.[5] Most of these fights were attempts by other powerful groups within the PRI to block a takeover of the party by a new strongman who would force the warring factions to cooperate under his leadership—Roberto Madrazo, a former governor of Tabasco and losing precandidate for the 1999 PRI presidential nomination.

After 2000, the national party presidency (the leader of the CEN) became a valuable post because it took over some of the roles and resources once held by the hegemonic president of Mexico and the Secretary of Governance, such as media exposure, campaign finances, and control over some of the closed-list PR candidacies: resources that could be harnessed to capture the party's presidential nomination for the leader of the party. One of the most serious problems for the PRI was that its national party leader from 2002 to 2005, Roberto Madrazo, also had presidential ambitions and he used the resources of the CEN to further his mission to win the party's nomination and the general election. Generally speaking, the entire party membership knows the CEN leader, and opposing groups within the party find it difficult to block a strong leader's presidential aspirations. Two groups fought to take over the CEN after the 2000 debacle: one tied to Roberto Madrazo and the other formed first around losing presidential candidate Francisco Labastida and later led by the northern PRI governors, which included many other groups opposed to Madrazo.

As one would expect if governors were to become central players within the party, the PRI state executives were active in these postelectoral crises: they made public statements about party unity, they supported one potential leader against her rivals, they formed blocks against each other and against the new PAN president of Mexico.[6] In the weeks following the July 2000 defeat, different governors quickly became part of a support base for one of the two main factional groups and they participated publicly in internal party politics for the first time in decades, while President Zedillo immediately lost his ability to lead the party.[7] While different PRI governors supported both

5. Interview subject 67, a former president of the CEN under Zedillo.

6. For more on the continued power of Mexican governors after democratization, see Gibson (2005). See Enrique Méndez, "Riesgo de fractura en el PRI," La Jornada, July 4, 2000; and Jorge Herrera and Alejandro Lelo, "PRI: presionan para cancelar la elección interna," El Universal, January 8, 2002. A governor at the time stated that the PRI was facing the worst crisis of its existence because it had lost its president; see "El PRI necesita una refundación," El Economista, July 23, 2001.

7. After the July 2000 election, many PRI leaders began to attack President Zedillo as a traitor. They were furious that Zedillo had publicly announced Fox's victory before the president of the IFE did so; see Méndez, "Riesgo de fractura en el PRI" (note 6 above). Zedillo reportedly wanted to place Jesús Murillo Karam or Labastida as the head of the CEN in July 2000, but was blocked, making it clear he was no longer the de

sides,[8] others tried to moderate the growing conflict because they worried that the entering PAN president of Mexico would attack their newly won fiscal privileges and preferred a united national party to protect them from executive attacks (which never materialized).

The PRI governors were split both on economic interests and personal alliances. First, some Mexican states are poor and isolated (especially in the impoverished south) and others, especially in the north, are well integrated into the international economy (Estévez, Díaz-Cayeros, and Magaloni 2008, 43). This split within the national PRI coalition formed one of the bases for the anti-Madrazo group of governors (formally named Unidad Democrática, but referred to by its nickname of TUCOM—the initials of All United Against Madrazo). This group of PRI leaders attempted to wrest the presidential nomination away from the leader of the CEN and those governors who supported his candidacy, mainly in the southern strip of the nation. This type of division is typical of a multiclass, multiregional party with a national electoral base, and it can be difficult to keep such an electoral coalition unified.

A battle within the PRI erupted over the election to choose the next leader of the CEN in early 2002, in which all registered voters (not only dues-paying party members) could participate. The choice of an open election to select the new leader of the CEN was an interesting concession to Madrazo, because with the support of his gubernatorial allies, it was believed he could win the contest. The new selection process to choose the head of the CEN would also give the impression that the party and its leaders were responding to the new realities of democracy by reaching out to its still large support base across the nation. Finally, Madrazo used democratization and decentralization of the candidate selection processes to gain support for his bid to win the CEN presidency. The governors, however, were critical actors in securing votes for their respective favorites by mobilizing the vote brokers in their states to work for one of the two rivals for the party leadership post.

In the 2002 battle for the presidency of the CEN, Madrazo and his opponent, Beatriz Paredes,[9] appeared to be enmeshed in a classic prisoners'

facto leader of the party; Esperanza Barajas and Daniel Moreno, "Derrotan en el PRI a gallos de Zedillo," *El Norte*, July 5, 2000.

8. The groups fought for months over *how and when* to choose the next president of the CEN. See Enrique Méndez, "Bartlett, Madrazo, and Roque se unen para controlar el PRI," *Jornada*, January 26, 2001; and "Pactan sucesión en dirigencia nacional," *Nacional*, May 2, 2001.

9. Paredes had a career that spanned four presidential terms. She was on good terms with sectoral groups, and had formed alliances with Salinas and Zedillo, and she was not tied openly to Labastida. According to one report, Paredes decided to run against Madrazo because she believed he had played dirty in the 18th National Assembly and was willing to destroy the party for his own ambitions; see Claudia Guerrero, "Corre PRI riesgos de ruptura," *Reforma*, January 13, 2001.

dilemma which put the party's unity at risk. Because the PRI's sanctioning rules were so weak and without its third-party enforcer neither competitor could trust the other not to cheat in the quest to win the party's leadership election. Both contenders used a subset of PRI governors to support their campaigns, which was prohibited in the statutes.[10] So, while fully conscious that the constant accusations of cheating in the press would further harm the PRI's image with voters, the two rivals could not change their strategies and compete fairly.[11] Once Madrazo proclaimed his victory, Paredes had to decide whether to continue to publicly question the validity of the internal election outcome, leave the party, or simply accept defeat. She chose the third option, and with that, helped save the party.[12]

The decision by Paredes not to leave the party can partly be explained by the personal history of the former governor of Tlaxcala and Undersecretary of Governance under President Salinas; but strategic calculations of the two contenders can also be taken into account. By accepting defeat in the 2002 CEN contest, Paredes knew she would forfeit control over the party, its resources, and its free press. What was worse, as president of the CEN after 2002, Madrazo could negotiate new candidates for governorships, enabling him to promote his allies as candidates for governorships in the quest to become the next PRI presidential nominee. He could also make himself popular amongst the party rank and file by using the CEN as a bully pulpit to publicly criticize the president's policies. The PRI had great name recognition (discussed below), financial resources, and, therefore, a promising future in competitive politics, as long as it avoided a major rupture. Madrazo offered Paredes a side payment of a leading party post if she accepted her loss. By remaining in the party, she could bide her time and either win an even better post if Madrazo became president of Mexico or, if he lost, take over the party. If she left the party, it would have divided profoundly and there would not have been much future as a member of the PRI. Paredes stayed and accepted the post she was offered.

The true split of the PRI came in 2003 and was a failure of then president of the CEN, Roberto Madrazo, to maintain party unity. Elba Esther Gordillo,

10. For more on the role of the governors in 2002, see Claudia Guerrero, "Piden gobernadores respecter contienda," *Reforma*, February 21, 2002; Guerrero, "Montiel pagó las despensas: Madrazo," *Reforma*, February 16, 2002. Montiel was governor of the enormous State of Mexico.

11. Beatriz Paredes for her part denied vigorously Madrazo's charges of skullduggery; see Fabiola Guarneros and Jorge Teherán, "Dividió elección interna al PRI, señaló Paredes," *El Universal*, March 1, 2002.

12. Paredes stated she did not leave in order to save the party. The official results of the election were extremely close, so had she left the PRI, it could have split the party down the middle. Paredes won 1,466,217 votes to Madrazo's 1,518,063. It is interesting to note that from the high point of ten million votes in the 1999 presidential primary only about three million people participated in the CEN election.

leader of the wealthy and numerous SNTE, ran on the ballot with Madrazo in the 2002 selection, and used her union members to help win the CEN leadership battle and so became Secretary General (second in command) of the party. In 2003, she ran for the Chamber of Deputies to become leader of the PRI's caucus in the lower house. She publicly promised to negotiate a new fiscal reform with the PAN president of Mexico that would have raised taxes on food and medicine, a move that was bitterly opposed by the bulk of her legislative caucus. Madrazo allowed the PRI's congressional caucus to rebel against Gordillo, who was stripped of her leadership post in the Chamber. Still, Gordillo attempted to become head of the CEN in 2005, when Madrazo had to give up the party presidency to officially begin his nomination quest, but she was blocked through a variety of statutory means. She formed a new party (the PANAL), using teachers as its base and the PRI formally expelled her in 2006. This split within the PRI was a factor in the party's third-place finish in the 2006 presidential elections: the PANAL used its teachers to campaign for the PAN's candidate; and it was once again clear that Madrazo would sacrifice any PRI politician in his quest to become the party's presidential candidate in 2006.

Even with Gordillo's exit and the loss of the SNTE's electoral support in several states, the fragmentation of the party did not come to pass, although the rupture did harm the PRI's results in the 2006 presidential election. The former SNTE leader was consigned to prison by the new PRI administration, and the PANAL remains a very small party whose deputies often vote with the PRI in the legislature. The exit did not place the PRI in real danger because its leadership was confined to close allies of Gordillo; other groups within the PRI did not join the new party and with his presidential defeat, Madrazo's political career was destroyed. And more importantly, the party had a popular candidate with which to face the 2012 elections.

A popular presidential candidate can act as a coordinating mechanism through which antagonistic party factions find ways to cooperate. If most group leaders believe the presidential candidate will win the election, they will support him, even if they are not his close allies. If he wins and they have opposed his quest for the nation's highest office, they will suffer the consequences, but if they supported his successful bid, they will likely receive at least some benefits. If, on the other hand, the leaders believe the party leader and presidential candidate will most likely lose the election, they can afford to sabotage his election bid, as we shall see below in the case of Madrazo.

The agreement between governors and PRI leadership broke down in 2005 and 2006, and the anti-Madrazo governors were able to sanction the presidential candidate. The Mexican presidency holds great value and it cannot be divided (there is no vice president in Mexico). Of course, if one of the internal party groups wins the general election, the victory helps the party's fortunes overall. But it can also upset the balance among the party's internal groups, because the winner would have overwhelming advantages in terms of money and posts due to its control over the federal bureaucracy. Therefore, all groups within the organization have incentives to work for the presidential nominee only if they believe he has a chance of winning the general election; and if they believe the new president will benefit them (or at least not hound them) once in office.

PRI party leaders' support for Madrazo was conditional on his popularity with voters and his willingness to negotiate candidacies. When PRI leaders believed that Madrazo had a chance of winning or that he would allocate candidacies to their allies, they publicly supported his presidential campaign. But when it became clear he could not defeat the PAN or the PRD in the presidential elections and after he reneged on his informal agreements over federal legislative candidacies, many of these leaders abandoned his campaign efforts (Langston 2009b; Madrazo 2006). Both the Madrazo campaign and the party's national legislative seat count were drastically reduced as the PRI went on to one of its worst national defeats in history, worse even than 2000.

In 2005, Madrazo was forced to compete for the presidential nomination against a coalition of mostly northern PRI governors. When this coalition decided on a common candidate (Arturo Montiel) to compete against Madrazo, information about the winner's questionable fortune surfaced within weeks, which immediately ended his bid for the nomination, and with it, any serious competition against Madrazo's candidacy for president from within the PRI.[13]

To withhold one's public support from the party's presidential candidate was and is a serious misdemeanor: it can harm the party's electoral fortunes and can bring the fury of the future chief executive of the nation if he wins the election. As mentioned above, the governors who did not support then-candidate Salinas in 1988 found themselves out of a job when he went on to win the presidency (Amezcua and Pardinas 1997). But because Madrazo was polling so poorly after January 2006, nonaligned and rival PRI groups did not fear him.

When the candidate lists were made public in March 2006, the governors discovered they had not won as many candidacies for their allies on the PR or SMD lists as they had reportedly negotiated, and Madrazo's support among his party elite fell dramatically from the end of March, 2006 through the July elections. His support fell from 75 percent to only 54 percent. Party leaders began to criticize the candidate and his campaign openly in the press, a practice that would have been unthinkable even six years earlier.[14] Once Madrazo was disgraced by his third-place finish in the presidential election,

13. Arturo Montiel constructed a long and successful career within the PRI, beginning in the State of Mexico as mayor of the large municipality of Naucalpan, then moving to ranks of the national PRI before becoming governor of the powerful State of Mexico in 1999.

14. Examples include: "Padece Roberto Madrazo "El Sindrome del Emperador": Bonilla Robles," *Notimex*, April 20, 2006. By early March of 2006, Madrazo was in serious trouble with the party's governors, as twelve of the then eighteen did not show up for the

the new PRI leader (Beatriz Paredes) reestablished the terms of the cooperative agreement between the CEN and the party's seventeen to eighteen governors.

Beatriz Paredes was an acceptable candidate to head up the CEN in large part because she was not seen as a potential presidential candidate.[15] Still, her record of negotiating among the powerful groups, especially in those states that did not have a PRI governor, was very good, and under her leadership, the PRI garnered an impressive record of electoral victories, most importantly, in the federal legislative midterms of 2009, in which the PRI coalition won 237 seats, almost double its 2006 result (at 121).

Since 2007, when it became obvious that the PRI had a popular candidate in the governor of the State of Mexico, Enrique Peña Nieto, the PRI's internal struggles calmed as many of the group leaders realized Peña Nieto was unstoppable in his quest to win the presidential nomination, and that he would have an excellent chance to retake the presidency in 2012. Because of these expectations of victory, leaders who might have fought to win the candidacy decided to wait another six years and support the probable future president of Mexico. At the same time, Peña Nieto was careful not to repeat the errors of Madrazo by supporting the candidacies and campaigns of several politicians who were not in his immediate political group.[16] And in doing so, he regained the presidency in 2012.

PARTY FINANCES AFTER 2000

Crucial resources that disappear after an authoritarian party's exit from power are government finance, social programs, and bureaucratic posts that the regime party employed, but the opposition could not. These resources made possible clientelist relations, patronage, and other forms of mobilization. At the end of an authoritarian regime, the new government normally cuts off these resources so that the former hegemonic organization is left to fend for itself. Very few authoritarian parties have the large set of investments and companies of Taiwan's KMT to ease its way into competitive elections. As discussed above, the hegemonic PRI had to depend on the Secretary of the Treasury for its expenditures and could not depend on members' dues. However, because of its governors' tax revenue and earmarked transfers from the federal government, and the electoral rules that had been negotiated in the waning years

party's anniversary celebration; Alonso Urrutia, "Madrazo vaticina que AMLO no acatará resultados de la contienda," *La Jornada*, March 6, 2006.

15. Interview subject 97, a PRI representative before the IFE.

16. For fascinating data on how many federal deputies have left the PRI before, during, and after their three-year stint in the Chamber since 1997, see Kerevel (2013).

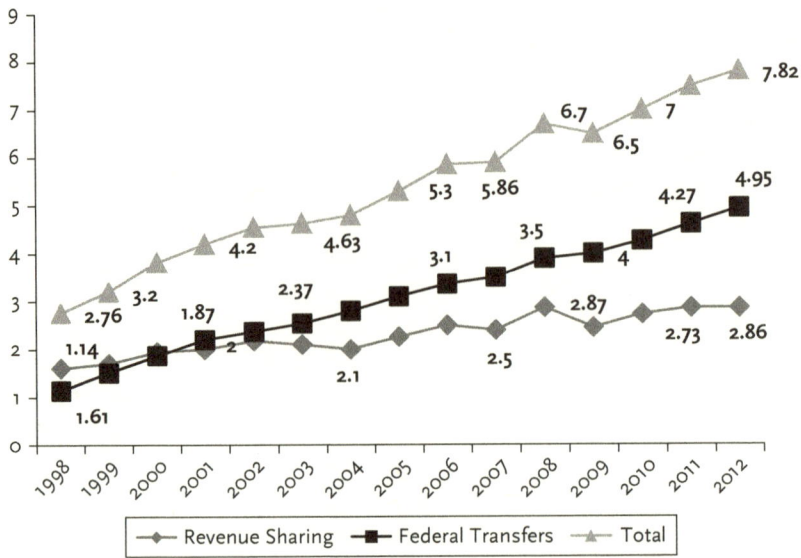

Figure 5.1 State government resources, in billions (2003 constant) US dollars, 1998–2012.
Source: Fuente http://www.transparenciapresupuestaria.gob.mx/ptp/contenidos/?id=29&page=Coordinaci%C
3%B3n%20con%20Entidades%20Federativas

of the transition to democracy, both the party's candidates in copartisan states and national party leaders had money with which they could campaign, maintain a voice in the media, and buy support in the Chamber, among other activities.

First, we look at monetary resources held by the governors and the national party leadership in Figure 5.1 below. Clearly, the PRI governors were far wealthier than party headquarters, collectively controlling from 27.6 billion US dollars in 1998 to 78.2 billion in 2012 (in constant 2003 US dollars). Even considering that only seventeen to twenty-one of the nation's governors were from the PRI, this is still an astonishing rise in state funds.

Almost 70 percent of federal transfers (which make up about half of the total) are earmarked for doctors' and teachers' salaries, which still allows 30 percent of the transfers and almost all of the revenue-sharing funds open to gubernatorial discretion. State executives are actors with resources, who work without the burden or benefit of strong oversight institutions.

The PRI received roughly a third of these public party funds shown in Figure 5.2, so the CEN controlled approximately 100 US dollars in electoral years and about 50 million US dollars in nonelectoral years (before the electoral reform of 2008). Compare this to the states' coffers and one sees the significant inequalities between governors and CEN.

One could argue that governors were in fact the informal leaders of the CEN president, and so should have been able to dictate the action of the national party boss, but this is not the case. First, CEN leaders were not always chosen in open national elections, as they were in 2002. Clearly, if the decision were

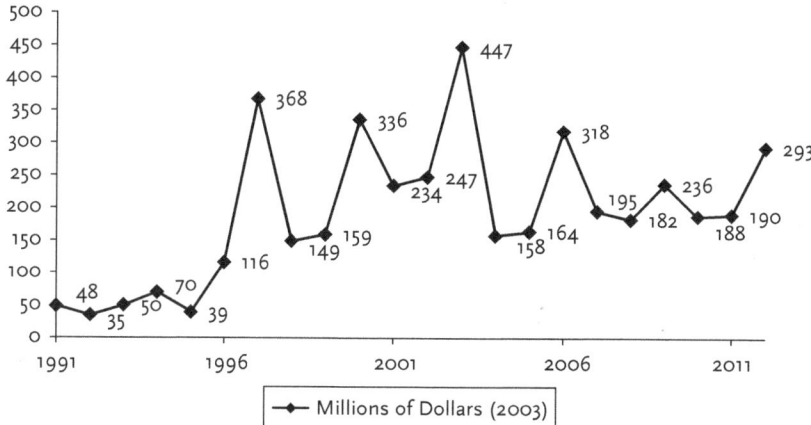

Figure 5.2 IFE funds to the parties, in millions (2003 constant) US Dollars, 1991–2012.
Table made with data from IFE, Mena (2010), Centro de Estudios Espinoso Yglesias and Integralia (2013).

open to party's rank and file, the PRI governors would have played a more important role because they mobilize voters within their state's borders. In fact, in 2005, 2007, and 2011, the CEN president was not selected in an open vote, but through a contested vote of the National Political Council (CPN), a large and open vote of all the party's local and state leaders (over 17,000).[17] In 2011, the PRI presidential candidate imposed his favorite for the post.[18] Governors, the exiting leader of the CEN, and, on occasion, the PRI's presidential candidate were involved in the negotiations to choose the new party leader, so the identity of the new CEN president was a negotiated outcome before 2011, not one in which only the governors participated. Second, only strong political figures can become leaders of the CEN, and once the leader is installed in her post, she is able to marshal the many resources held by the national party headquarters to shore up her position. Finally, governors do not always share the same interests in difficult policy disputes, which allows the party leader more leeway.

17. For an excellent discussion of the PRI's methods of choosing its leader between 2000 and 2010, see Pacheco (2013).

18. Humberto Moreira Valdés left the governorship of Coahuila to take over the CEN in March 2011 but lasted only through December of that year. He was followed by Pedro Joaquín Coldwell from December 2011 through November 2012, at which point César Camacho Quiroz, former governor of the State of Mexico, Peña Nieto's home state, took over the CEN through 2015. Emilio Gamboa Patrón, leader of the CNOP, had sought to lead the CEN in 2011, but it soon became clear that Peña Nieto wanted Moreira, and so Gamboa stood aside, according to one source, Nayeli Cortés Cano, "Humberto Moreira assume al cargo como president del opositor PRI," *Expansión*, March 4, 2011, http://mexico.cnn.com/nacional/2011/03/04/humberto-moreira-asume-al-cargo-como-presidente-del-opositor-pri. Moreira was designated by the Commission of Internal Processes (Comisión de Procesos Internos del PRI), which constituted a simple imposition.

During the 2000 to 2011 period, the leader of the CEN had resources with which to carry out party tasks, some tied to elections and others to keeping its state party offices active.[19] The party spent millions of pesos for public opinion polling, and carried out image studies for certain candidates, usually for executive posts. The national party paid the salaries for the PRI bureaucrats and the rent on the CEN buildings. It helped fund the state parties where there was no PRI governor, because these state parties have far fewer resources. The party continued to send its agents to the states to mediate candidate selection. In those states without a PRI governor, the CEN had to pay for their agents, although these agents often went to the state's business community to raise funds. The CEN also organized and paid for large party events, such as party conventions.

CLIENTELIST NETWORKS

Vote brokers are neighborhood leaders who are hired by a party to make connections with local residents so they will vote for the party on election day. They are well known in their communities, and build reputations that stretch across elections as "intermediaries" who can bring in the vote. The PRI had established lasting relations with generations of vote brokers, who were leaders of the markets, teachers, and neighborhood ladies who knew how to get people out of jail, and who protested in front of the municipal buildings to demand public lighting, better teachers, and more police. These were people who had skills and knowledge to deal with the government bureaucracy (Cornelius 1975).[20] The party, candidate, and governors are responsible for finding and hiring the vote brokers for the campaigns in the different elections. As this is a topic that is tightly linked to campaigning, it is treated at more length in chapter 7. It is enough to state here that once mass media advertising became free (as public service spots), the party had enough to pay their vote brokers with the resources controlled by the governors and by the CEN. Intermediaries are not necessarily party activists, or even members of the party, but their skills are necessary for electoral victory in modern Mexico.

19. Interview subject 70, a former advisor of a cabinet secretary.
20. Coppedge (1993) noted the differences between vote brokers with access to government leaders in authoritarian regimes in Mexico and those in (former) democracies, such as Venezuela in the 1980s. In the former, because there is no alternative employer, the vote brokers are less able to make demands from local government, while those in a democratic setting are better able to win access to goods and services.

THE COOPERATIVE AGREEMENT BETWEEN THE NATIONAL
PARTY AND THE PRI GOVERNORS

The conditional cooperative agreement between governors and the party headquarters can mutate into a hierarchical relation if the president comes from the ranks of the party, as is the case of Enrique Peña Nieto. After the disastrous 2006 presidential election, the PRI came back to victory in the presidential elections of 2012, after two terms out of office. Three reasons help explain this striking return to power. First, the governing PAN was not able to comply with many of its campaign promises, in some measure because it lacked experience and because the PRI had no interest in supporting PAN policy victories. Second, as noted above, the PRI never fragmented into several tiny parties. Third, Enrique Peña Nieto was an enormously popular governor of the large State of Mexico, and was a candidate acceptable to many groups within the PRI. As the previous section showed, the PRI governors and other leaders were able to sanction Madrazo after he reneged on his agreement with them. Peña Nieto, on the other hand, played the opposite role by acting as a coordination mechanism around which the different groups within the PRI gathered to avoid the divisions of 2006.

PRI politicians running for office in the same cycle would be able to ride the candidate's coattails, and if the party won election, others would have a chance to win bureaucratic posts for the first time in twelve years (Magar 2012). Because Peña Nieto's possibilities of winning the election were so high going into the nomination stage, no internal party rival competed against him, and almost all party and elected leaders supported him in the campaign, because it is not a winning strategy to anger the future president of Mexico.

Governors of the State of Mexico are considered potential presidential candidates because the state holds a large voting population, it is wealthy, and the state's six-year term closely mirrors that of the presidency,[21] and Enrique Peña Nieto was no exception. As early as 2007 (one year after Calderón's election in 2006), most PRI leaders anticipated that Governor Peña Nieto would be the party's presidential candidate, with a high probability of defeating the PAN and the PRD. As Peña Nieto's gubernatorial term wore on, and he became more popular in and outside the state thanks to an active publicity campaign, the incentives for other PRI rivals to compete against him for the nomination fell.[22] As Calderón's six-year term reached its midpoint, the combination of the US-led recession combined with the increasingly violent drug war, gave

21. The new governor of the State of Mexico is elected one year before the president of Mexico, so the governor leaves office just before the race to win the presidential candidacy begins.

22. Consulta Mitofsky reported that in January 2007, of 19.2 percent of respondents stated they would vote for the PRI in presidential election. By February 2009, that figure had risen to 34.4 percent.

the PRI an impressive victory in the 2009 legislative midterms. Governor Peña Nieto sent a close ally to run the budget committee in the Chamber of Deputies in 2009 to ensure that he could support his gubernatorial allies in the annual budget struggles in the two years leading up to his nomination, allowing him to knit together a larger coalition of PRI support. With Calderón's popularity dropping, the war against the drug cartels dragging on, and a weak candidate on the right, Peña Nieto won with a comfortable margin, despite many voters' fears of a return of the PRI.[23]

Despite his popularity, Peña Nieto was not considered a "modern" PRI politician: many political analysts knew of the close ties with his disgraced predecessor in the State of Mexico governorship, his membership in the powerful Atlacamulco political group, and his tightknit relations with the giant Televisa television conglomerate. In fact, the PRI candidate was questioned and criticized during the campaign because many wondered whether the traditional, corrupt, and authoritarian PRI regime would return to govern Mexico.

With the victory of the PRI and its return to the presidency, the dual agreement between the CEN and the party's governors was transformed. The president of Mexico is once again the informal leader of the party and has placed close allies to work as his agents in the CEN. The president has allowed the governors of the PRI wide latitude in overspending and taking on public debt many say because of the money they provided the 2012 presidential campaign. One of the last legislative initiatives of President Calderón was one to force governors and mayors to formally make transparent how they spend their federal transfers, a move to reduce discretionary state spending. The PRI's new caucus approved the bill with the approval of president-elect Peña Nieto, but the party's legislative leadership not pressed the Chamber to pass the enabling legislation.[24]

CONCLUSIONS

Governors have become leading political figures within the PRI because their mobilization efforts help win votes in internal party elections, federal legislative contests, and, of course, the presidential race (which will be shown in greater detail in chapter 7). Their support of vote winning allowed them to win more local and federal candidacies than they had enjoyed under hegemony,

23. The PRI candidate did not win with a 15 percent margin that questionable public opinion surveys had led voters to believe. The PRD-Morena candidate, Andrés Manuel Lopéz Obrador, performed better than most predicted.

24. The law was published in the Diario Oficial de la Federación in November 2012, http://www.dof.gob.mx/nota_detalle.php?codigo=5277259&fecha=12/11/2012. The new president is not sworn in until December 1 of the election year while the entering legislature is sworn in on September 1, which means the two houses of Congress work a full legislative session under the exiting president. For a good description of the bill, see Hilda Gómez, "Ley General de Contabilidad Gubernamental; ¿para qué?," *Milenio*, November 11, 2012.

allowing them to direct the future career prospects of thousands of ambitious PRI politicians. At the same time, the fiscal decentralization of 1998 was one of the most important policy changes of the 1990s for the governors, as the federal transfers and revenue-sharing monies now arrive yearly to the states' budgets in a formula-based manner. This money, which is difficult to audit, has been a boon to the political ambitions of the governors, both because they can better support their copartisan electoral endeavors and because they can spend on big-ticket items if they have ambitions beyond the governorship.

The distribution of party funds, negotiated in part by the CEN in 1996, delivers millions of pesos yearly to the coffers of the national party headquarters, which it then can spend with few guidelines. Candidacies, money, and the bully pulpit have allowed the CEN to negotiate, manipulate, and broker among the various groups within the PRI. These long-lived institutions all played an important role in determining winners and losers in the internal party battles over political resources during the 1990s and after the loss of Los Pinos in 2000.

After 2000, the relations of authority within the party changed dramatically. The PRI could no longer depend on the president of Mexico and the federal bureaucracy for its financial resources or its control over the electoral machinery of the state, although many informants reported that the party's governors from wealthier states did help the CEN with financial resources. During the period between 2000 and 2012, the PRI's governors were not obligated to obey either the president of Mexico (now from the PAN) or the leader of the party as they once had. At least during the first presidential term out of office, the CEN and the group of governors (some of whom were allies of Madrazo) found it difficult to cooperate because Madrazo used the post to pursue his presidential ambitions.

Once a PRI governor became the frontrunner to win the presidential nomination and was believed to have the popularity to win the general election, the relations of authority changed, as the leader of the CEN devolved into the agent of the eventual presidential candidate. But because of the ability and apparent willingness of PRI governors to spend on presidential elections, the president was less able to control the behavior of his party's state executives. Scandals involving governors have spiraled out of control: almost a half a dozen PRI state executives have come under intense judicial pressure because of the huge debts they have left in their states. Samuels and Shugart (2010) have written extensively about the relations of authority between the party and the executive in presidential systems once in office and argue that it is more difficult for parties in presidential systems to control their executives than in parliamentary systems. This argument is also true for the period before a politician wins the highest executive post of the land.

CHAPTER 6
Voting Behavior in Mexico

This chapter will lay out the basics of mass voting behavior in Mexico before, during, and after the transition to democracy and includes information derived from both aggregate voting data and individual preferences captured in opinion surveys. By exploring the various types of Mexican voters, one can better understand the PRI's ability to adjust to their demands by changing its candidate selection methods, transforming its campaign strategies, and by decentralizing its organization as its governors took over many responsibilities. Furthermore, because the PRI's brand name continued to offer Mexican voters the assurance of a certain type of pragmatic governing style, it made sense for many politicians to remain in the party. Finally, the nature of Mexico's pragmatic voters has allowed the PRI (and other parties) to rely (at least in certain areas) on clientelist practices rather than programmatic promises.

For historic reasons, both of the nation's two other major parties, the center-right PAN and the center-left PRD, do not enjoy national coverage, and must rely on regional bastions and other areas where they are able to compete with the PRI. The inability of the two former opposition parties to expand their competitive areas, especially the PAN, which held executive office for twelve years, means it is more difficult for them to win a majority in either of the two houses of Congress. Also, their candidates for the presidency must be very popular to vanquish their rivals. The basis of the PRI's national electoral coverage is its name recognition and its organization, as well as the ability of its governors to continue to support copartisan elections at the same time as its national party headquarters has successfully modernized the party's mass media appeals.

Because voters' partisan identification is relatively flexible and the number of independent voters (those with no reported attachment to any party) is high, campaign expertise and candidate image and popularity are of vital importance in election outcomes, especially for high executive office, such as the presidency and state governors. This has allowed the PAN and the PRD to either win the executive (the PAN in 2000 and 2006) or come close to doing so (the PRD in 2006). But when the PRI nominates a popular presidential candidate as it did in 2012, the party was almost impossible to defeat because of its wide territorial support.

This chapter is organized as follows: first, it explores aggregate voting patterns from the 1980s through 2012 to illustrate the nation's long-term voting trends. Then, it turns to different elements of democratic voting behavior, such as the PRI's continued strength of partisan attachments; the socioeconomic bases of party support, and regional support for the three parties. Finally, it explores the vital role of governors in promoting higher election returns for the PRI. The questions of why voters continue to support the PRI, despite its traditional reputation for corruption, economic mismanagement, selective repression, and electoral fraud, matter enormously for explaining why the PRI survived out of the presidential office for twelve years, and why it was able to return in 2012.

VOTING PATTERNS BEFORE THE 1988 ELECTION

Before the 1990s, the PRI won electoral contests with large margins in almost all elections, executive or legislative, at the municipal, state, or federal levels. Figure 6.1 shows that when the PAN was unable to forward a presidential candidate in 1976, the PRI won the election with 92 percent of the popular vote,

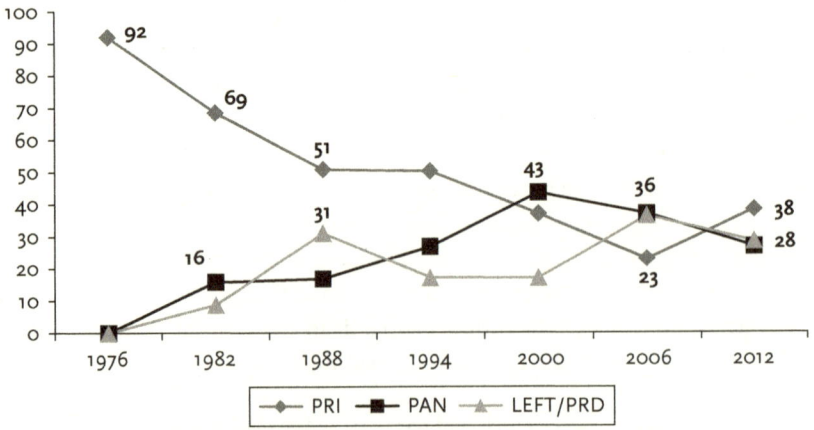

Figure 6.1 Presidential voting percentages in Mexico, 1976–2012.
Source: Vivero Avila (2007) and INE (http://www.ine.mx/archivos3/portal/historico//contenido/Historico_de_Resultados_Electorales/).

which fell to 68.5 percent against 15.8 percent for the second-place finisher PAN in 1982. In the mid-1980s, in the midst of terrible economic setbacks, the PRI still won over 80 percent of all the mayoral contests held in 1985 and 1986. The party won all gubernatorial elections until 1989.

Yet, by the 1970s, after several decades of economic and social modernization along with political stability, the PRI voting numbers began to fall in the nation's wealthiest areas, which were also the most urban, just as modernization theorists would predict (Ames 1970; Domínguez 2014, 43; Molinar 1991; Moreno 2009b). The party continued to do well in rural, agricultural areas whose population was poorer and less educated, which was known as the "green vote." As a result, the PAN began to win a higher percentage of votes in larger cities in the nation. But because of the SMD system for the Chamber of Deputies, which overrepresents the first-place finisher, the PAN did not win more plurality districts before the 1977 electoral reform which installed a mixed plurality and PR electoral system.

Attitudes about democracy and tolerance were not nearly as authoritarian as Almond and Verba had posited in their classic *Civic Culture* (1963)— which included Mexico as a case of authoritarian attitudes and culture. In one of the few public opinion surveys done in Mexico in the 1970s, Booth and Seligson (1984) ran a small poll to explore Mexico City's tolerance toward dissidence and opposition among workers and middle-class voters. What they found was relatively surprising: the urban population at that time supported civil liberties and the right to express opinions counter to those of the governing party, although the authors found differences between middle-class and working-class residents. Even so, workers held opinions that were still on the democratic side of the continuum (Booth and Seligson 1984, 114). Furthermore, PRI supporters were as tolerant of critics as nonsupporters. The authors stated (against Almond and Verba), that one could not explain the authoritarian system in Mexico as a consequence of an authoritarian political culture. This would become clearer as the economic crises of the 1980s rolled on.

THE BEGINNING OF THE END OF HEGEMONY: THE 1988 PRESIDENTIAL ELECTIONS

The 1988 elections demonstrated that the PRI was vulnerable to voter anger and could be turned out of office even with the rules and resources stacked against the opposition parties and their candidates. As shown in Figure 6.1, the PRI's vote between 1982 and 1988 fell from 68.5 to 50.97, a drop of almost 26 percent. The first cleavage of the 1980s and the 1990s for most Mexicans was whether the voter believed the PRI should stay in power or not (Domínguez and McCann 1996; Moreno 2009b). According to these authors, if the voter believed the PRI had done a good job or if she were afraid of the alternatives, then she would continue to mark the ballot for the hegemonic party. If the citizen thought that the PRI was incompetent and/or corrupt, then the voter made a second decision based on economic preference—toward either more government management and involvement in the economy (the PRD) or more free-market policies (the PAN).

Voters who rejected the PRI became aware of the possibility of strategic voting, which is viable only in systems with more than two strong parties and in elections which are won with a plurality of votes in a single district. Mexico, with its three strong parties and single-district plurality vote for the presidency, was and is a prime contender for the strategic vote. If citizens realized that their first preference had no chance of winning, they could turn to their second choice to avoid the worst outcome (the PRI). The classic example of the strategic vote was the high vote for Cuauhtémoc Cárdenas in Baja California in the 1988 presidential elections. In the governor's election the next year, the PAN's candidate solidly defeated both the PRI and PRD candidates. It is unlikely that the state's voters changed their political preferences in a year, which leads one to think that they were first and foremost interested in getting rid of the PRI, and when they thought the PRD candidate could do that in the 1988 elections, they voted for Cárdenas. But when the strongest opposition candidate for the governorship in 1989 was a member of the PAN, they threw their weight behind him, and have continued to back PAN candidates ever since (Moreno 2012, 574).

Voters in large urban areas went against the PRI in even larger numbers from 1988 onward. Domínguez (2014, 46) notes that regional patterns were linked to the dominant social classes in certain areas, such that a growing middle class that was especially hard hit during the economic crises in Mexico City and in northern cities voted heavily in favor of the opposition parties and against the PRI.

The typical election through the mid-1980s for almost any post was won with a large difference between the first-place PRI and the second-place finisher, usually the candidate running for the PAN. Yet, the very definition of Mexico's transition was the rise in electoral competition: in fact, Mexico's has been called the "voted transition," rather than one that was brought about through international pressure or massive social protests.[1] One might have expected that as competition grew, and PRI politicians began to exit the former hegemon, voters would reject the behemoth as antidemocratic, corrupt,

1. Merino (2003). There is no doubt that mass protests and the guerrilla movements led to an opening of the party system in 1977, helped drive the reform the electoral rules in the early 1990s, and clinched the final reform of 1996. But, in the Mexican case, mass protest pushed electoral reforms that allowed opposition parties to compete more fairly with the hegemonic PRI. Protests were never strong enough to bring down the PRI on their own.

and incompetent (given the disastrous economic crises from 1976 to 1995). But this was not the case.

During the course of the transition, Joseph Klesner (2001, 2005), among others, showed convincingly that while voters moved away from the PRI in the late 1980s and into the decade of the 1990s, most did not form strong ties with the two opposition parties. Instead, many became independent voters who could change their party preference for important offices in different elections, or split their vote down-ticket (vote for one party's candidate for the top office and then switch to other parties' candidates for lower-level offices). Because voters were less attached to the three major parties, campaigns and candidates' images for executive offices became crucial to election outcomes.

Mexican voters did not form semipermanent affective ties to the opposition parties for several reasons; principal among them was the regional weakness of the PRD and the PAN. Historically, the PAN grew up in the more conservative and Catholic central and central-west areas of the nation, in states including Querétaro, Guanajuato, San Luís Potosí, and Jalisco. The PAN also found electoral support in the Federal District (in federal legislative elections) and in the state of Yucatán. In the 1980s, however, the PAN took advantage of the anger of the small and medium-sized business people whose enterprises were growing in states of the north, such as Nuevo León, Chihuahua, and Baja California. These business owners had almost always supported the PRI; but when President José López Portillo nationalized the banks in 1982 in an effort to stave off economic disaster, one of the most affected sectors was these smaller businesses. The "Barbarians of the North," as they were known because they were not PAN members from earlier decades, began to run for mayoral posts under the banner of the National Action Party, and were able to fund their campaigns and use the anger of the population in several cities to defeat the PRI. Thus, the PAN began to build another base of operations in the northern tier of the nation. However, the center-right party was never able to extend its brand to the southern tier of poor states; nor was it able to capitalize on their initial gubernatorial victories in the northern states of Chihuahua and Nuevo León.

The PRD, as noted above, was born of three different groups: social movement leaders active in Mexico City; the small, left parties—most of which had little organizational base and also operated out of the capital;—and finally, some former PRI politicians who had been shunted aside as the top financial bureaucrats began to transform the nation's economy. The PRD was born in 1989 and it created a unified left, but it had great difficulty expanding out from Mexico City and the state of Michoacán (the traditional base of power of Cuauhtémoc Cárdenas).

The second problem for the former opposition parties is that they grew up as ideological options: center-left and center-right in opposition to the pragmatic PRI. The typical Mexican voter tends to be less rigidly ideological, especially on social issues. As a result, the parties' platforms, recruitment patterns, and candidate selection practices meant they had a relatively hard time being purely vote-seeking, making it more difficult to expand their base into the PRI's conventional strongholds or to forge links with voters who were unhappy with the hegemonic party (Bruhn 1997; Mizrahi 2003; Shirk 2005; Wuhs 2007).

PARTY IDENTIFICATION

Party identification has been defined as an affinity that a voter holds for one party over others in the party system (Campbell et al. 1966). This affinity is usually formed in an individual's childhood due to the influence of the parents' and family's affinity. Fiorina (1981) has noted that while this closeness to one party over others is formed while young, the voter's personal experience after coming to adulthood can change the affinity over time. Party ID can also be seen as an information filter: any positive information regarding a person's preferred party will be given greater weight, while negative information will largely be ignored. In the United States, for example, partisan affinity can remain stable over a lifetime and is often the best predictor of how the citizen will vote (Converse 1966). This stable identification with a specific party, however, can be far weaker in new democracies in comparison with their older counterparts (Greene 2011) because voters who grew up in authoritarian regimes did not socialize their preferences in their childhoods or because newer parties are not able to make strong connections.

One noteworthy point from Figure 6.2 is that the percentage of Mexican voters who identify with the PRI has not changed radically since the late 1980s: with the peaks and valleys common to this measure, across time, the former hegemonic party has maintained a connection with approximately 32 percent of the voting population. Even though the percentage of voters identifying with the PRI fell after 2000, it then recuperated with the successful candidacy of Peña Nieto. Even as the number of voters who are old enough to remember the Mexican economic miracle has fallen (Magaloni 2006), the cohort of voters who were not old enough to remember the last economic crisis (those born after 1990) has grown (Domínguez 2014).

Second, even though the PAN was in power from 2000 through 2012, roughly the same percentage of voters identified with the party as in the early 1990s, when it governed a single state and only a few state capitals. After the party's lackluster showing in the 2012 presidential elections, its support fell even lower, reaching that of the PRD. The center-left PRD traditionally had less support from voters, and depends on its popular candidates for president

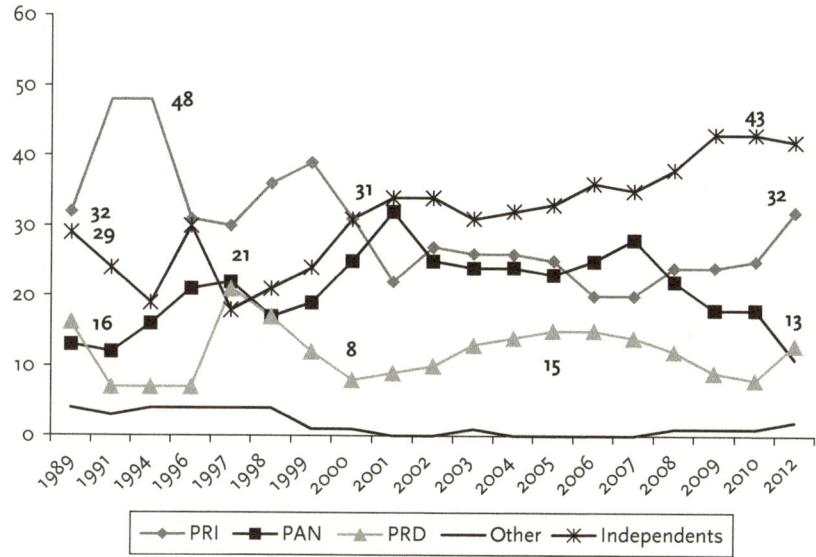

Figure 6.2 Partisan identification in Mexico, 1989–2012.
Source: Moreno (2012) and Somuano (2014).

both to compete nationally and to raise its federal legislative presence. Its high point of approximately a fifth of the population was due to the victory of its leader in the 1997 head of government elections in Mexico City. From there, its identification with voters leveled out at 15 percent.

These figures also demonstrate that despite the strength of the three parties through 2012, over 40 percent of Mexicans did not profess an affinity with any party; these are the independents. The percentage of nonidentifiers has grown from 29 percent in 1989 to over 40 percent after 2010, more than a third higher after twelve years of intense politicization thanks to the transition. Why has the percentage of independents grown during and after the "voted transition?" On the face of it, one would expect that as the three major parties battled to make elections fairer and more equitable, and as the ideological differences among these three became clearer, voters would connect to one over the other two. The answer goes back to the issue of de-alignment without a corresponding realignment: voters left the PRI but did not forge permanent connections to the PAN or the PRD, because of weaker family socialization, less than stellar government performance in office, and more extreme policy platforms.

The high number of independents means that campaigns play an important role in election outcomes (Beltrán 2007; Greene 2011). When voters identify strongly with a party option, then the central task of that organization and its candidates is not to persuade voters, but to mobilize them to turn out on election day. Independent voters, however, are more susceptible to campaign appeals, so that charismatic, experienced candidates and active campaigning can win them over. It also opens space to employ clientelism at the local level. This applies to all presidential, gubernatorial, legislative, and local candidates running under one of the parties' labels.

Still, as Moreno (2012) and Somuano (2014) argue, party identification in Mexico continues to form an important element of each party's vote: identifiers tend not to vote for another option when their party's candidate can win the election. PAN identifiers voted for their party's presidential candidates at a rate of 90 percent in 2000 and 2006 because they believed their candidates could win (Moreno 2012, 583). Even in the 2012 elections, when the PAN did not have a particularly strong candidate, six out of ten PAN identifiers voted for their party, while 70 percent of the PRI and PRD voted for their (stronger) option (Somuano 2014, 131). Furthermore, partisans are more likely to vote on election day than independents.

Though party identification is somewhat unstable, Figure 6.3 helps illustrate the power of the affinity between party and voter by demonstrating when voters decided on their party or candidate.

The same polling firm also demonstrated, using exit polls, that the PRI, PRD, and PAN partisans were far more likely to always choose the same party (at least in the 2009 midterm elections) than were those who selected the smaller parties, such as the Greens, the Citizens' Movement, or the Workers' Party. In 2009, 55 percent of those who voted for the PRI reported that they always voted for the same party, while 47 percent of the PAN supporters and 46 percent of the PRD voters did the same. Only 19 percent of the PRI voters reported they had decided to vote for the PRI candidate during the campaign, with 23 percent for the PAN and 20 percent for the PRD.[2]

A second consequence of a high percentage of independent voters is that they are more prone to punish poor performance by the incumbent party in government, both at the state and federal levels. So that even if the PRI loses a governorship or the presidency, a strong party candidate can return the party to office after a term or two, often because of disappointing performance of the other party.

What Figure 6.3 does not demonstrate is the volatility of personal identification during the campaign season and across elections. As Flores Macías (2009) and Beltrán (2007) have shown for the 2000 and the 2006 campaigns, a voter's attachment to one party or candidate can change during the course of the months of campaigning, especially due to the possibility of the strategic vote and successful media appeals. The percentage of voters who changed their party preference in the 2000 and 2006 presidential elections was 36 percent, or more than one in three voters (Moreno 2012, 583).

2. "¿Cuándo decidió el elector su voto?" *Parametria*, http://www.parametria.com.mx/carta_parametrica.php?cp=4156.

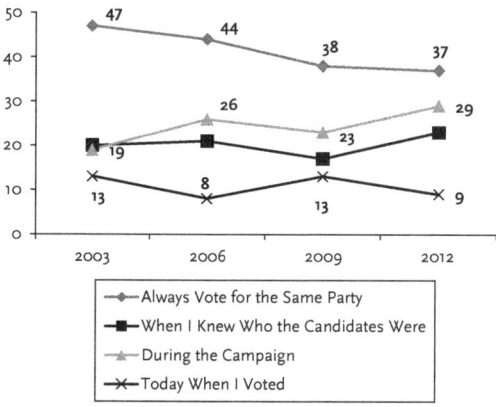

Figure 6.3 When did you decide to vote for the party or the candidate? All voters, 2003–2012.
Source: Parametria, Encuestas de Salida, Comparación de Resultados, 2003–2015.

THE SOCIOECONOMIC BASES OF PARTISAN SUPPORT

The PAN and the PRD are recognizably different parties in terms of their ideological platforms (Bruhn and Greene 2007; Moreno 2009a), while the PRI has been able to refrain from being too closely identified with either left or right policies because it has undertaken both. From de la Madrid (1982–1988) through Peña Nieto (2012–2018), the party's last four presidents (including Salinas, 1988–1994, and Ernesto Zedillo, 1994–2000) implemented promarket reforms which modernized Mexico's economy, but did little to alleviate serious problems of income inequality. At the same time, however, the PRI is seen as the party of the poor, of rural dwellers, and of the less educated.

Where do Mexican voters place themselves on the left-right economic dimension? According to a study carried out by Torcal (2014, 100), Mexican voters as of 2012 continue to be located slightly more to the right of the spectrum and are as conservative as they were in 2006 (Beltrán 2007; Somuano 2014). In 2006, PRI identifiers still placed themselves to the right and PRD to the left, but PAN voters had overtaken the PRI supporters to the right (Moreno 2012, 588). The typical PRI voter from the mid-1990s through 2006 was older, less wealthy, and lived in smaller towns or in countryside (Domínguez 2014; Klesner 2007; Moreno 2009). PRD voters, on the other hand, remain firmly in the center-left end of the left-right dimension, the PAN in the center-right (Somuano 2014, 130). The PAN voters, on other hand, were typically wealthier, younger, and better educated, while the PRD voters were more urban.

Klesner writes (2007, 3) that in the 2006 presidential elections, the PRI candidate, Roberto Madrazo, was most popular with voters over fifty, suggesting that the PRI base was ageing and that the party would find it difficult to regroup with younger voters. However, when the party placed a popular and young candidate (Enrique Peña Nieto was barely forty-four when he ran for office in 2012), younger voters with few memories of the PRI's economic mismanagement of the 1980s and 1990s were happy to vote for the PRI (Domínguez 2014, 54). Thus, the successful candidacy of Peña Nieto drew in new, younger voters to the party; this does not mean, however, that the PRI will be able to retain them if its president is unable to fulfill his promises in office. By 2012, 75 percent of PRD voters lived in urban areas, continuing that trend. What has changed in the urban, mixed, and rural party bases is that the PAN has been able to continue to win more mixed and rural voters, almost 40 percent of its total, according to Somuano (2014, 128).

Another important finding on where Mexican voters array themselves on the left to right dimension is addressed by Bruhn and Greene (2007), who find that federal deputy candidates are much more extreme than the typical voter. They write, "When we asked whether the government or individuals should be responsible for citizens' personal economic welfare, 75 percent of PAN candidates opted for personal responsibility while 68 percent of PRD candidates stated that the government should be partly or even fully responsible for citizens' welfare (2007, 34). PRD voters, however, were less likely than their party's candidates to demand government welfare projects. But in terms of liberal and conservative views on social issues both PAN and PRI partisans tend to be more conservative, whereas PRD partisans and independents are generally more liberal (Moreno 2009).

The PRI in 2012 lost its advantage with women (perhaps because the PAN's candidate was a woman) and the PAN was able to reach poorer voters, in part because of its social policies such as Popular Health Coverage (Seguro Popular), which was targeted to the poorest rural and later urban residents. Religion continues to play a role in attracting voters and they place themselves to the right in the ideological spectrum (Somuano 2014, 129). It is still not clear whether these changes are permanent or if the gains made by the PAN outside their traditional sociodemographic bases will fade after six years out of office.

REGIONAL ASPECTS OF VOTING

While an electoral realignment did not occur during the decades of the 1990s, other variables, such as social class and region, do have recognizable effects on the likelihood that an individual will feel an affinity to one party rather than another (or none at all). In terms of regional differences, the PAN was strongest in the center-west and competed with the PRI successfully in the northern fringe of states, while the PRD was dominant in Mexico City and the western state of Michoacán, and competed with the PRI in the poor south (Klesner 2007; Molinar 1991). In the 2006 presidential elections, for example, the regional element was so strong that the PAN's candidate Felipe

Calderón won the north and center-west regions of the nation, even when taking into account the social class of the voter. The PRD's strongholds do not overlap with those of the PAN in 2006: the center-left presidential candidate won Mexico City and did well in the south, but did badly with left voters in the north (Klesner 2007), again underlining the importance of the regional dimension in voting, as well as the regional nature of the PAN and the PRD.

The PRI, in large part thanks to its governors, has been able to stay competitive in all regions of the nation, for all levels of elections: municipal, state, and federal. For example, the PRI's vote in 2006 did not demonstrate a strong regional dimension (Klesner 2007, 7–8) as did those of the PRD and the PAN. In terms of independents, Moreno (2012, 587) writes that nonaffiliated voters were found in higher numbers in the central region in the 2000 presidential elections, but by 2006, there were more in all areas except the south. By the 2012 elections, the PRI's strong candidate was able to win in all regions, except for the center of the nation where Mexico City (heavily PRD) is located. Once again, the importance of the PRI's inherited popularity together with constant electoral work of its governors is evident.

However, the typical sociological indicators explain only about 20 percent of variation (Klesner 2007, 21), which makes economic performance, voters' evaluations of the incumbent president, and the qualities of candidates important factors in citizens' decisions in elections. These short-term factors play into election outcomes because so many voters are not closely identified with a party, although the PRI has managed to hold on to its historical lead.

THE IMPORTANCE OF GOVERNORS FOR PRI ELECTORAL VICTORIES

The PRI continued to win federal elections, and ultimately retook the presidency in part because of the electoral dominance of its governors. As Figure 6.4 shows, the PRI went from holding 100 percent of the thirty-one states in 1985 to eighteen of thirty-one states and the Federal District in 2001. From that point on, however, the downward spiral was arrested. The PRI ended its twelve years out of power holding nineteen of thirty-two states, more than the other two parties combined.

Because Mexican voters are not particularly ideological, even when the PRI lost states to the PAN or the PRD, it has been able to recapture many of them in future elections. As of 2012, the PRI had never lost the states of Tamaulipas, Durango, Coahuila, Veracruz, Campeche, Quintana Roo, the State of Mexico, and Hidalgo. Of the fifteen different states the PAN has won,

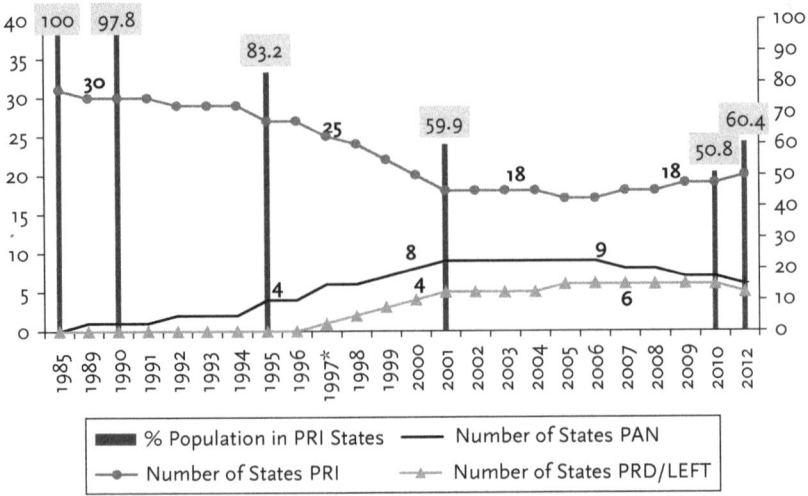

Figure 6.4 The number of governorships per party, 1985–2012, and percentage of population living in PRI states.

*In 1997, the Federal District (Mexico City) began to directly elect its head of government. The Federal District is normally considered a state because of its population and wealth. The right Y axis is the percentage of Mexico's total population that lived in a PRI-governed state. Sources: CIDAC (http://cidac.org/base-de-datos-electoral/) for the governors' elections and INEGI (http://www.inegi.org.mx) for several years of census data.

it lost ten of them back to the PRI, one to the PRD, and held the rest.[3] The PRD has won nine states, and later lost six to the PRI and one to the PAN. From 2010 to 2012, when Peña Nieto won the presidency, the PRI's governors' influence grew; in total, they went from governing 50 percent to 60 percent of the nation's population.

Magar (2012) has produced evidence suggesting that Mexican gubernatorial coattails: that is, their ability to raise the vote for copartisans candidates, are powerful—even more so than those extending from the presidential candidate. In concurrent races, state gubernatorial candidates were able to raise the vote of their copartisan brethren running for a concurrent federal deputy race. Magar argues that the electoral results for federal deputy are influenced as much by local forces as they are by national politics, and that parties and their candidates are able to win votes in the federal deputy elections that are similar to the outcomes in the gubernatorial race, even though they run in considerable smaller districts.

Finally, because many voters in Mexico tend to be pragmatic, they are not averse to selling their vote in return for small gifts or services from the

3. The states of Aguascalientes, Chihuahua, Jalisco, Nayarit, Nuevo León, Querétaro, San Luís Potosí, Sonora, Tlaxcala, and the Yucatán (the PAN lost Morelos after two terms to the PRD).

candidates and from the party. This subject will be explored in greater detail in chapter 8.

CONCLUSIONS

This chapter has explored the different aspects of Mexican voting behavior from late hegemony onward. One of the most important findings is that while the number of independent voters has grown, the PRI has been able to maintain a link with a third of the electorate, making election victories easier, but not automatic. The former opposition parties were never able to establish such strong links with their newly conquered voters, leaving their candidates more vulnerable to short-term electoral conditions. Second, the PRI has retained its ability to win elections in all regions of the nation, unlike the PAN and the PRD, which are regionally based and compete with the PRI in their respective strongholds. Finally, many Mexican voters are more pragmatic than programmatic, which benefits the equally pragmatic PRI, because it can continue to employ its wide networks of local allies and contacts to mobilize voters with clientelist goods (see chapter 8). However, if the PRI cannot show to citizens that it is capable of successfully running the nation, its advantages in that dimension may well end. If voters are pragmatic and the PRI cannot deliver on its promises, then it too will be rejected at the ballot box.

CHAPTER 7

Changes to Candidate Selection and Political Recruitment

Candidate selection illustrates the relations of power within any given party because it demonstrates which groups and which level of party hierarchy are able to control this vital selective good (Epstein 1967; Gallagher and Marsh 1988). In authoritarian parties, candidate selection is even more important than in their democratic counterparts because the judicious distribution of nominations allows regime elites to reduce internal challenges and thereby enhance the stability and durability of the hegemonic regime. In fact, one can argue that candidate selection in authoritarian party regime augments the duration of these types of government (Brownlee 2007; Geddes 1999).

This chapter examines how the PRI's candidate selection and recruitment changed from the hegemonic to the democratic eras to capture how electoral competition strengthened the governors at the expense the corporatist sectors and other PRI groups. The vote-winning capacity of the party's state executives allowed them to obligate the regime's leaders to devolve power over many federal candidacies to them and in doing so, decentralize the party's organization. National party leaders did not lose out completely, however, as they won a good deal of control over the closed-list PR candidacies for both the Chamber and the Senate. Most of the party-affiliated unions and party activists were unable to maintain or increase their candidate quotas because they were unable to choose popular candidates or procure electoral victories, or because their volunteer labor was not necessary to win victories at the ballot box.

The chapter concentrates on nominations for federal deputies and governors. PRI candidate selection during hegemony was designed primarily to distribute selective benefits to a large number of groups within the party to reduce the probabilities of internal divisions and ruptures. Since the opposition parties were so weak, the fights over elected office took place at the nomination stage within the ranks of the PRI, and, thanks to single-term limits, all had to look to their political superiors to make these decisions—rather than voters or party activists. Each president and his two closest political agents—the Secretary of Governance and, to a lesser extent, the leader of the national party—made many candidate decisions for federal legislative posts and oversaw the decisions made by its governors for local and state elected positions.

In hegemonic Mexico, the autocrat did not delegate total control over candidate selection or spoils to a separate organization, such as the party. Magaloni (2008) states that autocrats need their elites to remain loyal in the long term and so must commit in a credible fashion to distributing posts and rent-seeking opportunities. An effective way to do so is to establish a party and shift responsibility for career advancement to that organization.[1] But, as this chapter shows, each authoritarian president of Mexico carefully maintained a final veto over all candidate selections, *and* gave his cabinet Secretary of Governance a larger say in the final decisions instead of the leader of the party, precisely to maintain overall control of the sticks and carrots needed to keep his unruly regime unified.

Since the onset of full democracy, however, the PRI's candidate selection process has the central objective to choose candidates who can win fair elections. Even after 2000, and despite the demands from the party's rank and file to participate in candidate decisions (and promises from party bosses to allow them to do so), nominations for federal legislative posts have remained firmly in the hands of the national party leaders and the party's governors, while gubernatorial selection processes have veered from national party impositions of the candidate to primaries, to negotiated agreements among the PRI candidate hopefuls to select a single "unity" candidate without a primary or convention.

Candidate selection is defined as the formal or informal rules that determine which citizen will represent the party on the ballot, as well as the actors who make this decision (Norris 1997; Protsyk and Lupsa Matichescu 2011; Siavelis and Morgenstern 2008). Political recruitment centers on how citizens are brought into the formal political arena, and what types of citizens tend to be drawn into the electoral process (Norris 1997). Legislative recruitment is used in this study because it allows us to examine group membership and the political arena (local versus national) of politicians who run for the federal

---

1. Reuter and Turovsky (2014, 665) simplify Magaloni's theory of commitment and delegation. They hypothesize that elites who have demonstrated loyalty to the party, that is, those who joined earlier rather than later, will receive more opportunities in the future. It is not clear, however, whether the authors can separate the variable effects of loyalty, networks, and professional competence in their model.

Chamber of Deputies to test different hypotheses about changes in candidate selection in particular, and party change more generally.

Ranney (1981) classifies candidate selection across two dimensions: the level of centralization at which the selection takes place and the inclusiveness of the process. In the most centralized form of selection, the national leadership—with little or no advice from subnational affiliates—selects the party's standard bearers. This is followed in terms of centralization and openness by national selection with subnational input. A less centralized form, and the most common around the world, is selection at the level of the constituency (the level at which the election takes place) with national or regional supervision. In the most decentralized form, which is seen in the United States, candidates are chosen at constituent level by voters with no regional or national supervision by party leaders. Ranney's second dimension looks at who participates in the selection process, from registered voters, to delegates who are chosen by other party members, to the decision of a single party leader (see also Hazan 1996).

In the hegemonic PRI, candidates for federal legislative posts were chosen by national party leaders (not party members or voters) with subnational input, while those for subnational posts were selected by state party leaders (the governors) with national supervision and input.

After 1994, as shown in Table 7.1, candidate selection has been decentralized for many posts, most importantly for governors and the presidential candidate, while high slots in the closed-PR lists are reserved for the national party, but negotiated with governors. This chapter helps explain why one sees these changes and in doing so, it illustrates how institutions helped determine intraparty winners and losers.

The first part of the chapter offers a one-of-a-kind glimpse of how legislative selection actually took place during the hegemonic years, and is based in part on over fifty interviews I conducted with local, state, and national party leaders, high-ranking bureaucrats within the Secretariat of Governance, and former governors.[2] The interviews cover many types of PRI politicians—including those from high and low posts, those from the municipal, state, and national levels of office, those who became national leaders, and those who never left their home towns. I conducted in-depth conversations about how candidates were chosen and by whom, following a general script.[3] These

2. Thanks in part to a grant from the Consejo Nacional de Ciencia y Tecnología (CONACYT).

3. The typical questions for the candidate selection interviews were: who participates in the candidate decisions, and for which type of elected post? I have heard the president makes all these decisions, is this true? Has this changed over the past decades? Why? Is Gobernación involved in deciding candidacies? Why? Do politicians who are passed over protest? How do party leaders respond? What role do the party agents play in candidate selection? What is the relation between the agents and the governors? When do governors have more influence over candidate selection? What role

Table 7.1 INFORMAL CANDIDATE SELECTION PRACTICES IN THE PRI, HEGEMONY TO DEMOCRACY.

Post	Hegemonic form	Form under democracy
President	Presidential decision	First, a conflict-ridden open primary. Later, a conclave, a convention, and an imposition.
Governor	Presidential decision with input from Governance and CEN	First primaries, then multiactor negotiations for a unity candidate. CEN more active in non-PRI states.
Federal deputy	Negotiated among many groups and sectors with presidential veto	Governors choose plurality candidates, CEN chooses PR with gubernatorial input. CEN active in non-PRI governor.
Senator	Presidential decision with input from Governance and CEN	Negotiated among governors, CEN, and state groups.
Local deputy	Governors with CEN oversight	Strong governor influence; negotiated with local factions, CEN active in non-PRI states.
Mayor	Governors negotiated with local groups, with CEN oversight	Strong governor influence; negotiated with local factions, CEN active in non-PRI states.

Source: Author interviews and party statutes.

interviews began in 1995 with party leaders who had been active from the early 1980s when the PRI was still in power, and continued until 2013, when the party had just returned to Los Pinos. Other sources include the party statutes and newspaper accounts from the 1980s and 1990s. Party statutes hold the formal rules of these candidate selection processes, and allow one to understand how the party manipulated the rules to control the outcome (Langston 2006). Newspaper sources, even with the artful control the hegemonic regime held over newspapers (Lawson 2003), can still be used to understand basic changes in the regime's strategy for candidate selection.

To understand political recruitment, I based my findings on a different source of empirical data: the political career information on federal deputy and gubernatorial candidates who won the right to represent the party at election time. This chapter presents data on almost all PRI congressional candidates from two hegemonic legislatures (1982–1985 and 1985–1988) and compares these to a random and representative sample of the professional

did the sectors play in candidate selection? Who chooses the leaders of the state party branches? How do you believe that candidate selection will change now that electoral competition is climbing? Do you believe the governors will win more influence?

backgrounds of 300 PRI candidates from two plural legislatures (2006–2009 and 2009–2012). The legislative recruitment data help show the relative weight of each intraparty group, and places the corporatist sectors in a more reasonable dimension to demonstrate changing patterns over time. The chapter also discusses how gubernatorial selection and recruitment changed. Finally, I collected background experience on over 120 PRI gubernatorial candidates from the hegemonic and democratic periods.

HEGEMONIC SELECTION AND RECRUITMENT

The first challenge of hegemonic selection and recruitment was to knit together the widest possible group of coalition politicians by selecting members from as many party groups and factions as possible (Fagen and Tuohy 1972). During late hegemony, one saw federal deputies from all social classes and education levels who incorporated the interests of peasants, workers, federal bureaucrats, governors, and municipal political bosses. With more groups included in the distribution of candidacies, the probability of a concerted effort to bring down the president from within the regime was reduced. Many politicians won elected posts, and because of single-term limits, those who did not had another chance in three years' time.

Selection to elected posts was controlled from above because the president either chose the candidate or had a final veto, which tightly linked the ambitions of PRI politicians to regime leaders who controlled ballot access. Because the president of the nation—who was the final arbiter in most selection disputes—was at the apex of this pyramid, loyalty and discipline of the subordinates were more assured (Camp 1980; Centeno 1994; Marván 1990; Smith 1979; Willis Garman and Haggard 1999). The regime's leaders also attempted to choose competent executive candidates (for governors and the presidency), who were closely matched to their preferences so as to require less monitoring of their behavior in office or sanctioning for incompetent or prohibited behavior.

The second objective of legislative selection was to channel policy experts to chair the Chamber's committees and guide the president's initiatives through congress in an expedited fashion (which will be discussed more fully in chapter 9). Finally, regime leaders wanted to choose PRI politicians who would vote the party line and cause few problems in the Chamber. As a result, under hegemony, one should see many different types of politicians recruited to the Chamber, from both the national and the subnational level.

The lack of electoral competition creates serious problems for candidate nominations because it reduces the flow of information from voters and politicians in the local political arena up to the party leaders. Other works, especially Landry (2008), have considered how the problem of vertical control and agency loss in a closed, noncompetitive regime can be solved via recruitment rules and control over political advancement. However, that study does not take into account the severe problem of information asymmetry between regime leaders and subordinates—and the costs of overcoming this issue. If one of the objectives of candidate selection under hegemonic conditions was to fashion a workable coalition, then national PRI leaders had to acquire information about the politicians they were selecting for different posts: their group identification, abilities, enemies, and indiscretions. The problems of information gathering and candidate selection in hegemonic Mexico are tightly linked, and were solved via political recruitment (or agent matching, in principal-agent terminology). But choosing agents whose interests were at least somewhat aligned with those of the principal was not enough—the principal also had to be able to credibly threaten PRI politicians who lost out in the candidacy fight if they protested, at the same time it distributed side payments to losing precandidates. This section provides an explanation of how the hegemonic presidents overcame these serious problems of information scarcity by delegating some nomination responsibilities to the Secretary of Governance and the leader of the national party.

The formal rules of candidate selection changed several times during the many decades of PRI rule, but the basic outline was as follows: candidates were formally chosen in party conventions at the constituency level, with party delegates selected according to rules specific to each selection process. In practice, rank-and-file members had little power over candidate selection because their participation as delegates was limited to ratifying the single candidate party leaders had placed on the ballot, which made any real competition among precandidates impossible (Langston 2001). In general, the formal statutory rules were written to allow national party leaders or governors to impose candidates.

When one thinks of candidate selection during the glory days of PRI rule, the word *dedazo* immediately comes to mind—that is, the informal prerogative of the president to single-handedly designate his successor in the presidency (Arnaut 1997; Brandenberg 1964, 92; Hansen 1971; Reveles Vázquez 2003a). But the president of Mexico did not single-handedly choose PRI candidates to all elected posts; rather, he was directly in charge of selecting his own successor in the chief executive's office,[4] but other candidates for top elected posts—governors and senators—were chosen with the information, advice, and at times the participation of the Governance Secretary. In the case of federal deputies, the president of the CEN was more involved. The president personally nominated the candidates for several elected posts, including most of the governors and senators, and he had a veto over the coveted PRI

---

4. See Casteñeda (1999) on the presidential succession, and also González Casanova (1965) and Hansen (1971).

candidacies to the rest of the offices. His direct subordinates—Governance and to a lesser extent the CEN—were fully involved in the lengthy process of choosing hundreds of federal deputy candidates every three years, while governors were responsible for negotiating and choosing candidates for subnational elected posts, always under the watchful eye of regime leaders, who could overturn these decisions made if necessary. It is important to remember that the president hand selected both the Secretary of Governance and the leader of the PRI and could remove them at any time.

Chapter 3 presented the reasons behind the dual involvement of the Secretary of Governance and the leader of the CEN in candidate selection, especially in the large-scale selection of federal deputies every three years. Involving these presidential agents improved the president's ability to control the coalition by giving both actors instruments with which to manage the enormous and, at times, unruly coalition, providing more information to the president from two sources; and finally, employing two agents weakened the powerful Governance Secretariat by allowing the CEN president some space to place and negotiate candidacies.

The first step in both legislative and executive candidate selection under PRI hegemony was to gather information on the thousands of PRI politicians who were potential candidates for elected office. Then, for federal legislative posts, the Secretary of Governance and the president of the CEN managed the multilevel negotiations among groups and sectors to decide the party's standard bearers; however, the president always held veto power over the final candidate list. In gubernatorial selections, the president of Mexico and the Secretary of Governance were the central actors involved. Finally, an important part of the selection process was the postselection clean-up, in which the losers were given lesser posts or promised future positions to keep them within the regime's confines. Because competition within the coalition over candidacies and other posts was so fierce, it had to be regulated, monitored, and resolved peacefully. The *pax priísta*—that is, the stability and loyalty of the wide-flung political class over the course of several decades—was not easy or automatic; it was worked at, negotiated, and worried over constantly.

For potential legislative candidates, regime leaders gathered information to maintain a balance among different groups within the regime, and to assure the party and government leaders that the legislators would vote "correctly" in the Chamber, that is, with the president's preferences. Information gathering on gubernatorial candidates was more vigorous, as the regime's leaders had to know whether the candidate had the backing of important political and economic groups within the state and so would be capable of governing.[5] The regime's leaders needed to answer one main question about all potential

5. Interview subject 19, a former leader of the CEN under Zedillo.

candidates: Who is this person?[6] Both the Secretary of Governance and the CEN sent their subordinates to the states and districts to uncover the basic profile: to which faction or group the politicians belonged; the number of supporters each group had; their enemies; their personal indiscretions (debts, addictions, etc.); and finally, any acts of corruption.

To uncover this information on thousands of potential PRI candidates at both the local and national levels, the CEN of the PRI sent to the states the infamous party agents (called *delegados*),[7] who, unsurprisingly, were often distrusted by the local political elite because of the information they gathered and their influence over candidate selection. Conflicts often erupted between the PRI's state party branches (State Directive Committees) and the CEN's agents because the leaders of the state committees were placed by the governors, while the party agents answered directly to the president of the CEN. According to a former state politician, the agent of the national party "keeps the governor under control, mixes up the chips in the selection game, and plays up the interests linked to the president."[8] Another local politician remarks that the party's agents were the channel through which the governor negotiated with the CEN over candidacies, especially for federal races.[9] The party agents were almost always former federal deputies or party leaders from other states who had a great deal of experience with internal party affairs. To avoid agency loss, they were moved around quite a bit and normally did not originate in the states in which they were working so they would not be tempted to favor one group over another.

The party was not the only organ responsible for information gathering in the hegemonic regime. The Secretariat of Governance also gathered political intelligence on both members of the revolutionary family and the political opposition (Tucker 1957). The Secretariat had agents all over the states, the Congress, and the National University of Mexico (UNAM), to collect this information.[10] There did not seem to be any great differences either in the type of information that was sought on PRI politicians or in its quality. Furthermore, many sources mentioned that the CEN and the Secretariat

6. Interviews with subjects 11, 9, 4, and 5. Much more information became public in 2002 when the files from the Dirección General de Investigacion Políticas y Sociales (DGIPS) and the Dirección Federal de Seguridad (DFS) in the Mexican National Archives became public; see Sergio Aguayo (2001).

7. These agents who were sent from the CEN to gather information on the local politicians should not be confused with the delegates to the party's nominating conventions or with the delegates the federal ministries sent down to the states. For more on candidate selection under late hegemony, see Rodríguez Hernández (1991).

8. Interview subject 36, a former rector of the state university and former federal deputy from Baja California.

9. Interview subject 20A, a former member of the state PRI in Jalisco, April 17, 1997.

10. Interview subject 6, a political analyst.

of Governance shared information during the candidate selection phase, but that each was responsible for gathering its own.[11]

The following section describes how party leaders negotiated candidacies for different sorts of elected posts for the Chamber and governors.

NEGOTIATION AND SELECTION OF FEDERAL DEPUTIES UNDER HEGEMONY

The president's two agents—the Secretary of Governance and the leader of the national party HQ—were not only responsible for gathering information on potential PRI candidates; they also participated in the actual selection of federal legislative candidates, although the president was ultimately responsible for the politicians chosen. The president, according to a former leader of the PRI in the early 1980s, constructed a governing coalition of allied PRI leaders to support his project and to defend him in the face of a political or economic crisis.[12] Thus, candidate selection was an instrument of not only elite circulation and job placement, but also of placing allies and forming governing coalitions within the wider authoritarian regime.

The party agents sent down to the states by the CEN were responsible for making up the initial lists of possible federal deputy candidates, which made it in the interests of state politicians and the governor to be on good terms with agents of the national party.[13] The party prepared the profile of the ideal candidates based on what the president's wishes.[14] The CEN and Governance[15] were always especially active in making up lists of potential candidates,[16] but many other groups did the same: members of the president's closest circle, members of the cabinet and corporatist leaders all made lists of their allies to win a spot in the Chamber.[17] In the weeks leading up to the selection,

11. Interview subjects 9 and 4, both former members of the CEN.
12. Interview subject 4.
13. Interview subject 11, a former member of the CEN.
14. See Francisco Cárdenas Cruz, "Pulso político," *El Universal*, February 11, 1985, 1, in which the head of the PRI states that the party is looking for candidates whose "ideological formation, prestige in his area, and vocation to service guarantees the platform of principles that we uphold."
15. Interview subject 8, a former General Director of Governance under President Zedillo.
16. According to interview subject 2, who was a president of the CEN during the early 1980s, José López Portillo wanted almost no part in choosing the candidates for the 1982 deputy races, which contrasts greatly with President Luis Echeverría in the races at the end of his term in 1976. Subject 2 says that no candidate got on the final list that went to the president unless he knew about it and at least in part approved it.
17. M. A. Granados Chapa, "Plaza Pública," *Jornada*, January 15, 1988, 1, states that the sectors, the governors, and of course, the presidential candidate (in a concurrent

corporatist groups and affiliated unions made public "demands" to the party leadership about the number of candidacies they wanted.[18] These demands were often accompanied by the promise of the millions of voters that the sector in question would mobilize come election day, numbers that were usually wildly inflated.[19] Often, these sectoral groups fought among themselves to win more seats.[20]

After several different lists had been produced and were circulating around Mexico City, there came a series of negotiations among representatives of the president, Governance, and the CEN.[21] Many factors could help determine whether the chief of Governance or the leader of the CEN did better in the candidate placement phase, but most important was the agent's relation with the president of Mexico.[22] Normally, the outgoing president could place some deputy candidates, so only the midterm candidacies belonged completely to the president. Then the lists were whittled down by the representatives of the Secretary of Governance and the president of the PRI, each with his own information sources, before a final list was presented to the president. The president would then give his final decision on the lists, and place some of his favorites.[23]

According to a former leader of the CEN under President Zedillo, the governors attempted to place as many allies on the federal deputy lists as possible, but there was no guarantee of success.[24] Most governors were awarded between one or two federal candidacies, and one of the jobs of the Secretary of Governance was to make sure these candidates were of sufficient quality

electoral year) made the candidate decisions, with a few left over for the outgoing president. According to one count, around 10,000 PRI politicians competed for 1,261 elected posts in a concurrent election year; Francisco Parra, "Alrededor de 10 mil Priistas luchan por mil 261 Lugares," *Financiero*, February 1, 1988, 6.

18. See J. Miguel Segundo, "Lista de 18 Aspirantes de la CCI a Curules Priístas," *Nacional*, January 23, 1985, 2.

19. Juan Guzmán, Carlos Velázquez, and Rodrigo Santiago, "12 millones de votos, el poderío electoral de la CTM para las elecciones de julio: Ramírez Gamero," *Uno más uno*, January 21, 1985, 4.

20. Guillermo Correa and Salvador Corro, "Curules y escaños, grandes metas actuales de líderes priístas," *Proceso*, November 20, 1987, 20; "Bloquea la CTM la nominación de candidatos de la CROC," *Universal*, January 20, 1988, 13.

21. Interview subject 55, a former member of the CEN under Salinas and a former federal deputy.

22. Luis Medina notes that a former Secretary of Governance, Jesús Reyes Heroles, had an especially strong role in choosing the candidates for the midterm elections of 1979, the first after the 1977electoral reforms. On the other hand, subject 4 relates that Hector Olivares Santana, as head of Governance in 1982, did not have such an important part to play in candidate selection except as a provider of information, because President López Portillo did not want to participate much in the selection process.

23. Interview subject 2.

24. Interview subject 9.

and loyalty.[25] Governors wanted their allies in the federal Chamber to groom at least one ally to possibly replace them, which meant running from a Senate seat, and most senators had prior experience as federal deputies. The state executive also wanted to support the other political groups within his state, so they would not cause damage to the party's chances at the polls.[26]

Thus, candidate selection for the Chamber of Deputies was not as top-down as many believed: requests, demands, and information were gathered on potential candidates in the states and cities and sent up to Mexico City, where the final negotiations and decisions took place.

LEGISLATIVE RECRUITMENT UNDER HEGEMONY

This chapter has argued that one of the most important objectives in candidate selection for legislative posts under hegemony was to include as many groups within the coalition as possible and that the decision-making process to select Chamber candidates was less centralized than gubernatorial selection in that subnational groups were more involved in the outcomes. These two claims cannot be tested directly with the data available, but I can generate testable empirical implications. This section also dispels certain myths about the overwhelming power of the corporatist sectors to select their candidates and places them in a context that balances their weight against that of governors, other state factions, and national bureaucrats. These data are the base from which one can track changes to candidate selection during and after the transition to democracy.

Most of the literature on deputy candidate selection under PRI hegemony has used the *official* data on sectoral affiliation provided by the party instead of background information on the deputies themselves, information that over-represents the power of the sectors in the distribution of candidacies (Pacheco 1991; Pacheco and Reyes del Campillo 1989; Reyes del Campillo 1990, 1992).[27] Table 7.2 presents data on the professional backgrounds of most PRI deputy candidates from two hegemonic legislatures from the 1980s. These data demonstrate that governors and high-level federal bureaucrats, as well as the sectors, were capable of placing allies in the

25. The CEN could not allow candidates who were actually hated by local voters, according to interview subject 8, a former General Director of Governance. While most governors got to place one to two people, those closest to the president could place more, and the governors who were on the outs with the president received none; interviews with subjects 55, 18, a former member of the CEN and 3, a former leader of the CEN under de la Madrid, April 1996.

26. Interview subject 26, a former governor of Chihuahua during the 1980s, and subject 7, a former leader of the state party in Baja California Sur.

27. For an important exception, see Pacheco and Reyes del Campillo (1989, 63).

Table 7.2 GROUP IDENTITY OF HEGEMONIC
PRI CANDIDATES FOR FEDERAL CONGRESS,
1982–1985 AND 1985–1988

	Number	Percentage
Sectoral		
Workers'	134	24.0
Peasant	69	12.3
Popular	64	11.4
Subtotal	267	47.7
Nonsectoral		
Federal government	112	20.0
State govt/governors	173	30.9
National party	7	1.3
Subtotal	292	52.2
Total	559	

Source: *Diccionario biográfico del gobierno mexicano* (1984, 1987).

Chamber. As a former leader of the CEN explained, the leaders of the sectors could suggest names of potential federal deputy candidates, but they were not involved in the final choice.[28]

I assigned the PRI's federal deputies to one of the mutually exclusive categories based on the political posts they held *before* winning a seat in the Chamber (and because the PRI lost so few plurality races during hegemony, we can speak of *candidate* profiles, not only deputy winners).[29] Regardless of which sectoral label the PRI employed to nominate the candidates officially, this table only takes into account prior posts; so to be considered a representative of the CNC, one had to have held a leadership post in one of the peasant centrals or be a state leader.[30] For example, according to one informant, the Peasant Sector was pure bureaucracy, and held leaders who had little or no contact with the rural voters of the communal landholdings. They were the sons of peasants who had studied to become lawyers, and then gone on to rise in the bureaucracies of the Peasant Sector, the Secretary of Agrarian

28. Interview subject 2. The CNOP held many smaller organizations and had little identity as a sector.

29. The PRI lost a single SMD race in 1982 and only 8 in 1985, in the midst of a profound economic restructuring.

30. CNC leaders complained publicly that non-members were placed on the candidate lists under the label of the Peasant Central. See "Malestar entre cenecistas por los nombres de los candidatos," *Uno más uno*, May 28, 1991, 7, which reported that of the seventy-five supposed members of the CNC who had been nominated, *twenty-five*, or 33 percent, *did not belong to the sector.*

Reform, or the Secretary of Agriculture. Members of the state government bureaucracy won some of the CNC candidacies.[31]

To be included in the state governor or government category, a politician had to have held several state posts before winning the Chamber candidacy. The total number of PRI deputies in the sample of hegemonic candidates is 559 out of the total universe of 600, taken from the 1982–1985 and 1985–1988 legislatures.[32]

Nonsectoral politicians (at the bottom of the table) are more common at over 52 percent than are those from the corporatist sectors.[33] The corporatist organizations were certainly powerful, but did not control all deputy candidacies. Governors and leaders of the federal government also placed candidates in the federal congress: state executives and state factions were able to place almost 31 percent of all deputy candidates, the single highest percentage among all groups. Despite the PRI's functional affiliation that was based on one's work place (worker, peasant, or professional), the nation's electoral system has always given precedence to geographical representation because of the plurality seats in the Chamber—this institutional reality affected the party's hegemonic organization in fundamental ways.[34]

Aside from territorial considerations, the president allowed his cabinet ministers and other high-ranking federal bureaucrats to send "their people" to the Chamber to assure that their bureaucratic interests would be paramount when considering legislation in their issue areas (see chapter 9). Twenty percent of all candidacies were allocated to those who had carried out their career

31. Interview subject 16, a former member of the state party leadership in Jalisco in the 1990s.

32. The numbers presented below are supported by newspaper accounts at the time, in which the CNC received thirty-six candidacies in 1985 and the Workers' Sector seventy-four. See Guillermo Cantón Zetina, "A Costa de CNC, la CTM Suma Postulantes: CNOP, Igual," *Excelsiór*, March 1, 1985, 1. Because the CNOP was the least homogenous sector, up to 142 federal deputy seats that were supposedly from the Popular Sector in fact went to groups that were not tied to a specific sector. Because many of the CNC deputies are from the federal bureaucracy, our CNC numbers are lower than the newspaper's.

33. For more on sectoral quotas, see Diaz-Cayeros (2006), Nacif (1995), Pacheco and Reyes del Campillo (1991), as well as Rodríguez Araujo and Lehr (1984). The figures of different authors do not coincide. The problem with the official numbers is twofold: first, the CNOP numbers include everything from SNTE leaders, who are true sectoral deputy candidates, to allies of the governors, who are not. Second, many of the agrarian sector candidates actually came from the federal bureaucracy (the Secretariat of Agriculture and the Secretariat of Agrarian Reform). Pacheco and Reyes del Campillo do the best job disaggregating the CNOP data, but do not separate the agrarian candidates. They state that in 1985, 24 percent of the candidates were workers, 16 percent peasant, and 60 percent from the Popular Sector (Pacheco and Reyes del Campillo 1989, 63).

34. The introduction of PR in 1977 did not allow the PRI to win PR seats, a rule that changed in 1988. Therefore, in this sample the PRI candidates are only plurality candidates.

in federal bureaucratic posts, and almost none of these had a true sectoral affiliation.

Another important point one can draw from this table is the enormous strength of the local political arena, taking into account both those from the corporatist sectors and those who are gubernatorial allies or are from other state groups. Approaching these same data in a different way, 62.3 percent of the federal deputy candidates (regardless of whether they were from a sector or not) came from a subnational background, versus only 37.7 who came from a national career path. Despite the single-term limits, and the weak opposition challenges at the ballot box, the force of federal institutions and plurality races can be seen in these recruitment numbers. Many party groups existed in local and state politics, despite the centralized nature of candidate selection and policy making. Thus, it is not surprising that when faced with growing electoral pressures in the 1990s that the subnational political arena would take on greater importance, and the party would decentralize as a result.

HEGEMONIC SELECTION OF PRI CANDIDATES FOR GOVERNOR

Under hegemonic rule, gubernatorial nominations within the PRI were crucial because of the powerful political role played by the state executives. Those governors who could not avoid or mitigate political conflicts in their states caused problems for the national leadership, as did those who failed to secure local and federal electoral victories in their states (Rodríguez Hernández 2008).[35] Because the president and his direct agents did not and could not tell the thirty-one state executives how to confront a thousand different problems, the incomplete contractual relation allowed enormous room for gubernatorial initiative. Governors were also responsible for implementing many of the president's policy directives, which they could interpret in different ways than federal bureaucrats (Fox 1994a; Grindle 1977; Rubin 1990).

The president of Mexico did not always have a personal favorite for each state who trumped all other potential gubernatorial candidates. If he did not, the Secretary of Governance had more influence in the process. The leader of the CEN was less involved in the gubernatorial selection process. The sitting governors also had a say in who would succeed them but there was no guarantee that their choice would be respected. The process of gathering information was open to many interests within the state and at the national level, but there

35. As subject 34, a former PRI governor of Baja California, explained, a "good" governor and his people should not be caught in outlandish acts of corruption; he should not embarrass the president with white-elephant development projects; and he should win both local and federal elections in his jurisdiction.

was no negotiation as there was for the Chamber of Deputies; the president chose each state's candidate with input from the Secretary of Governance.

What factors did the president take into account when he chose the thirty-one gubernatorial candidates during his six-year term?[36] First, the governor had to have the support of the political and economic groups within the state, because "to become governor is an expression of group interests."[37] Other political calculations were also involved in the selection: the wishes of the sitting governor, the group or factional membership of the potential candidates; how long a PRI faction had "run" the state; whether the state usually placed a corporatist leader as governor; and finally, and most importantly, the opinion of the president.[38]

A final issue for the president and his closest advisors when choosing gubernatorial candidates was the role the state executives played in the presidential succession. Up through the 1950s, the governors had been central actors within the party; but were much weakened by the 1980s (Hernández Rodríguez 2014). So, even though the governors could not play such an important role in the succession as their predecessors had, their support in presidential elections helped generate the huge margins of victory of which the PRI was so fond. Proof of this can be found shortly after the 1988 electoral disaster, when several governors (all were from the PRI until 1989) were "fired" by President Salinas for having been lax in their vote-winning duties (Amezcua and Pardinas 1997).

PRI governors normally attempted to place their allies as successors in the gubernatorial post. If they were involved in determining who would succeed them in the state post, they would be able to command the loyalty of a wide range of political actors during their six years in office; and their political group would stay relatively powerful into the near future.[39] Sitting governors normally groomed at least one favorite ally to succeed them by sending favored politicians to different posts at both the state and the national level. Yet, even in the best-case scenario—when the governor was good friends with the president, for example, his ability to place his own successor was not guaranteed. As a former governor of Baja California stated about a successor, Roberto de la Madrid, "Everybody likes Bob. He's a great friend of José López Portillo. He was such a good friend that Bob felt like a national politician. Cabinet secretaries came to see him. But as strong as he was, even he couldn't place his own successor."[40] If the governor were considered an underperformer or if he

36. The Federal District did not elect a head of government until 1997.
37. Interview subject 9, former leader of the CEN under Zedillo.
38. Interview subject 9 and with subject 63, a former governor.
39. Many of the political groups at the state level are based on governors and former governors, although others can exist, for example, those based in the state university; see Langston (2003).
40. Interview subject 34.

did not have a good relation with the president, then it was even less likely he would be allowed to place an ally.

To better illustrate the risky nature of gubernatorial candidate selection, it is worth examining a failed case at the end of hegemony and the beginning of the transition. Baja California was the first governorship lost to the opposition in Mexico's hegemonic history. The PAN defeated the PRI in part because voters were far more willing to reject the PRI than in other states and in part because the president of Mexico and his leader of the PRI did not handle the selection process well. As explained by a former leader of the state party during this period, first, the president had removed the sitting PRI governor just before the state elections because he had not won the state for Salinas in the 1988 presidential elections. Second, the president imposed a PRI candidate for governor that did not correspond to any of the political groups within the state PRI. She had few links to local groups, so few leaders supported her election bid. In the PRI terminology of the day, the president and leader of the CEN had to "invent" her because she was not a major figure in her own right. She was tied to a former governor, but he had not taken the time to build up her political force within the state, which would have been possible had she worked with women, teachers, students, and other groups. Had they demanded a candidate with her characteristics, she might have been better supported by political groups in the state.[41]

HEGEMONIC SELECTION FOR MAYORS AND LOCAL DEPUTY POSTS

While the Governance Secretariat and the CEN maintained a watchful eye, it was the governors who actually selected most candidates at the municipal and state levels. The governors were given this instrument so they could better control their states politically, since subnational politicians had to look to their governors to allow them to continue their careers in the state and local political arenas.[42] Former leaders of the party readily admitted that the governors controlled their state party branches and that the strength of each state affiliate depended on how active the governor was.[43] The governors guaranteed

41. Interview subject 37, a former head of the state party in Baja California during this period.

42. At times the gubernatorial candidates had to share this power with the former governors of their states; Jaime Mariscal, "Que no intervengan funcionarios en procesos priístas de selección," *El Universal*, February 18, 1986, 23.

43. Interview subject 18. Also, with subject 40, a former governor, and with a former leader of the state party in Jalisco, subject 14. Eduardo Huchim, "Lucha por el poder en Campeche," *Uno más uno*, March 3, 1985, 1; and Arturo Lino, "Necesario, que no influyan al seleccionar candidatos," *El Sol*, October 1, 1984, 1, which quotes Tulio

electoral victories, and so they were allowed to decide the candidacies for most mayors, the local assemblies, and at least a few federal deputies.

Through local candidate selection, the governors managed the conflict among PRI groups over positions. The governors knew when to say to their state politicians, "It is not your turn, just wait a bit." The governors "offered something and everyone knows the state executive can comply," because he (the governor) controlled the selection of candidates.[44] Mayors were among the most important candidates the governors had to place: but not all of these positions would be filled by their personal allies.[45] "He (the governor) had to integrate other groups, and give something to the losers, and bring them to his cause."[46] As Gillingham (2014) notes, these positions were negotiated—not imposed by the governors. In the small municipalities, governors had to decide among contending families. The large municipalities required different handling: the rival groups were not families, but rather leaders of different economic or political groups, so agreements had to be made among the business leaders, former mayors, and landowners.[47] Using archive data, Gillingham (2014) has shown that in the 1960s—when the nation was still rural, but modernizing quickly—only 2.4 percent of the municipal president candidates came from the Workers' Sector, while almost 40 percent were identified with the Peasant Sector.

CANDIDATE SELECTION UNDER DEMOCRACY

Increasing electoral pressure changed both candidate selection and legislative recruitment in profound ways from 1988 onward. The case of the PRI closely mimics that of the KMT in Taiwan in that both had time prior to their ousters to modify internal practices to deal with growing electoral competition (although regime leaders also reformed the economy in Mexico). This contrasts to the communist successor parties in Eastern Europe that were forced

---

Hernández, then governor of Tlaxcala, "The governors influence the candidate selection decisions of the PRI."

44. Interview with former governor of Baja California, subject 34.

45. Gillingham (2014) reports that over 40 percent of candidates for mayors in the 1960s did not have a strong relation to the party or government. When competition began to grow in certain areas in the 1980s, many argued that democratizing candidate selection was the best way to choose better candidates. However, it was clear that the governors often stood in the way of this and de la Madrid was not ready to force them; Luis Gutiérrez, "El PRI ante su lucha más difícil: democratización," Uno más uno, September 9, 1985, 1.

46. Interview subject 29, former member of the municipal PRI committee in Chihuahua.

47. Interview subject 26, a former governor.

to react much faster due to the almost immediate exit from power after the fall of the Berlin Wall.

When opposition party candidates began to win gubernatorial elections in the 1990s, the president, the CEN, and the Governance Secretariat faced a dilemma: if they chose the best candidate, but one who was not a close ally of the president or another national leader, they might have to deal with a less loyal state executive. Yet, if they did not allow the most popular PRI politician to contend for the seat, she might leave the coalition and run for an opposition party and win. Governors were able to wrest some control from the national regime leaders even before 2000, as authority slowly and painfully shifted away from the president and the Secretariat of Governance, and was transferred to the PRI governors.

Federal institutions helped decentralize the party under democratic conditions as governors and states provide political space for politicians in their quest to construct political careers (Montero 2007; Riker 1964; Samuels 2003). Mixed-member electoral systems, with a strong plurality element, should also decentralize the party's organization because district-level campaigns and elections should privilege local politicians and their parties, at the same time candidate-centered campaigning promotes the interests of office seekers and holders, rather than the party leadership. However, the constitutional prohibition of consecutive reelection mitigates the effects of the electoral system, as office seekers must cast about after a single term in office for another post, destroying the politicians' incumbency advantage and weakening (but not eradicating) the personal vote in the plurality districts, as will be discussed in the next chapter.

The 2008 version of the PRI statutes states that the Political Council at the level of the election chooses the method of candidate selection in each selection process.[48] The Political Council is a deliberative body of the party and exists at the local (municipal), state, and national levels. The Political Council in question can choose from three different selection methods: open primaries, closed primaries, or conventions with democratically elected delegates (Art. 181).[49] For federal posts, such as the president, senators, and federal deputies, the CPN decides on the selection method (and for which proportion

48. The most recent version of the PRI statutes can be found at http://pri.org.mx/SomosPRI/Documentos/Estatutos2014.pdf. The present work uses the 2008 statutes which have not changed dramatically.

49. In conventions, at least 50 percent of the delegates must come from the territorial structure, while the other 50 percent is made up of both members of the local Political Council and sectors. So only roughly 25 percent of the delegates are now members of one of the party's mass organizations, far less than a majority. These delegates now vote individually (Art. 184), and no longer use "economic vote," in which the single name is called and each sector is asked sequentially if it agrees with the nomination, to which all respond with a roar, "¡Sí!"

of the legislative districts—the same method does not have to be used in all districts or states in the same selection process). To make it onto the ballot, the candidate hopeful must have participated in an opinion poll (but not necessarily have won that poll) and demonstrated support from at least a few of the different groups within the party, such as the territorial base, a mass organization, political councilors, or accredited individual members of the party (Art. 187).

While the party's governors influence both local and federal candidate selection in their respective states, the CEN formally controls the candidacies for PR slots, as evidenced by Art. 194, which states: "in the case of the PR candidates, the CEN will present to the Permanent Political Commission (CPP) of the CPN the proposed list of candidates and alternates to be voted upon."[50] Thus, the CEN chooses the candidates and decides their spot on those lists, and usually, ten to fourteen of the names at the top of each of the closed lists for the nation's five circumscriptions can expect to make it into the Chamber, and about ten or eleven of the thirty-two names on the Senate's closed-PR list. The CPP can give only a yes/no vote to these lists: its members cannot replace names and or shuffle their order.

In those states in which the governor is not from the PRI, the CEN shares control over deputy selection with the strong groups within the state PRI.[51] Where there are strong state party organizations, as there were, for example, in Jalisco and Nuevo León in the late 1990s and into the early 2000s, the state party leaders are able to negotiate more successfully with the CEN and place candidates who are not tied to national groups. But in the states with weak or fractured state PRI affiliates, the CEN has more power to impose candidates.[52]

Under hegemony, the PRI governors had been allowed to place one or two allies, after 1994 and with growing force in the 1997 midterm congressional nominations, they were able to select more candidates in the 300 plurality races (although they were still monitored by the leader of the CEN until 2000) in return for their work in assuring electoral victories in the states.[53] However, it is clear that while democratization implied decentralization, it did not imply more openness, at least after 2003. The promise of opening candidate selection within the PRI (Casillas Ortega 2000) was lost. In the PRI's

50. Article 194.
51. Interview subject 49, a former local and federal deputy from Guanajuato, April 21, 1999.
52. Interview subject 67, a former leader of the CEN in the Zedillo sexenio.
53. Interview with former CEN presidents, subjects 66 and 67. Subject 67 states that the usual actors were present in the 1997 selection process: SEGOB, the CEN, and Esteban Moctezuma as Zedillo's representative in the process (who was also a leader of the CPN). Although the president of the CEN, Humberto Roque Villanueva, had the final say, the real selector was Hector Hugo Olivares, another member of the CEN. Zedillo did not want to participate too directly. The role of the governors was greater than in 1994 (interview subject 23, a close ally of Elba Esther Gordillo).

2009 selection, forty-nine percent of a sample of 200 (of the 300 total) congressional candidates were selected through open nominations. However, in 2012, less than 3 percent of the candidates were chosen in open or democratic selection procedures. Compare this to 68.5 percent of the PAN congressional candidates who were selected through democratic procedures in 2009 and 82 percent for the PRD.[54]

If the statutes call explicitly for the participation of either voters (open primaries), party activists (closed primaries), or low-level party leaders (the delegate conventions) in nominating federal Chamber candidates, then why was it so easy for the governors and the CEN to impose their favorites? First, the statutory rules are easily manipulated;[55] and second, there was no overarching power to obligate the governors to comply with the rules before 2012.

The PRI governors are not completely without national party supervision when making their selections: the CEN can replace any candidate with few statutory constraints (Art. 191). Further, all specific nomination rules or procedures that the lower-level Political Councils emit must have prior approval of the CEN before they are published (Art. 192 and 193). However, if the CEN oversteps its bounds, the governors can respond in kind, as seen in chapter 5, when Madrazo did not deliver as many deputy candidates to the governors as they had agreed to informally.

GUBERNATORIAL SELECTION UNDER DEMOCRACY

The push toward more open and democratic selection methods for governors that failed under Salinas (chapter 3) succeeded under the new administration of President Ernesto Zedillo. After an attempt to write democratic convention rules for gubernatorial selection in three states in 1995, the party experienced a new political crisis in early 1998: the PRI was the dominant party in the state of Zacatecas, but the national leadership failed to manage the gubernatorial selection process properly, and a disgruntled pre-candidate left the party, ran under the PRD's label, and soundly defeated the PRI's candidate, converting that state into a PRD haven for two six-year terms.[56] In the next state to choose a candidate, instead of creating a conflict by imposing one

54. These numbers taken from the author's database on campaigning.

55. For example, if the PRI runs in a partial electoral coalition, the districts which make up the coalition are not required by its statutes to hold democratic selection procedures. Since most of the party's districts are included in a coalition, the party was able to avoid both primaries and fair delegate conventions after 2000.

56. The 1998 gubernatorial election in Zacatecas was the first failed selection of the 1990s that led to a defeat by a former member of the PRI; see Eisenstadt (2004) and Langston (2003).

gubernatorial candidate over another, the CEN organized a primary to select the candidate, who went on the beat his PAN rival and take back the state for the party.

The primaries in the PRI were not new: the party had attempted to open candidate selection procedures for mayors and governors first in the mid-1940s, then in the early 1960s, then in the 1980s, and finally in the early 1990s, all of which had been deemed failures and had been abandoned.[57] But these gubernatorial selections were different in large part because the pressures of electoral competition were growing quickly in the late 1990s. The party leadership decided to use primaries for gubernatorial selection to achieve several objectives: first, as an informational device to convince losers in the selection battles that they were not as popular as the primary winner with regular voters; second, to signal voters that the PRI was interested in democratic procedures and in modernizing; and finally, to choose winning candidates without causing ruptures (Langston 2003).

Through the late 1990s, the party used gubernatorial primaries, but encountered a serious problem: by the end of the 1990s, the Secretary of Governance was no longer strong enough to obligate its copartisan governors to hold fair nomination proceedings,[58] and after 2000, there was no longer a third-party enforcer in the form of the president. As a result, the party once again cast about for a viable selection method to avoid serious internal divisions, while selecting a winning candidate. With the loss of the presidency and the party's extra-official Leviathan in 2000, the party's nineteen to twenty-one governors shared power with the CEN over candidate selection.

THE ATTEMPT TO DEMOCRATIZE LEGISLATIVE SELECTION IN 2003

The more decentralized and democratic rules used by the party in the 2003 midterms to select its candidates for federal deputies were a sharp divergence from traditional practice. In the 2003 Chamber races, all the party's SMD candidates were supposed to be selected in closed party primaries, except those that were part of the electoral coalition with the Green Party (PVEM), (97 of the total of the 300 districts), leaving the remaining 203 in hands of the party's activists. However, according to many experts and members of the PRI, the primary experiment in many of these districts was a failure, as they had

---

57. See Gillingham (2014) for more on the primaries in the late 1940s; also Leonardo Zaleta, "San Ignacio, Sinaloa; Pueblo chico, infierno grande," *El Sol de México*, March 15, 1990, 2, and Edmundo González Llaca, "Democracia Contra Cacicazgo," *Excelsior*, May 25, 1989, 7.
58. Interview subject 66, a former president of the CEN.

only one potential candidate on the list, or in other cases, a well-known candidate ran against a political nonentity.[59] The governors had enormous influence over at least half of the remaining candidates to the SMD slots in their states.

The die had been cast: the 2003 legislative midterm election had the first set of candidacies for which there was no PRI president of Mexico or Secretary of Governance dictating the PRI's selection procedures. The party statutes allowed the full participation of the activists in choosing their candidates; yet, the party's leaders—both national and subnational—did not relinquish their hold over candidacies to the party's activist base.

While the CEN and the governors split the universe of legislative candidacies between them, lower-level party politicians did not give up hope on democratic selection mechanisms. PRI candidate hopefuls between 2000 and 2007 used several methods of protesting specific abuses by their leaders during the selection process, most commonly, street protests after a selection had ended, or attacks in the press against the offending party leader.[60] Party politicians also had a solid rule-based ally: the legal authority of the Federal Electoral Tribunal (colloquially known as TRIFE), which was charged with assuring that the parties respected their own statutory nomination rules. For example, in 2005 several party members hauled their own party leaders up on charges before the TRIFE under the argument that the candidate selection procedures of the Alliance for Mexico (the PRI's electoral alliance with the Green Party) did not clearly state the requisites for winning a federal candidacy. The TRIFE resolved in their favor and party leaders were forced to clarify the procedures. The victory was short-lived, however, as the TRIFE ruled that the public opinion polls were only one element to be considered in the final nomination decision.[61] The problem of using the TRIFE to force the leadership to be more transparent and rule-bound in its selection processes was solved in 2008 when the party's leaders took advantage of a wide-reaching electoral reform to curtail sharply the TRIFE's role in internal party affairs. Over time, it became clear that the PRI members were less willing to use this legal tool against their leaders than the PRD or the PAN.[62]

59. A former CEN leader (subject 67) estimated that 90 out of the 203 party primaries had only one candidate.

60. For a typical article on the subject, see Juan Balboa and David Carrizales, "Tramposo modo de elegir candidatos de PRI-PVEM al Congreso: CTM-Oaxaca," *La Jornada*, March 12, 2006.

61. Article 7 of the TRIFE clarification states that the outcomes of the poll must be turned into the TRIFE to be considered. And even if the precandidate in question won the candidate opinion poll, the Alliance was not statutorily obligated to nominate him. This is much like the KMT statutes, in which the primaries are only one element of the final decision.

62. Ávila Ortiz (2012, 113).

As we have seen, party leaders decided they did not need the volunteer labor of rank-and-file activists to win elections in large part because IFE monies and gubernatorial support can be used for large-scale media appeals and underwriting the cost of the ground campaign.[63] The secretary of finance of each party's CEN takes the money and distributes it discretionally (although an article was added to the PRI's statutes in 2007 stipulating that half of the money from IFE must go to the state affiliates).[64] In the 2003 race, almost 80 percent of the IFE financing was spent on national media appeals, not district-level campaigns.

The 2006 electoral races continued the informal arrangement between the governors and the CEN.[65] The formal 2006 set of rules for the Chamber selection allowed the "Governing Body" of the Alliance for Mexico (the electoral alliance constituted by the PRI and the Green Party for that specific election only) to choose the candidates for senators and federal deputies for the 300 plurality races; there was not even the appearance of internal party democracy. The governing body was made up of only three members of each party, one of whom was the president of the CEN and the other two who were chosen by the Permanent Political Council of the CPN.[66] The only participation of the regular party militants and leaders who formed part of the CPN was to validate the choices made by the small governing body of the Alliance.[67] Something close to the same procedure was used for the candidates for senator and federal deputies for the PR lists: the governing body of the Alliance put the list together, sent it to the CPN, which could only emit an up-down vote on the list. The CPN could not change names, or their order in the closed list. Thus, the candidacies for federal deputies are shared between the party's governors and the CEN leaders.

63. As Aguayo (2010, 239) notes, the party does not need to concern itself with the preferences of the militants because it receives only 2.3 percent of its income from them, as reported in the IFE figures.

64. I do not have enough information to know whether this rule is respected in practice.

65. In 2006, 4,182 members of the party competed for a candidacy; see Balboa and Carrizales, "Tramposo método de elegir candidatos de PRI-PVEM al Congreso" (see above, note 60).

66. "Convenio de coalición total que celebran por una parte, el Partido Revolucionario Institucional," http://www.ine.mx/documentos/PPP/docs_pdf/Alianza_por_Mexico. pdf. There was a alliance in all 300 plurality districts between the Greens and the PRI in 2006.

67. Dictamen al acuerdo del órgano de gobierno de la coalición "Alianza por México" por el que se elaboran las propuestas de candidatos a senadores de la república y diputados federales al congreso general, por el principio de mayoría relativa, para ser sometidos a la validación, en su caso, de los consejos políticos nacionales de los partidos revolucionario institucional y verde ecologista de México. March 20, 2006. Accessed October 12, 2009.

LEGISLATIVE RECRUITMENT
UNDER DEMOCRATIC CONDITIONS

Because of the nation's plurality district races, one should expect to see federal legislative recruitment become more localized under democracy than it was under hegemony, even without consecutive reelection or candidate-centered campaigns. First, PRI governors now choose many candidates for their respective state and federal races and they tend to select those who are active in the municipal and state arenas, not national politicians. Even those who are chosen by the CEN for SMDs are usually local-type candidates. Local politicians are good candidates for plurality districts because they know or build contacts with the neighborhood vote brokers and because they are better known by constituents. As we will see in chapter 8, democratic electioneering has a strong component of both candidate-led local voter mobilization and party-based media appeals. The PR lists allow national leaders an easier path to the Chamber and the Senate as they require no campaigning (voters have only one ballot for both tiers, unlike other mixed-member systems).

Table 7.3 shows that electoral competition and exile from Los Pinos has decentralized candidate recruitment, in large part because of the new strength of the governors *and* the pressures of electoral competition that favor candidates with more local political experience. A random sample of PRI candidates for two plural legislatures in the democratic era (2006–2009 and 2009–2012) helps demonstrate that the professional backgrounds of PRI's congressional candidates have become more local than their hegemonic counterparts. The first column of the table below holds the immediate prior post of the hegemonic PRI federal deputy candidates from the 1980s[68] and the second contains that of a random and representative sample of 300 from the total of 600 PRI SMD candidates from the 2006 and 2009 legislatures. Because we examine candidates, not winners, we can better identify what the PRI leaders at each point in time were looking for in their deputy candidates.

The 2006 and 2009 data consist of a random sample of 386 PRI deputy candidates (300 SMD candidates from two legislatures and 86 from the PR lists). From Table 7.3, one sees that municipal-level candidates, that is, those who came directly to the Chamber from a municipal-level job (city council, mayor, local party, or local government) have doubled in strength from the 1980s to the present (from 9 to 18 percent), a finding consistent with the demands of district campaigning. The state politicians (local deputies, state government and party) have maintained their position from hegemony to democracy, an interesting finding considering how centralized the hegemonic PRI was supposed to have been. Politicians with national political backgrounds (national

---

68. Because so many of the hegemonic deputies won their elections, we consider them candidates and compare them to the candidates in the democratic era.

Table 7.3 IMMEDIATE PRIOR POST, PRI DEPUTIES, HEGEMONIC COMPARED TO DEMOCRATIC ERA

Hegemonic era		Democratic era	
(SMDs only)*		(SMD and PR)	
1982 and 1985 legislatures		2006 and 2009 legislatures	
	Percentage		Percentage
Municipal	9	Municipal	18
State	55	State	54.7
National	32	National	12.5
Nonpolitical	4	Nonpolitical	14.8
Total Percentage	100	Total Percentage	100
N = 582		N = 386	

Source: For the hegemonic era, *Diccionario biográfico del gobierno mexicano*. For the democratic period, newspapers contained in *Infolatina*, a cuttings service.
*Up to 1988, the PRI did not compete for the PR races because of legal restrictions.

party, corporatist sector boss, or federal bureaucrat), have become less prevalent, as demonstrated in Table 7.3: 32 percent of SMD candidates were national politicians under hegemony versus 12.5 for the combined full sample that includes *both* plurality and PR list candidates, where far more national politicians are able to enter the Chamber. One obvious reason for this collapse is that the PRI no longer holds the federal bureaucracy and so the number of national posts available to PRI politicians has fallen. Another cause is that national political leaders are not good candidates to win district races, and so must win their place in the Chamber through a smaller number of closed-list PR seats. Finally, the prevalence of nonpolitical figures is notable, many of whom are local business people who are recruited because they are well known and can pay for a part of their campaign activities.

If the general argument presented above is correct, then those groups within the party that are unable to react successfully to growing pressure at the ballot box should not do well in winning or continuing to control candidacies. Union density in Mexico has fallen from 22.4 percent of the economically active population in 1992 to 15.4 percent in 2000, to 13.6 in 2013.[69] There is a great deal of variation within these figures, however. The Table 7.4 shows the change in formal union members between 1984 and 1998, which were the most formidable years of union decline.

From the table, one sees that many industrial unions, especially in manufacturing, were hard hit by the profound changes to the development model

69. Source: OECD.org, https://stats.oecd.org/Index.aspx?DataSetCode=UN_DEN.

Table 7.4 PERCENTAGE OF UNIONIZED WORKERS
IN DIFFERENT MEXICAN INDUSTRIES, 1984 AND 1998.

Industry	1984	1998	Percentage difference
	%	%	%
Mining and petroleum extraction	.50	.49	−2.0
Food products, beverages, and tobacco	.35	.18	−48.6
Textiles, apparel, and leather products	.28	.16	−42.9
Paper, paper products, and printing	.19	.16	−15.8
Chemical substances, petroleum and coal	.43	.28	−34.9
Basic metal industry	.50	.26	−48.0
Other manufacturing industries	.32	.13	−59.4
Electricity, water, and gas transmission	.65	.57	−12.3
Restaurants and hotels	.9	.9	0.0
Transportation and communications	.54	.20	−63.0
Public administration, defense, and health	.37	.29	−21.6
Education, social service doctors	.65	.57	−12.3

Source: Fairris and Levine (2004, 14).

in Mexico from the mid-1980s onward. For example, in food products, the decline was from 35 percent union coverage to only 18 percent, a fall of roughly half, which is similar to textiles, from 28 to 16 percent. In basic metal industries, again, the union density fell from half of the companies' employees to 26 percent. In the transportation and communication industries, the drop has been more pronounced from 54 percent to only 20 percent union membership. With far fewer union members, these groups that were affiliated with the PRI were no longer able to demand as many candidacies in the Chamber.

However, in education and oil production, the unionized members have remained steady, dropping only from 65 to 57 percent in education and public sector doctors, and from 50 to 49 percent in mining and oil extraction. These numbers help explain why the PEMEX workers' union still wins candidacies in the PRI and why the Teachers' Union (SNTE) was so powerful it was able to win candidacies both within the PRI and within its own party (PANAL) once Elba Esther Gordillo had split with the PRI.

Table 7.5 shows that candidates from the corporatist sectors have done badly in the distribution of candidacies since the onset of democracy, especially those from the CTM (Workers' Sector), a figure that fell from 23.6 percent of the PRI's deputies to 4.9 percent. The Popular Sector deputies dropped from 17.3 percent to 10.9 percent of deputies. Interestingly, the Peasant Sector has not lost as many candidacies, in large part because it can still win races in rural areas.

Table 7.5 SECTORAL AFFILIATION OF PRI DEPUTIES
CANDIDATES, HEGEMONIC VS. DEMOCRATIC ERAS.

Part 1: PRI Federal Deputy candidates from the hegemonic
period.

	1982	1985	Total	Percentage
Peasant Sector	38	31	69	11.7
Popular Sector	53	49	102	17.3
Workers' Sector	73	66	139	23.6
Total sectors	164	146	310	53
Total number deputies	299	289	588	

Source: *Diccionario* biográfico del gobierno mexicano.

Part 2: Random Sample of PRI Federal Deputies Candidates
from 2006 and 2009.

	2009	2006	Total	Percentage
Peasant Sector	14	15	29	9.6
Popular Sector	18	15	33	10.9
Workers' Sector	8	6	14	4.9
Total sectors	40	36	76	25.2
Total number deputies	150	151	301	

Source: Information taken from *Infolatina*, a wire cutting service.

The difference in the percentages of sectoral representation in the SMD districts versus the PR candidates illustrates the problems the sectoral groups now have in placing their allies in the Chamber. Of the 300 SMD candidates in the democratic sample, only 25 percent were identifiably sectoral; while in the PR sample, almost 32 percent were from a corporatist sector. Thus, the national party and those few unions that continue to control resources use the closed PR lists as a way for leaders to reach the Chamber, while the SMD candidacies are no longer distributed for elite maintenance, but to assure electoral victories.

GUBERNATORIAL SELECTION AND RECRUITMENT UNDER DEMOCRACY

The political weight of the governors in Mexico means that these candidates are of higher quality in terms of their prior career trajectories than their federal deputy counterparts. With increasing political competition, powerful state politicians can use their personal popularity to oblige the party's leadership to negotiate their successors in office rather than impose the gubernatorial candidates from the top-down.

In the period from 1995 to 2012, the PRI has used party primaries, conventions, and negotiated "unity" candidates (selection processes with only one precandidate) to select gubernatorial candidates. Of all gubernatorial selections, 33 percent have been competitive (mostly primaries, but also some convention of delegates with more than one precandidate) and 67 percent have been noncompetitive.[70] Since 2005, almost all candidates have been chosen through a system in which all the candidate hopefuls are brought together, and then a single winner is determined, who is termed a "candidate of unity." This type of selection tends to create fewer splits from the party and is far less expensive than a primary.[71]

Executive office seekers and holders have decidedly more power than their legislative counterparts for two reasons. First, voters have a strong identification with the executive office. It is clear what a mayor, governor, or president does, but few voters understand how a local or federal deputy spends her time. Second, the form of voting for an executive office is far more intuitive: one ballot in a single round of voting contrasts with the mysterious assignment of PR seats in a two-tiered system with a fused ballot, in which the legislator cannot return to ask for the voters' support in future elections.

The power of executive candidates in the democratic era tends to manifest in splits or threats of splits from the party: if a gubernatorial hopeful does not win the nomination, she can threaten to leave the party, run against the PRI candidate, and win the state. In the period from 1995 to 2012, of all PRI gubernatorial selection processes, fully twenty-four out of ninety-seven (almost 25 percent) ended up in a member of the party exiting the ranks, winning the nomination for another party in and running against a former PRI colleague. Party splits can cost gubernatorial elections, and a great deal of effort goes into avoiding them.[72]

While the onset of competition over the gubernatorial nominations opened the doors to more open selection methods for some years, it has also had a profound decentralizing effect on the backgrounds of candidates that run for the state's highest office. In Figure 7.1 below, one finds the prior political experience of the PRI's gubernatorial candidates in both the hegemonic and democratic periods.

After 1995, instead of national-type politicians, as characterized by prior jobs in the national party (a figure that dropped from 51 to 23 percent) or

70. Data gathered from newspaper sources by the author.
71. In Mexico, primaries are organized by the parties themselves, not state government.
72. These figures are taken from the author's database on governors. See Bruhn (2014) and Garrido (2014) as well.

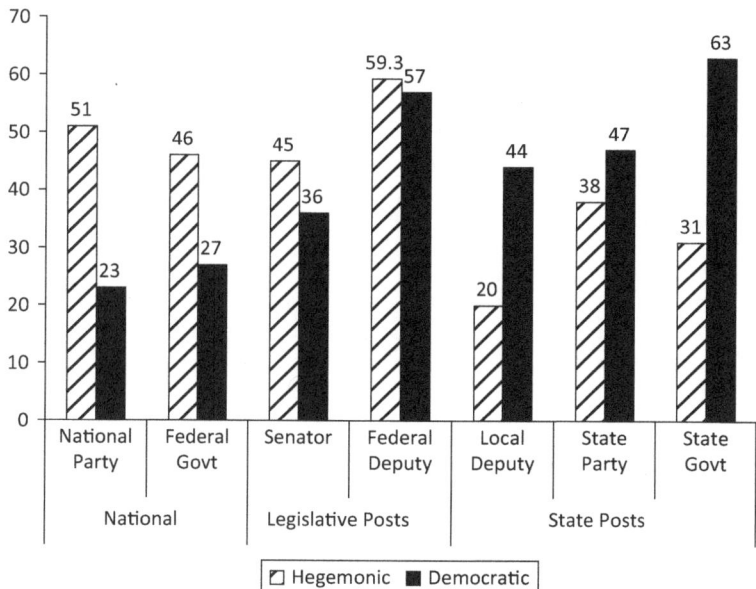

Figure 7.1 Prior experience of PRI gubernatorial candidates, 1960–1995, compared to 1995–2012, in percentages.*

N = 221: 124 governors from the hegemonic era, and 97 from the democratic period, which is counted from 1995 to 2012.

Source: Camp (1995) and newspapers for candidates before 1995. *Infolatina* from 1995 to 2012.

*Numbers do not add up to 100 percent because most gubernatorial candidates held several offices before winning the nomination.

the federal government (from 46 to 27 percent), the party began to nominate politicians with more subnational experience. Those who had been local deputies before winning the nomination rose from 20 to 44 percent (more than double), and the percentage of those who had worked in the state government grew from 31 to almost 64 percent (more than 100 percent increase). As expected, electoral competition drove decentralization in gubernatorial recruitment, just as it had in legislative recruitment.

CONCLUSIONS

With the PRI absent from the presidency between 2000 and 2012, political opportunities for ambitious PRI politicians in the states grew, strengthening the governors thanks to their influence over subnational and many federal candidacies. Because of the growing power of the governors, the party's organization decentralized even before 2000, but especially after the onset of democracy. Furthermore, governors of the large states (from all parties) are excellent candidates for the presidency. All this leads to greater power for the states' executive office holders. Since the PRI retook the presidency in 2012, the president of Mexico is once against first among equals in the party's gubernatorial nominations; still, the process of arriving at a candidate implies more negotiation than imposition.

CHAPTER 8
Changing Federal Deputy Campaigns

This chapter addresses how the PRI and its federal deputy candidates changed their methods of congressional campaigning from the hegemonic to the democratic period. In doing so, the chapter will pinpoint which party groups were able to take advantage of growing electoral competition in order to grow more powerful, helping to explain why the party survived its twelve years out of the presidency. PRI governors (the number of which varied from nineteen to twenty-two of the nation's thirty-two states in the period after 2000) have strong incentives and copious resources to support federal (and local) campaigns in their respective states, pushing up their party's seat totals, which maintained the PRI as a major political actor in national politics between 2000 and 2012 because of its large congressional caucuses. Further, the party's public financing depends on the deputy seat count. During the twelve years out of office, the national party leaders had fewer resources than the governors, but controlled national media appeals. The two groups that were involved in voter mobilization and campaigns before the end of hegemony were able to adjust quickly to new demands at the ballot box, and they gained new resources to do so during the protracted transition period.

The federal deputy candidates had always run active campaigns in part because they enjoyed the support of the PRI mayors and governors, and in part because they were obliged to do so by their superiors in the national party. The PRI did not use overt repression to force voters to the polls, and while they could simply make up vote totals, normally, the party obligated its candidates to work for their votes. After the onset of competition, candidates were driven to transform their campaign tactics as well. Still, they do not control many resources, cannot not hire their own radio and television spots (after the 2008 electoral reform), or run for the same office in the next term. Despite this, the congressional candidates have run even more active campaigns since democratization.

In Mexico's federal system, candidates to the Chamber of Deputies can win a seat either through a single-member district (SMD) plurality race (60 percent of the 500 seats) or through a slot on one of the five closed forty-person PR lists (40 percent, or 200 PR seats). They hold their office for only one term, although they can run again after a period out of office.[1] Voters have only one ballot that determines both tiers; they vote for their favored candidate in the plurality race, and these district votes are aggregated up to one of the five multimember regional PR districts to determine the number of seats the party wins on each of the five closed lists. Because of the fused ballot and closed lists, candidates to the PR lists do not run campaigns; they depend on the popularity of the sixty SMD candidates in their regional forty-member closed PR district.[2] This makes the outcomes of the campaigns in the 300 SMDs that much more important for the party's overall Chamber seat count.

Vote winning is one of the most important tasks parties undertake in their quest to win control of government, so understanding campaigns and the party's role in them helps capture the true nature of a party's internal organization and how it changes. First, the type of campaigning that the candidates and parties carry out helps determine whether office seekers are stronger than the party leadership or vice versa (Cain, Ferejohn, and Fiorina 1987; Carey and Shugart 1995). If candidates do not need party workers to communicate with the electorate and mobilize voters, and instead depend mostly on their own resources and image, they will enjoy greater autonomy from the party's strictures once in the Chamber. But if their personal image and reputation do little to sway voters and parties manage and fund campaigns using programmatic appeals broadcasted through mass media outlets, then individual office holders are weaker in congress compared to their party leaders.

The way that parties and/or candidates carry out their campaign activities also illustrates whether the party has an organizational presence on the ground or not. In the Mexican context, the study of campaigning illustrates that the PRI did not have strong municipal affiliates and that it depended on its governors and mayors to support the efforts of the deputy candidates.

Two factors by and large explain changes to congressional campaigning between the hegemonic and democratic eras: first, growing electoral competition and, second, new electoral rules that made the contests fairer and more

1. This rule was changed in the 2013 electoral reform. Now the candidates who run in 2018 will be able to stay in office for up to three terms, as long as they are renominated by the same party.

2. In the fused ballot, voters have only a single ballot to vote for their plurality candidate; they do not have a second ballot to decide their PR representatives. The second tier is decided by the number of SMD votes in each of the five regional multimember districts (m = 40) for each party. To the author's knowledge, this is the only mixed-member system in the world with a fused ballot, excepting South Korea from 1988 to 2000.

equal. The electoral rules were negotiated between the regime's leaders and the opposition parties to made electoral fraud more costly; to distribute campaign resources in a rule-based manner to all registered parties; and finally, to make mass media accessible to all competitors.

One can trace over time the connection among electoral competition, electoral rule changes, and PRI congressional campaign strategy. Before the onset of competition, campaigns were largely run by the candidates themselves with the support of the governors, the mayors, and the sectoral groups in those districts in which they existed, with oversight provided by the party's national office. The two central activities of the federal deputy campaigns were rallies and smaller meetings with local notables. Advertising and communication consisted of painting walls and hanging posters, with some radio and newspaper interviews. The party did not run national mass-media appeals until well into the 1990s. Instead, it monitored the individual candidates to make sure they did not shirk in their electioneering duties. Candidates had reason to shirk because the margins of victory were consistently high (on average, above 30 percent). But if all campaigned as little as possible, the collective outcome would have resulted in a far lower proportion of votes for the PRI than if each of the candidates had campaigned actively. The work they did during campaign season as political intermediaries (delivering selective goods to their districts and renewing alliances with local leaders) was fundamental in keeping the regime afloat with as little outright repression as possible. As one former PRI senator and deputy remarked, "The PRI would not have been as hegemonic without these alliances. . . . It would have simply been a regime built on acts of authority and force."[3] As long as the candidates held the requisite number of rallies (with large crowds) and meetings with the local leaders, the CEN normally left them alone, and demanded little in terms of issue pronouncements.[4]

This is the forgotten story of the PRI's remarkable electoral outcomes. Magaloni (2006) and Greene (2007) correctly surmised that high electoral returns for the PRI were produced by government subsidies and preelectoral economic outlays. But through the individual efforts of hundreds of PRI candidates during their ground campaigns, many of the lowest-level selective goods were disbursed to the poor, and promises were made to local entrepreneurs, helping create these margins for decades.

To understand campaigning during the hegemonic period, the chapter uses the interviews the author conducted with over forty PRI deputy candidates

3. Interview subject 54, a former federal deputy and senator from the hegemonic era.
4. A typical ideological appeal during an election from 1982: "We will win these elections because the people of Jalisco know that the governments of the Revolution have brought them peace, tranquility, and free education for more than 50 years; because they are conscious of the nationalistic ideology of the PRI, one that is very Mexican," *El Informador* (Jalisco), June 27, 1982, 3A.

and party leaders from both the hegemonic and democratic eras, as well as newspaper articles from the early to mid-1980s. I spoke to candidates who were winners and losers, from urban and rural districts, from competitive and bastion areas, and from sector-held districts and those that had no corporatist presence.[5] The interviews with state and national party leaders from both periods help to compare and contrast the information provided by district level candidates, who tend to exaggerate the importance of their campaigning efforts. For each of the two periods, I look at several aspects of district campaigning, including the efforts to reach and mobilize voters, techniques to communicate with voters, and the role of the CEN in congressional campaigns to understand how competition changed campaigns, and how these new campaigns strengthened certain groups within the PRI, while harming others.

For the democratic period, I rely on both interviews with PRI, PAN, and PRD candidates and a database consisting of a random and representative sample of 200 of the party's 300 SMD candidates for the 2009 and 2012 races for a total of 600, which captures a series of activities from newspaper reports and YouTube.

CAMPAIGNS UNDER PRI HEGEMONY

Scholars largely ignored federal legislative campaigning in Mexico under PRI dominance.[6] Yet, authoritarian electioneering was extremely important for the PRI and the regime's leaders during the Mexico's hegemonic heyday, as it generated and renewed vital links between the national authoritarian regime and local leaders through the exchange of selective access to government benefits. Authoritarian campaigning allows autocrats to remain in power because it generates a great deal of information on local politics in the absence of electoral signaling and opinion polling. Campaigning for the federal Chamber of Deputies was decentralized in that deputy candidates ran their campaigns largely as they saw fit, within the limits established by the party's resource advantages, limited use of technology, and single-term limits. The governors obliged their mayors to support the campaigns of their copartisan federal deputy candidates knowing that if they did not win "their" elections, they could be punished.[7]

5. The interviews considered the follow questions in the same order: What type of activities did you carry out; how many people worked on your campaign; how many were paid; what role did the local party play; did you hire experts; how much did the campaign costs; how much did you receive from IFE; how did you finance the rest?

6. For two important exceptions, see Schmitt (1969) and Taylor (1960).

7. The PAN often accused the PRI mayors of aiding copartisan candidates; see "Evidente, el apoyo económico de los ayuntamientos a candidatos priístas," *Dia*, August 11, 1991, 12.

Electioneering efforts were not completely party-based, because the PRI did not have strong party branches in every municipality or precinct in the nation. Many municipal party branches did not control selective goods and so did not function as US party machines did in the late nineteenth century or the Taiwanese local affiliates in the second half of the twentieth. However, these campaigns were not candidate-centered either, because of the lack of consecutive reelection and electoral competition. Rather, they were a combination of candidate activity, the party's ability to intimidate opposition candidates, and, in some areas, mobilizing work carried out by workers from the Peasant, Workers', or Popular Sectors.

Many authors assumed that the mass organizations of the party had mobilization capacity that reached throughout the length and width of the nation (Collier and Collier 1991; Hamilton 1982; Murillo 2002; Samstad and Collier 1995) and that the party's territorial branches helped organize campaign activities. But in reality, both the territorial and corporatist structures of the party were weak in many areas of the nation, making it imperative that the candidates manage their campaigns and that the CEN monitor them, even though their personal images mattered little.

Programmatic promises over national policies were not the centerpiece of congressional campaigns. Instead, candidates acted as political intermediaries, who expedited the exchange of selective goods between the national party and/or federal bureaucracy and local leaders, such as local businesspeople, priests, school principals, doctors, and leaders of the neighborhoods. Brokering under noncompetitive conditions meant the candidate had to triangulate among the state and municipal governments (almost all of which were governed by the PRI), which controlled access to government resources, and channel these selective goods to neighborhood leaders, who would then bring residents to the voting booths on election day.[8] These local demands included installing public lighting and sewage, castigating corrupt policemen, and forcing public school teachers to show up for class. The deputy candidate could go over the head of the mayor and gain access to the state or federal government, if necessary.[9] Most admit that the brokering was done before the election, and little attention was paid the district after the deputy reached San Lázaro.[10]

---

8. The term *gestoría* or political brokering became connected with the communal lands and the CNC in the 1930s. All those who wanted to get their land claims legalized had to do so through official government channels, and needed help from people who could read and deal with the bureaucracy. The term later meant that popular representatives offered to broker government services or permits for those who were organized within the PRI. Luis Javier Garrido, "La tráfica de influencias," *La Jornada*, April 4, 1986, 5.

9. Interview subjects 54 and 76. Interview subject 76 won his districts in both the hegemonic and democratic eras, and states that he made alliances with local leaders, and offered them solutions to their problems within the community that other elected PRI officials refused to solve. Also, author interview subject 60, a former federal PRI deputy and leader of the CEN.

10. The common explanation for why the deputy did not return to her district after winning the election was that the deputy had little to gain from "taking care of his

Political brokering helped create or renew alliances between the national regime leaders in the federal bureaucracy and national party and local leaders; and because all of the governors and most of the mayors were from the PRI, it was easier to channel resources to the candidate. This was the glue that kept the party operating at the local level. In return, local leaders were expected to organize meetings, lunches, and smaller rallies during the campaign. But most importantly, local leaders controlled the neighborhood brokers who were charged with getting voters to the booths on election day. Because these local leaders offered such an important commodity to the PRI regime, those from rural areas were given wide latitude in how they ran their localities—at times using violence and intimidation; although not all local leaders were caciques. The former Secretary of Electoral Training for the CEN of the PRI, Hector Hugo Olivares, stated in 1985 that if the CEN proved successful at organizing a then new program of voter mobilization using *party members* in the localities instead of local notables, "then this method of vote promotion would end the problem of *cacicazgos*, because there would no longer be the need of going to the local 'strongmen' who offered a certain number of favorable votes."[11] Beginning in the early 1960s, the PRI's leaders made several attempts to strengthen the party's territorial apparatus, most of which failed, and so the PRI continued to depend on local leaders and caciques.

The literature on rural caciques from the 1960s and 1970s recognized the importance of local leaders in electoral duties.[12] Paré (1975) wrote about one rural area in the 1960s, and explained that local strongmen were given political prerogatives over the internal economic market in rural areas that allowed them to control economic gains (1975, 48–51). The caciques also worked with the governors to help bring in the vote and acted as an intermediary between the peasants and state government.

Still, many political scientists believed the corporatist sectors were mostly responsible for voter mobilization. Craig and Cornelius (1995, 254) write, "The mass organizations were charged with mobilizing voter supporter for the regime, and aggregating interests of the constituents to the government bureaucracy. "Elections, as a result, were 'secondary affairs' because the interests of the organized masses were aggregated and transmitted through the sectoral organizations" (Arnaut 1997, 18). Murillo (2002, 14) writes of Mexico and Argentina, "Union leaders provided electoral machines for labor

voters" because of single-term limits. However, interview subject 61 offers another: if the deputy showed too much interest in his district once in office, the governor or other local power holders might think he was trying to place his own ally as the PRI's candidate in the next round, which was informally prohibited.

11. See Miguel Angel Rivera, *La Jornada*, March 30, 1985, 2.
12. Among many others, see Friedrich (1965) and Ugalde (1973).

based parties and social consensus in return for political influence."[13] This chapter presents evidence that the sectors were in fact not present across many of the nation's districts, and the influence of sectors over election-eering was limited to "their" districts; that is, districts in which they were traditionally able to place a leader or member of their group as candidate. Finally, even where the sectors were active, the candidates—together with the governors—were still personally responsible for winning their races and were crucial elements of the PRI's hegemonic success. This distinction between sectoral mobilization and neighborhood vote brokers is crucial: since the Workers' Sector was largely active in urban areas (where industrial and craft unions were located), it was easier to replace their faltering work-ers with neighborhood leaders that the governors and mayors hired. On the other hand, the rural-based Peasant Sector was better able to continue to win votes and seats, because it worked in rural areas.

Campaign Mobilization under Hegemony

In an authoritarian regime in which public opinion surveys were not used, both candidates and voters worked in an information-poor environment. A second crucial responsibility of the PRI deputy candidates during their two-to three-month campaigns was to collect information about voters' opinions about regime performance and deliver information to voters about the suc-cesses of the PRI.

Mass rallies and small meetings with local notables were two central aspects of hegemonic campaigning. Large rallies brought together anywhere from 1,000 to 10,000 residents in the central plaza of a town or city to listen to speeches and music.[14] Rallies had two objectives: first, to show the party's agent in the state, and therefore the CEN, that the candidate could mobilize voters (with the support of mayors or sectors in those areas in which they were active). This was a crucial way to signal higher-level leaders within the PRI that the candidate was mobilizing voters to show up on election day.[15] Second, rallies helped demonstrate to opposition candidates that the PRI

13. According to Camacho Solís (1980, 111), the CTM had several political duties in the first decades of the regime; first, it contributed to writing the programmatic platform of the party; second, it recruited some politicians, notably in the local arena; third, it constituted an integral part of the electoral process, because its districts tend to vote heavily for PRI candidates; and finally, the CTM's state federations supported the governors by mobilizing voters.

14. Interview subject 64, a former PRI deputy from a rural district who had won elec-tions in both the hegemonic and democratic periods.

15. Interview subject 53, who was a former secretary of organization of the CEN, senator, and leader of the Peasant Sector.

enjoyed overwhelming support and so it was not worthwhile investing scarce resources in that particular district (Magaloni 2006). These rallies were filled with peasants and locals who were trucked in from nearby localities, and they were normally organized by the mayor, the local party, or a union where one was active.[16]

The second most important aspect of campaign organization consisted of the small meetings that the candidate held with local economic and social notables of the district. The purpose of these smaller meetings was to listen to the demands of local leaders; in this way, they were intimately linked to clientelistic exchange. Depending on the type of district for which one was running, the deputy would meet with neighborhood leaders, those responsible for the markets, teachers, business leaders, and the local corporatist leaders, if there were any. Many former deputy candidates mentioned that the mayors were fundamental in organizing these meetings, because they knew the area and its leaders better than the candidate.[17] A former deputy reports that while she used local party leaders to organize small meetings with neighbors, she was careful that they did not bring the same neighbors to meeting after meeting, giving the candidate the impression they were working to mobilize new voters.[18] On election day, these local leaders moved voters to the polls.

HEGEMONIC COMMUNICATION TECHNIQUES

Aside from the small meetings with local leaders and the large rallies, the candidates from the hegemonic party had a variety of other instruments to reach voters. The first and most notable were the famous painted public walls in cities, towns, and villages.[19] The painted walls provided very simple information that was largely invariant across time and space: the candidate's name, the post for which she was running, the date of the election, and the party's name and emblem.

Newspapers reached a more educated, elite audience, and were used mostly to interview the PRI candidates, although sometimes advertisements were

16. Interview subject 76 mentions that in 1985 when he ran for office, the sectors in his district (the CTM and the FSTSE) helped organize his campaign events because he was a member of the FSTSE. But when he ran in 2003, the sectors were no longer present. Interview subjects 67 and 61 offered the same observation in their interviews.

17. Interview subjects 60 and 61. At times, the party structure would help the candidate, although this did not seem to be the norm; see Ivan Restrepo, "Testimonio de una visita domiciliaria," *La Jornada*, April 8, 1985, 7.

18. Interview subject 59, who was a member of the CTM, and candidate under both hegemonic and democratic conditions.

19. In Mexico, instead of houses or commercial strip malls, many buildings in the center of town and side streets present a wall to the street, which can be painted.

taken out. Some PRI candidates had to pay off the newspaper columnists and reporters so they could be assured that they would be given a certain number of positive interviews and stories during the campaign.[20] If the politician refused to pay off the newspaper, he could expect some negative press, even though he was the PRI candidate. The newspapers usually ignored opposition candidates.

Mass media strategies, such as television and radio, were not used by the PRI (or any other party) in campaigning efforts before the 1990s, either at the national or local level. Rather, the Office of the Presidency in Mexico City made deals with the owner of the single private television network, Televisa, so that the nightly newscast would simply cover the PRI campaign for the Congress, and ignore the opposition's efforts (Hughes 2006; Lawson 2005). The PAN and other opposition parties fought to get equal treatment and access to both state-owned and private television, but before the electoral reforms of the 1990s, it was close to impossible.[21]

Most PRI deputy candidates organized their own campaign teams, although in some areas, a sectoral group would take over much of the organizational work.[22] As a former federal deputy and former leader of the CEN stated, if a sector were present in the district, and had a role in nominating the candidate, its members would work for the deputy hopeful; otherwise, the candidate was on her own.[23] For example, in a district of Tamaulipas, the sugar cane cutters' union was powerful, but in the 1988 congressional election cycle, it could not place an ally or leader as the deputy candidate of "its" district, and so did not support the PRI candidate.[24]

The PRI's hegemonic campaigns for the Chamber can be termed "candidate-managed" because the corporatist sectors had strength in only about half of the nation's single-member electoral districts as the legislative recruitment data presented in the previous chapter showed. And as several interviews with former party leaders and deputy candidates attest, the sectors were active only in those districts in which they could place one of their own or a close ally as candidate. Candidates, however, could not rely on their personal images or reputation for performance in office because of a lack of mass media and single-term limits, so one cannot term these candidate-centered efforts, either.

20. Interview subject 61.
21. See James Fortson, "Tiempo a la Oposición en la TV Estatal Pide AN," *Excelsiór*, April 9, 1985, 1.
22. Interview subjects 76, former deputy 67, former deputy and losing candidate 59, and former deputy in the hegemonic era 68. Interview subject 59 reports that the CTM ran in the same districts for decades, increasing the expertise and information about their bailiwicks.
23. Interview with former hegemonic federal deputy subject 68.
24. Interview with former hegemonic deputy subject 61.

The Party Branches in Hegemonic Campaigning

One could assume that where the sectors were weaker, the territorial structure of the party, which is made up of committees at the precinct, district, municipal, and state levels, would do a great deal of campaign work precisely because of their privileged position "on the ground." However, many hegemonic federal deputies report that the territorial offices of the party in several districts and municipalities were abandoned between elections, with little or no money, physical headquarters, or leadership.[25] In an extreme example, in 1987 a PRI gubernatorial candidate complained publicly that the party had no committee offices in the state's eighty-four municipalities.[26] Dale Story (1986, 79) reports that only 35 percent of the party's municipal committees met regularly during the early 1980s, in a period of intense interest in strengthening the local organizations.[27] A former editor of a PRI-sponsored newspaper *El Nacional*, interview subject 44, stated that the state PRI in Guanajuato "had no reason to function" between major campaigns and that outside of campaign season, the leader of the state PRI *should not* play an active role in strengthening the party's municipal affiliates. But under other governors, the state and local parties were more active, and interview subject 29, a former federal deputy, stated that in Chihuahua, the campaigns were run from the formal structure of the party, and even the precinct committees played a role.

Although no other party in Mexico could come close to competing with the official party's geographical coverage of its organization, it was surprisingly sparse in terms of a permanent presence, especially in more rural areas.[28] It was cheaper and more efficient to have candidates do the campaign work in those areas that did not have a strong sectoral or territorial presence, a finding that is confirmed by Cornelius's 1975 work on urban settlements in the 1960s and 1970s. Urban brokers exchanged votes and campaign support for access to selective benefits, such as regularization of the takeover of the lands and the provision of local services. While national regime leaders might have

---

25. Interview subject 18, a former Secretary of Electoral Action of the CEN, who states that the CEN did not know the names of the leaders of the precinct committees, or who had named them, and that they often had no party documents recognizing their authority; see Ismael Romero, "No hay archivos confiables . . . ," *El Universal*, September 1, 1990, 5.

26. Miguel Angel Rivera, "Lugo encontró desorganizado y sin sede al PRI en Hidalgo," *La Jornada*, January 18, 1987, 9.

27. A former leader of the state PRI in Guanajuato in the early 1990s noted that close to the elections the precinct committees would begin to work very superficially, and that generally, the territorial part of the party was weak (interview subject 47).

28. A former local deputy and member of the state PRI in Jalisco, interview subject 20A, stated that in many rural municipalities in the state, they had no idea who the militants were, and it was difficult at times to find the building that housed the municipal committee.

bemoaned the existence of rural and urban brokers, party leaders and low-ranking government officials supported them because "Eliminating the caciques would require lower level officials to invest much more time and energy in grass roots political organizing" (Cornelius 1975, 164).

GOVERNORS, MAYORS, AND THE TERRITORIAL BASE OF THE PRI

The governors and mayors, almost all of which were members of the hegemonic party, were central pieces of the overall campaign strategy for the PRI, and the governors were expected to support their co-partisan candidates or suffer the consequences.[29] The governors had several electoral tasks in campaign season: first, they made sure their state's mayors helped organize both rallies and smaller meetings.

Governors also gave the PRI deputy candidates some access to selective state resources with which they could conduct brokering with local leaders. They encouraged state employees to volunteer to take part in district election-eering, and offered financial help, transportation, materials for posters, and even folding chairs for larger meetings and rallies. One former governor from the 1980s noted that he decided where to place some of the polling stations.[30] Finally, governors ran promotional campaigns: every time they opened a hospital or inaugurated a public works project, they boasted "This is what the PRI does for you."[31] A candidate from the hegemonic period went as far to say that if the governor placed or supported a candidate's nomination for a district in his state, that candidate would need little help from the CEN in the campaign.[32]

National Party Leadership's Role in Hegemonic Campaigning

The CEN's role in congressional campaigning was to oversee the national effort which consisted in monitoring individual deputy races to assure regime

29. For the 1988 presidential succession, the governor of Colima had supported Manuel Bartlett as a candidate for the PRI, but his rival, Carlos Salinas, won the nod. When Salinas placed an ally to be candidate of a district in Colima, the governor refused to support her campaign efforts (interview subject 60). Another deputy candidate from the same election cycle stated that because his state's governor was against his nomination, the local party would not help with his campaign (interview subject 61).

30. Interview subject 63, a former PRI governor in the 1980s.

31. Interview subject 88, a former PRI governor.

32. Interview subject 76.

leaders that no districts would be lost. The national party, as we have seen, had an army of agents in the states. These agents were charged with quantifying the candidates' campaign efforts in their region by counting the number of meetings held, the number of rallies (and how many people attended), and the number of meters of painted walls as well as banners and posters swinging from utility poles.[33] If the deputy chose not to perform her duties up to standard, she could expect a visit from the concerned party agent. As a result, it was in the interests of the local party leaders and the candidates to exaggerate their efforts.[34] In the worst case, the party had the ability to threaten to remove its support from the candidate in the middle of a campaign, although this occurred very rarely.

Because of the dire economic situation in 1985, the PRI began to elaborate more serious campaign strategies, centering on door-to-door canvassing and neighborhood mobilization led by party workers rather than the candidate. This is a clear indication of the early and ongoing interest in the national PRI leadership in assuring PRI victories using more modern technologies and information (which does not negate their use of fraud). The CEN also provided electoral information for the candidates on their districts, a practice its leaders instituted in the 1980s because of the electoral effects of the economic downturn.[35] This information included sociodemographic data on the residents of the precincts within the district, as well as data on past electoral returns.

The PRI established a vote target for the legislative 1985 midterm elections of 16.5 million votes and promised to train thousands of activists to promote and defend the vote across the nation. The PRI stated would use its party base, defined as the unions, small-business people, and government workers to get out the vote.[36] Furthermore, the party promised to press its former office holders into service during the campaigns. This was one of the first nationally organized mobilization strategies.[37]

33. Interview subject 57, a former polling expert with the CEN during the early 1990s.

34. Former leader of the state PRI in Baja California, subject 32, relates that local party leaders informed agents sent down by the CEN in 1989 that everything was in shape to win the elections, right before the party was defeated for the first time ever in gubernatorial elections.

35. The party sent pamphlets to its candidates in the 1985 electoral year explaining how they should deal with criticisms of the regime's handling of the economy. See José Ureña, "Aumentar salarios, contra intereses de mayorías: PRI," *La Jornada*, March 25, 1985, 7.

36. See Angel Trejo, "Movimiento Millonario de Militantes Priistas," *El Sol*, March 26, 1985, 9, and Miguel Angel Rivera, *La Jornada*, March 30, 1985, 2.

37. Interview subject 68, former Undersecretary of Organization of the CEN in the mid-1980s, explained the 1985 voter mobilization program: first, the national party did not carry out a national media campaign; second, local *party* activists mobilized voters, and this was volunteer work. Finally, the sectors and members of the territorial structure participated in this vote promotion.

Most Mexicans voted for the PRI of their own free will, yet fraud and manipulation were crucial elements of the Mexican electoral landscape. However, for obvious reasons, it was difficult to quantify and measure.[38] One can never know for certain what percentage of the PRI's massive vote stemmed from its successful macroeconomic policies, its mobilization advantages, the lack of serious opposition alternatives at the ballot box, or its ability to steal votes and pad the vote totals. But one can speak in general of the kinds of fraud and electoral manipulation that were perpetrated upon the electorate in Mexico for decades. The first type of vote manipulation was that the federal government financed PRI campaigns with public resources, which were unavailable to the opposition (Magaloni 2006; Schedler 2006). The party received money from the federal government, and it also was able to disburse to its candidates such goods as access to municipal and state services, building materials, licenses, and contracts (Greene 2007).

The second type of fraud was rigging the actual vote count, either by padding the vote totals, or stealing votes from the opposition.[39] Members of the PRI "filled the ballot boxes," or sent out the "flying brigades" of party or campaign workers who went from voting station to voting station fulfilling their civic duty by voting early and often, which was possible because they were registered in more than one precinct (Lawson 2000). The voting lists were purposively out of date, and many dead people came back to life to vote on election day.

The party representatives of the voting stations were extremely important for "protecting the vote" and PRI deputy candidates were usually responsible for placing their own representatives. Once voting ended, the official ballot tallies left the polling station, after which, they passed "customs" where the polling officials could change the tallies, before they arrived at the electoral district's central counting office. The PRI was able to exclude the opposition representatives from the stations by a variety of legal and bureaucratic means. So, if the party had control over the polling station officials, it could better control the electoral results, which explains why PRI candidates were so

---

38. See Craig and Cornelius (1995, 255) for a list of the PRI's fraudulent activities and Eisenstadt (2004) for the most complete work on fraud in Mexico.

39. An excellent source is Jorge Casteñeda, "El fraude moderno," *Proceso*, 773–17, August 26, 1991. Deputies did not want to win fewer votes than the historic average in their district, but in a strange act of courtesy, if one were running in a concurrent presidential election, it was also seen as bad form to win more votes than the president. Interview subject 67, a former federal deputy and president of the CEN.

interested in placing their own polling station representatives if they were not politically aligned with their PRI governor.[40]

Another unfair advantage was the constant abuse to which some opposition candidates were subjected during the campaigns. A two-time losing congressional candidate for the PAN from Jalisco reports the following forms of intimidation that occurred during his 1976 run for office in a rural district.[41] First, somebody shot over his head outside a municipal building when he was speaking to a small crowd. Second, the mayor of a town cranked up the municipal loudspeaker when the candidate tried to give a speech outside a church. Third, local PRI leaders falsified the identity of representatives of his party at the polling stations. Fourth, local PRI rowdies tore down the PAN candidate's posters and chased him and members of his team out of neighborhoods, and painted over their walls.[42] Finally, soldiers were posted outside the voting booths, so the opposition candidates could not stop many fraudulent PRI tactics. It was not that every opposition candidate was subjected to this sort of abuse, but enough were as to make it difficult to run in many districts, especially those located in rural areas.

As prevalent as fraud and electoral manipulations were, they were costly to carry out, and as a result, it was much better to win each election with as little open and contestable fraud as possible. Many have simply assumed because the PRI was so vertically organized that if a candidate were in trouble, the party's fraud experts would find out about the problem and automatically fix it. However, the true contractual nature of internal party relations becomes clearer if one examines the role of the party's fraud experts, called "raccoons."[43] At times, a party fraud expert would tell a PRI candidate she would lose her election unless she used his services. Because the candidate had no independent picture of voter preferences in her district, she had to rely on her instinct to know if the expert was telling the truth, and pay the fraud expert should she use his services.

More serious fraud was revived in the 1980s because of the economic crisis, and the electoral pressures this placed on the PRI's unpopular sectoral candidates (Reyes del Campillo 1990, 157).[44] The use of overt fraud to change electoral outcomes, rather than to pad vote totals, created costly problems for the

40. Often the deputy candidate could not trust the governor or a powerful sector within the district to man the polling stations because they could steal votes from the PRI candidate to make him look bad before the CEN (interview subject 60).

41. Interview subject 80, a candidate of the PAN in the hegemonic era.

42. Marta Anaya, "En Pleno Apogeo, la Guerra de las Bardas," *Excelsiór*, March 29, 1985, 4.

43. *Mapache*, or raccoon, refers to the animal that steals things in the dark but is difficult to catch.

44. The PAN printed a pamphlet in the 1985 midterms detailing how to avoid the PRI's fraudulent activities. See Antonio Gil, "Libro del PAN para Evitar los Fraudes Electorales del PRI," *El Sol*, April 14, 1985, 1.

PRI, as the PAN became more successful at blocking this type of vote stealing (although the PRD was not as successful in this area). One of the battles that was waged and won during the 1990s was the creation and strengthening of an autonomous electoral court system, which allowed opposition parties to contest many of these fraudulent practices (Eisenstadt 2004).

ELECTORAL COMPETITION AND THE BEGINNING OF MODERNIZED CAMPAIGNING: 1990S

A dramatic transformation in the PRI's congressional campaigning began after the 1988 electoral catastrophe, when the party lost forty plurality races (of 300) instead of the customary one to ten. The regime leaders realized that campaigning (and candidate selection) would have to be reformed if the party were to maintain its hegemonic position. The PAN in Chihuahua had already begun to test more modern campaign techniques, such as more modern publicity and campaign consultants.[45] The PRI's national leaders realized that the classic campaigns were no longer enough, especially in more middle-class, urban areas as competition continued to grow during the 1990s.[46]

The legislative midterm campaigns of 1991 saw the emergence of a new kind of electoral strategy that was based on paying an army of political operators to work in the competitive precincts to raise the vote and win the district.[47] However, the PRI's national organization still did not use modern media appeals.[48]

The first step taken by the CEN in 1991 to modernize the party's district-level campaign strategies was to take over the management of the most competitive districts from the candidates, and in doing so, centralize some aspects of campaigning. The CEN gave itself the task of reaching and registering potential voters: it renewed the voting lists in the districts, began to use public opinion polls, targeted assured voters, and then channeled the party's resources accordingly.[49] Most importantly, it kept a count of how many SMDs had to be won, given the different percentages of the national vote in the PR

45. René Delgado, "Elecciones: pérdidas del PRI y triunfos importantes del PAN," *Uno más uno*, November 14, 1983.

46. Pacheco (1997) argues that by 1988, the PRI had turned its attention to more urban districts. Overall, however, the 1988 concurrent legislative and presidential elections were very traditional, with little use of mass media to target messages to voters.

47. Interview subject 68.

48. In 1991, the president's team used the popularity of the chief executive in the nightly newscast on Televisa to shore up the vote of the deputies—not an advertising strategy.

49. Interview subject 58, a former Undersecretary of Elections for the CEN in the transition years.

seats that the PRI could expect, in order to capture as many Chamber seats as possible.[50]

For the 1991 midterm races, the CEN created a map for each of the nation's 300 districts that discriminated between the precincts that were easiest and hardest to win, and then concentrated money and manpower on the competitive precincts. In 121 priority districts, the CEN focused on voter mobilization, the installation of voting stations, and hiring loyal representatives for the polling stations. This army of paid political operatives was sent to different areas within a precinct to find residents who would promise to vote for the PRI candidate, get their names and addresses, and make sure they were registered to vote. Each secretary of the CEN was responsible for a region of the country.[51] Federal deputy candidates from more competitive districts had less autonomy and were obligated to follow the priorities established by the CEN and to submit to far more oversight. The preelection tactics were followed up on election day with a type of small-scale clientelist exchange, referred to as *Operación Tamal*, in which party mobilizers handed out small incentives, such as breakfasts, so voters would mark the ballot for the PRI (Bruhn 1997).

The party depended economically on the federal government from its foundation in 1929, and the opposition could not hope to match these resources until after the 1996 electoral reforms.[52] To mitigate this dependence on government financing, the party began to ask for donations from business, which was done in parallel with public party finance reforms.[53]

The 1991 electoral mobilization model was an enormous success, and the PRI lost far fewer districts in 1991 than it had in 1988. The model continued to be used in the concurrent 1994 presidential and legislative elections, and even though the PRI's vote fell from its historic levels, the party was in no danger of losing the presidency or its absolute majority in the Chamber. Then, as

50. Interview subject 57 stated that it was easier to win a difficult majority district than to raise the national vote by 1 percentage point. The CEN had these numbers in mind, but individual candidates did not (interview subject 53).

51. The electoral mobilization model used in 1991 was based on the Chihuahua model, first employed in the 1986 municipal and state races in the state of Chihuahua. The fundamentals were: nominate a smaller number of sectoral candidates; place more money and people to work in the territorial structure, particularly the precincts; obligate state bureaucrats to work in the precincts during the campaigns, and especially on election day; invest almost nothing in media; put money into buying tamales or breakfasts on the day of the election; pay people to mobilize voters and take care of the voting station. This money would be provided by the federal and state governments through the CEN. Paid vote promoters, not lower-level activists, were the base of this strategy (interview subject 2A). The leader of the party denied that government funds were spent on PRI campaigns; José Ureño, "Niega Colosio . . . ," *La Jornada*, July 30, 1991, 1.

52. For example, Marco Rascón. "Un minuto en Televisa," *La Jornada*, June 18, 1991, 9.

53. See Saúl Vázquez Granados, "Gran Influencia Política Tienen los Empresarios que Financian al PRI, Reconoce Sales Gutiérrez," *El Financiero*, January 14, 1992, 12.

discussed in chapter 2, the 1994–1995 economic crisis exploded, and the PRI saw the end of the hegemonic era as one set of the regime's leaders began to negotiate a far-reaching electoral reform with opposition party leaders.

AFTER 1996: MODERNIZED CAMPAIGNING
UNDER COMPETITIVE AND FAIR CONDITIONS.

As shown in the section above, the PRI leadership did not wait until the 1996 electoral reform or the 2000 defeat to adjust to competitive elections. Leaders within the party knew they would be indispensable if they managed different aspects of campaigning. The party organization now had resources to spend on mass media appeals, allowing it to modernize quickly by designing mass media appeals and using public opinion surveys.[54] The PAN and PRD leaders followed suit. There was no longer a collective-action problem—deputy candidates now had to campaign vigorously. In the twelve years the PRI spent out of the presidency, the party's governors also strove to win elections in their respective states to enjoy more influence in the federal chamber.

Even before 2000, national party leaders were divided into one group that strongly believed that national media appeals are more effective in winning votes (and that ground campaigns are largely an excuse for party leaders to enrich themselves) and another that insisted mass media had to be supplemented with large numbers of paid vote promoters working in the districts. This conflict was resolved for the 2000 race because the CEN had money to spend both on media and on vote promoters,[55] even though many of its leaders believed district campaigning was a waste of time. Between 2000 and 2006, a good proportion of IFE money was spent on media advertising: for example, Mena (2010, 15) reports that the PRI spent almost 57 percent of all its campaign money from IFE on radio and television in the 2006 presidential elections. The national party headquarters today hires polling and marketing firms, organizes television strategies, and plans an overall marketing strategy for congressional candidates. However, district candidates believe that homogenized advertisements, made by paid professionals in Mexico City and designed to sell the party label across the nation, are not sufficient to convince local voters, and as a result, they campaign vigorously in their localities. A two-pronged approach has been established, one based on the media work of the CEN, and the other based on the candidates' efforts in the districts.

---

54. President Salinas had begun to use polling in the late 1980s in the Office of the Presidency, and it quickly spread to the CEN.

55. Interview subject 67, president of the CEN at the end of the Zedillo term, stated that despite this conflict, national party headquarters spent on both.

Table 8.1 COMPARATIVE ACTIVITIES IN DISTRICT CAMPAIGNS, 2009 AND 2012

		Full sample	PAN	PRD	PRI
Activities		%	%	%	%
Interviews		54	48.7	45.5	68
Rallies		60.8	42	42	87
Videos		51	49.25	38.7	65
Social media	FB/Twitter	55.6	42.8	42.8	72.5
Canvassing		66.5	61.2	52.2	86
Number of candidates		1200	400	400	400
Av. # of video views		517			

* Source: Author's data. This is a random and representative sample of 200 of the 300 SMD candidates from the three major parties taken from YouTube, Google, and newspaper cuttings services, such as *Infolatina*.

Under a simple plurality system with consecutive reelection, one could have expected that the onslaught of democratization would modernize congressional campaigns along the lines of their American counterparts: modern, media-driven events that are heavily dependent on the ability of the candidates to sell their image to district voters (Agranoff 1976; Ceasar 1990; Wattenberg 1991). However, modern congressional campaigns in democratic Mexico have developed differently. First, one sees greater candidate-voter contact during the campaign season, but less image-based campaigning than in the United States, because of single-term limits imposed on all elected officials. Deputy candidates do, however, organize rallies, neighborhood tours, phone banks, leafleting, and door-to-door canvassing. Further, as Table 8.1 shows, more than 70 percent of the PRI candidates invest in some sort of social media, and half of them produce YouTube videos extolling their personal integrity and outlining their promises for local service provision.

Mexican parties receive IFE money for both regular party activities (every year) and campaigning for electoral activities every three years. In 2008, a nonelectoral year for federal elections, all parties together received over 182 million US dollars, giving the parties the resources to support a permanent bureaucracy and state affiliates. In the 2009 legislative midterms (held under the new electoral code), the parties received the equivalent of 236 million US dollars, and did not have to pay for their television or radio spots.

The CEN negotiated the electoral reforms of the 1990s and 2000s with the national leaders of the other two major parties so it could establish its authority over public campaign finance. It does not leave the party's total seat count in the Chamber of Deputies to the individual, noncoordinated actions of 300 majority candidates as it might under a simple majoritarian system. These two factors help explain why the CEN modernized its campaign strategies more fully than the plurality candidates and resisted their pleas for more funds. The PRI governors, on the other hand, continue to support their copartisan campaign efforts in their respective states.

Under the 1996 electoral code (which lasted until 2008), all registered parties divvied up 30 percent of the total finance pool, while the remaining 70 percent was allocated according to each party's previous showing in federal congressional elections. The overall pool of resources for each election depended on the number of registered parties multiplied by the cost of a typical federal deputy campaign, which was computed by IFE bureaucrats. However, while the party received money based on this calculation, IFE resources were not sent automatically to the deputy candidates to run their SMD campaigns; rather, they were sent (and still are) to the Secretary of Finance of each party's CEN. The parties are not obligated by law to allocate a specific amount of campaign funds to Chamber candidates.[56]

The amount of federal money spent on Mexican federal elections has skyrocketed since 1991 from 46 million dollars for all parties to over 445 million dollars in the 2003 midterms, to 293 million in 2012 (*without* the costs of advertising), which has allowed the CEN to play an important role in campaigns. Now that the party no longer has to buy media time, it has much more money to spend on local mobilizing, which is difficult to track and monitor.[57] Furthermore, state electoral institutes allocate funds for local and state elections, and are not obligated to report this money to the IFE (Harbers 2010, 142). According to Mena (2010, 21), the state electoral institutions (resources separate from those of the IFE) allocated to the parties the equivalent of over 380 million US dollars in the 2009–2010 *subnational* elections.[58] Finally, and most troubling, most of the PRI candidates for federal deputy received roughly MXP$400,000 from the CEN for their campaigns in 2009, the equivalent of

---

56. Personal communication with Arturo Sánchez, IFE councilor. Individual deputies have few reasons to comply with spending limits because, as Poiré (2006, 4) has pointed out, only political parties are legally accountable to IFE. Furthermore, before the changes to COFIPE in 2008, it was extremely difficult to audit actual spending in the districts.

57. Evidence of this was the related electoral scandal involving the MONEX or prepaid gift cards that PRI voter promoters allegedly handed out in return for votes. The PRI's lawyer, Jesús Murillo Karam, stated that the cards were bought to distribute about six million dollars to pay for the PRI's organization, not votes; http://www.animalpolitico.com/2012/07/si-usamos-tarjetas-de-monex-pri/#ixzz2YkG662vA.The PRI was later absolved in a questionable vote in the IFE; see http://www.cnnexpansion.com/negocios/2013/01/23/penanieto-pri-monex-ife-elecciones-voto.

58. Mena (2010) presents data on spending per capita of the IEEs, which we have translated into per state spending in 2010 dollars by multiplying the per capita spending figure given by Mena by the INEGI census figures for 2010 for the twenty-seven states that reported. This is then translated into dollars.

US$37,000. Federal deputy candidates cannot win competitive or bastion districts with $37,000. A study conducted by Centro de Estudios Espinoso Yglesias and Integralia (2013) estimates that underreporting on campaigns is endemic; and the true spending figures are several times higher than the official numbers.

District Campaigns under Democracy

One can test the proposition that higher levels of electoral competition drive district-level campaign modernization; with its correlate—less competition causes less modernization. As expected, even today, one finds that in rural areas with less competitive elections, campaigning has not changed dramatically since the hegemonic party held sway. In rural areas of the country, such as Durango (a state still held by the PRI), rural campaigns remain largely unchanged.[59] But in competitive districts of the nation, campaigns are more modern, with new technologies, such as videos in YouTube that have been quickly adapted by the district campaign teams.

More candidates now receive professional training or hire professional campaign managers, or are forced to accept a campaign specialist sent down by a copartisan governor. Mass mailings are now a part of modern district campaigning in Mexico, unlike thirty years ago.[60] Those who used them stated they were usually sent to loyal voters to strengthen the likelihood of voting on election day. In the 2003 legislative midterm election,[61] 33 percent of Mexicans report they had received some sort of information or contact from a federal candidate or party, while in the 2009 races, this figure had risen to 40 percent. Robocalls now form part of modern campaigns as well, and more than 16 percent of respondents report receiving a call in the 2009 midterms.[62] Before 2008, paid professionals worked to improve the candidate's image with voters through advertising spots. Those candidates who are business people are now more popular with the PRI than before in part because they can pay for a good portion of their campaigns by themselves (or with their friends) and in part because they are well known and willing to use modern electioneering

---

59. Interview subject 65, a former federal deputy.

60. Interview subject 78 stated that he paid for three mass mailings during his campaign, for which he used a voter list that he had put together. The mailings went out in different stages: the first was to notify the voters that he was a priísta; the second asked the voters to support his candidacy; and the third thanked them.

61. CSES Opinion Survey, Mexico, 2003 and 2009, which can be accessed at http://lnpp.cide.edu/.

62. Unfortunately, this question was not asked in 2003, and so cannot be compared.

techniques.[63] Of the major parties competing in 2009 and 2012, 16 percent had business experience; the PAN was highest at 22.3 percent and the PRI was slightly above average at 17.25 percent (the PRD only had 9 percent of its candidates with backgrounds in the private sector).

A second difference between PRI congressional campaigns in the two eras is the prior electoral information that candidates have, in which they carefully distinguish between losing, competitive, and bastion precincts to employ different strategies of voter contact.[64] Many candidates, such as a former deputy (interview subject 78), mentioned that they had prior experience in the general area of the district for which they had run, and that they were able to take advantage of this to raise funds and organize meetings.[65]

The power of many of the sectoral organizations has been greatly reduced, except for the SNTE and, in some areas, the CNC.[66] One deputy winner states that in her urban district in Hidalgo, "The *voto corporativo* no longer exists."[67] But candidates in indigenous areas still rely on blocks of voters in rural districts in some states.[68] Because the corporatist vote has largely disappeared in those districts where it had been powerful, other means of voter mobilization have sprung up.

Candidates now rely on several methods of direct voter contact: door-to-door canvassing, small meetings with neighbors, and walking tours of neighborhoods.[69] In a strange twist in what is considered modern and traditional campaigning techniques, in Mexico, house-to-house canvassing has become a far more important element in competitive campaigns than it was before the 1990s.[70] People want to meet and greet the candidate.[71] House visits are

63. Interview subject 78.
64. Interview subject 53, who was then Secretary of Elections in the CEN.
65. See Langston and Aparicio (2012) for empirical proof that prior political experience can help one's electoral fortunes.
66. Interview subject 79, a federal deputy from a rural area, who stated that he won his district because he is a school teacher and member of the SNTE. As a result, much of his campaign work was organized and supported by the SNTE in the district.
67. Interview subject 93.
68. Interview subject 75, from a poor, rural district, relates that in the rural areas, the indigenous people vote in blocks, following the orders of their local strongman. He worked closely with these leaders in the indigenous communities because "they had to have the capacity to get people together, and get them to the voting booth on a certain day."
69. Interview subjects 53 and 68, both former members of the CEN of the PRI, state that door-to-door canvassing began in the 1980s, but that it was not a widespread practice.
70. Interview subject 74, former federal deputy, from a wealthy, urban district. Interview subject 76A stated that mass rallies and the sectors no longer were a factor in campaigns and that canvassing became important in both larger and smaller towns. Also, interview subject 91, a PRI winner from a wealthier urban district in the Estado de México.
71. Interview subjects 73A and 72, both federal deputies for the PRI. Another PRI campaigner for a poor urban district (Ecatepec), near Mexico City tells a similar story (interview subject 92).

considered more important for urban districts than they are in their rural counterparts, and can be organized by both the candidate and the party, where it is strong.[72] Most candidates concur that canvassing provides closer contact with voters and creates a multiplication effect as those who were visited tell their friends and family. Twenty-three percent of respondents in a 2003 national, postelectoral opinion survey report having received a visit to their home by a candidate or a party worker.[73] Eighty six percent of all PRI deputy candidates had canvassed their districts during the federal campaigns under study (see Table 8.1).

In the author's federal deputy candidate interview set, one finds a surprising consensus among both winning and losing PRI candidates that large rallies are no longer efficient mechanisms of voter mobilization, although one is normally held at the beginning and end of the campaign. The arguments against rallies are basically the same across deputies: large-scale gatherings are expensive and there is no longer any guarantee that the attendees will vote for the candidate.[74] Despite these statements, data on federal campaigning reveals that candidates continue to organize mass rallies, whether on their own, or in coordination with co-partisans running conterminous campaigns in the same area. In the sample of campaign activities, 87 percent of the PRI's federal deputy candidates held at least one rally.

As can be seen from this table, the PRI federal deputy candidates continued to be far more active campaigners, even in the years (2009 and 2012) that their party did not hold the presidency. The PRI congressional candidates were more than twice as likely to have appeared in a video, the majority of which were self-produced (87 percent as opposed to 42 percent for the PAN and PRD candidates). This is a surprising result because videos are not that expensive—most used in Mexican congressional elections are not professionally produced, but are instead videos of the candidate smiling and meeting with constituents, speaking at rallies, and speaking of their prior experience. The same result is shown for social media, which consist of Facebook pages dedicated to the candidate and Twitter accounts: 72.5 percent of the PRI candidates had some

72. Interview subject 93 stated that she, together with the precinct-level party operators, organized small meetings of fifteen to twenty people who would go to a neighbor's home to show a video of her political proposals; she often did not attend these events.

73. CSES postelectoral opinion survey, Mexico, 2003, available at http://lnpp.cide.edu/.

74. Interview subject 70, a former deputy from a rural district, relates two problems: first, people are no longer willing be trucked long distances to attend a rally; and second, the candidate has to pay for both the buses and the food. Interview subject 59 reports that by the 2000 election, the PRI could not hold rallies in Mexico City because people came to boo and insult the candidate. Interview subjects 65 and 72 revealed the same concerns. Both were representatives of the Peasant Sector running from rural districts. The only deputy who admitted he wanted a rally was interview subject 77, from a poor mountainous region.

sort of social media presence against less than 43 percent for the opposition candidates. If monetary resources explained differences among the campaigning efforts of the three parties, then these measures should be more equal, as they cost so little. Instead, it appears that PRI candidates (who run in more competitive districts because of the national scope of their party) are willing to expend more effort on modern techniques, and are pushed to do so by their leaders.

Vote brokers in the neighborhoods are now extremely valuable political resources in SMD campaigns, and successful candidates are those with greater prior *local* experience who are able to make credible commitments to these local brokers (Langston and Aparicio 2012). Much of the work once done by party or sectoral volunteers is now carried out by paid workers.[75]

Vote promoters must be paid with money and some access to public services before election day. There appear to be two kinds of vote promotion: the first is part of a professional team that makes phone calls, talks to local leaders, and helps with transport on the day of the election. The second type is more home-grown and involves nonprofessionals, who are neighbors with a natural talent for acting as brokers with local government. Candidates still do not offer many programmatic promises and, given the tight control over bill initiation in the Chamber, it is difficult for an individual deputy to hope for legislative victories, as we shall see in the next chapter.

To communicate with voters, walls are still painted and posters still hung (before the most recent 2008 electoral reform which prohibited hanging electoral material from public property). Before 2008, radio was a crucial element of district-level campaign tactics to reach voters. Between 1997 and 2008, almost all the candidates I interviewed reported that they had used radio advertising, whether they were in urban or rural districts.[76] After 2008, the candidates communicated with voters in two ways: either the candidate convinces the state party branch to pay for a number of spots on local radio or the candidate requests the station to conduct an interview. Newspapers are still used, although it is impossible to calculate how many candidates continue to pay off the owners or editors to guarantee favorable coverage.[77]

75. Interview subjects 59, 68, and 97.
76. Almost every candidate and deputy interviewed for the democratic era mentioned that radio was a crucial aspect of his or her strategy to reach voters. In the 2009 CSES poll, almost 33 percent of respondents remembered an electoral advertisement on the radio. Whether these ads were paid for by the candidates or the party is unknown. Available at http://lnpp.cide.edu/.
77. Interview subject 65, who ran in the democratic era in a very rural area, refused to pay a newspaper a bribe, but since so few of his rural voters read the newspaper, it was not a problem.

Midterm legislative elections (held every three years) are very different from those that are concurrent with the presidential race (every six years). In concurrent elections, active deputy campaigns support the presidential effort because the presidential candidate cannot reach the roughly 143,000 precincts that make up the 300 SMDs that district candidates traverse in the course of their campaigns. In the concurrent race, the presidential candidate's team controls more money, decision-making power over the message, and the use of attack advertisements. The national party dedicates to the presidential candidate many of the spots that are supposed to advertise the federal deputy candidates. The CEN is usually out of the loop in terms of the presidential media strategy, but is still allowed to put a mobilization army into play. Because the parties enjoy free media time for their television and radio spots, public campaign financing is chasing fewer outlets, particularly in the local arena, leading one to believe that paid neighborhood mobilization (as it is euphemistically called) is even more important than it was before 2008.

Governors and Federal Deputy Campaigning

Mexican elections, especially those below the level of the presidency, are not oriented toward programmatic or ideological issues. Many voters in Mexico do not have access to paved roads, running water, or secure property rights, which leads to clientelistic exchange rather than programmatic platforms. As we have seen, the particular fiscal decentralization regime in Mexico has given state executives financial resources from the federal government under a weak accountability regime, so governors have both the incentives and the resources to spend on supporting copartisan candidates in their states (Mirón Lince 2011). The state executives have many resources at their command: they can send out state bureaucrats to help hand out pamphlets at major intersections; they advertise the improvements made during their administration and that of their party just before the federal legislative elections; they can distribute money to buy small bundles of goods that are distributed on election day; and they can obligate the PRI mayors to help the candidate, among other activities. As such, governors can secure selective goods for their copartisan candidates during the campaigns. If the PRI deputy candidate is lucky enough to run for a district with PRI mayors, the chances are better that she will enjoy their support, which is especially important in setting up meetings with local notables.

State PRI affiliates are not totally dependent on copartisan governors to support the campaigns. The state PRI affiliates have other sources of legal funds, including transfers from the CEN and public financing for regular party operations and campaigns for state-level races that come from state electoral institutes (which are the state equivalents of the IFE). The PRI, however, on average has sent only 15 percent of its IFE resources (for ordinary party activities) to its state branches, as compared to 55 percent for the PAN and 22 percent for the PRD (Harbers 2010, 149).

The Role of the National Party Organization

The role of the CEN in competitive congressional campaigns has become strikingly more modern than it was under PRI hegemony. According to my interviews with members of the CEN and candidates in the democratic era, the national leadership's most important role is to manage the national mass media appeals (largely television and radio spots, although the use of social media is becoming more sophisticated) and to hire public opinion firms. For example, in the 2006 presidential elections, the PRI (together with its electoral ally, the Green Party) had roughly 102 million dollars to spend (Mena 2010, 15). The millions of pesos that are funneled through the CEN and the availability of advanced technologies of communication obligated all parties to focus on devising or improving their media appeals. And the desire to maintain control over party finances and to raise voting numbers across the nation convinced the party's leaders not to devolve advertising responsibilities to the deputy candidates.

The second most important task of the CEN is to provide the candidates with information that takes two forms: the first is precinct-level voting histories, and the second is district-level opinion polls run at various points in the campaign (it is rare that the candidates hire their own polling firm). The national leadership is also active in unifying campaign styles and messages, and develops congressional hopefuls strategies that are suitable for different types of districts. Candidates, however, are allowed to pick and choose what national messages they will emphasize in their individual campaigns and which they will ignore.

Electoral competition in Mexico is more local in part because gubernatorial popularity and local issues now influence congressional elections (Magar 2012), and plurality candidates from the PRI run active campaigns. Stronger PRI governors are sometimes capable of homogenizing video clips for copartisan candidates running for the federal legislature. Both of these factors point to greater party decentralization. Nonetheless, as Weldon (2005) has shown, legislative discipline remains high for all three parties even as the PRI lost its majority in the Chamber, which points to the strength of the national party leadership in directing the voting behavior of its deputies. The following chapter will show how—despite growing localism in plurality campaigning—the national party leadership, with input from the governors, has been successful in keeping control over its legislative caucuses into the democratic era.

CONCLUSIONS

This chapter presented several surprising results; first, despite high vote margins and assured victory, the PRI's leaders under hegemony obligated their deputy candidates to actively campaign, because campaigns knit together the vast and variegated network of local leaders to the national authority regime via the exchange of select government largesse in return for votes. Second, the sectoral coverage across districts was weaker and patchier than many authors have stated previously; the corporatist unions shared mobilization tasks with caciques, local producer groups, mayors, and governors, among others. Local party organization—that is, the permanent manpower and resources ensconced in local and state branches—was weak in many areas of the nation. It was often cheaper for the party to use its candidates than to pay for a more permanent presence. Voter mobilization was carried out by local leaders and neighborhood brokers who were more permanent fixtures of the political landscape. Mayors, governors, and sectoral groups all had a role to play in this mobilizing activity.

When electoral competition began to climb in the late 1980s and into the 1990s, the party's state executives were well equipped to continue to support copartisan campaigning in their state. With the resources from the decentralized revenue sharing and federal transfers, the governors enjoyed a new source of financial wherewithal to carry out these tasks. The urban-based workers' groups were unable to adjust either their mobilizing tactics (because of the changing economic development model) or revamp their lists of possible candidates. The Peasant Sector, on the other hand, continued to deliver votes.

The effects of the political institutions, such as federalism, a two-tiered electoral system with a fused ballot, plurality races in SMDs, and single-term limits have allowed both governors and the national party headquarters to take the lead in mobilizing voters, running campaigns, and winning votes. The power these groups have over elections explains the shape that the organization took: more decentralized but still less attuned to the needs of legislative office seekers. The demands of district campaigning, and autonomous access to resources allowed both the CEN and subnational leaders to cooperate around the shared goal of vote winning. Both sets of leaders have strong interests in seeing more PRI politicians seated in the Federal Chamber, and both had the means to support campaigns. This helps explain why governors and the CEN found common ground in deputy campaigns and why they could cooperate in legislative strategies once these candidates won office.

CHAPTER 9

Authority and Delegation in the Chamber of Deputies

The last area of party activity that concerns us is how the regime and, later, the PRI's leadership, controlled and guided the collective activities of its caucus members in the Chamber of Deputies (the lower house of Congress), comparing the hegemonic and the democratic eras. This chapter's findings support the general argument presented in this study: political competition strengthened national party leaders and the party's governors, allowing them to take over the party. Electoral competition decentralized legislative candidate selection (especially for the SMD races), as well as political recruitment, because governors could place their allies in the Chamber. National leaders, meanwhile, continue to coordinate the legislative effort of the party caucus, together with the leader of the PRI in the Chamber. The identity of these national leaders has changed from the successive presidents and their Secretaries of Governance during hegemony to the leaders of the CEN and other party factions under democracy. With the exception of the 2003 split, the two sets of leaders and different party groups cooperated within the Chamber, in part because of shared interests and in part, because of the willingness of the PRI's leaders to deliver more resources to their governors.

To better understand the relations of power and delegation within the PRI's legislative caucus during hegemony and democracy, this chapter uses a unique measure: the political and professional backgrounds of those PRI deputies who became committee chairs as compared to those who did not, across the two periods. Committee leaders were and are responsible for "taking care" of pieces of legislation that pass through their panels and are placed in their posts by party leaders, although the identity these leaders have changed. So, by understanding who these committee leaders are, and how their group identity has (or has not) changed due to electoral competition, one can pinpoint the new areas of power within the PRI. I use the career backgrounds of almost 1,000 PRI federal deputies from both eras to understand how the identity of principals and agents has changed and how delegation within the PRI's legislative delegation has been transformed as well.

The Mexican legislature was famously weak compared to the executive during the years of hegemony because the president ruled over a party that was confronted with very little electoral competition and deputies who were limited to a single term (Bejar 2006; de la Garza 1972; Lujambio 1995; Nacif 1995; Weldon 1997). PRI deputies found it difficult to legislate against the executive's wishes because if they did, they soon found their political careers had ended.

However, if one examines the pattern of committee leadership allocation before democracy, one finds that Mexican presidents were deeply concerned about the representatives of different PRI factions and their ability to use the committees in the legislature to modify or amend bills that would benefit their specific constituency (be it corporatist or territorial) to the detriment of the administration's overall policy direction. Even in the context of legislative weakness, the Mexican committee system held some formal prerogatives over the legislative process that could make it problematic for the administration's legislative goals. The Mexican president and his direct subordinates in the Chamber placed closely matched agents as committee leaders to further reduce the autonomy of the representatives of other groups within the PRI coalition so they could not modify administration policy. Instead of relying exclusively on the threat of ex post punishment, the regime's bosses also used ex ante agent matching.

In 1997, the PRI lost its simple majority in Congress for the first time and since then, the legislative branch has evolved into a full-fledged governing partner, ending the decades-old legislative capitulation to the executive (Alarcón 2006). Legislative office holders, however, continue to be weak vis-à-vis their party leadership, and while the role of the committee system has changed somewhat, deputies still do not have seniority advantage, and so do not have specialized knowledge to craft better policy. But electoral competition has changed the identity of the principals who influence committee and voting behavior of the PRI deputies in democratic Mexico: the president of Mexico and his agents have been replaced by national party leaders (both the leader of the CEN and the caucus leader) and copartisan governors, although they influence legislative voting under different circumstances.

In the twelve years out of office, the CEN and caucus leaders took the lead in most legislative issue areas, coordinating the efforts the PRI's deputies (which varied in size from 25 to 45 percent of the 500-seat Chamber, as compared to 75 percent in the early 1980s) and negotiating with the party's governors on relevant bills. The governors are most active during the annual budget negotiations, which affect their state revenues directly because of Mexico's particular fiscal federalism (Díaz-Cayeros 2006) or when tax policy is under consideration. As in the case of Argentina, the governors delegate much of the legislative authority to national party headquarters, with the exceptions of important tax reforms and the annual budget bill (Jones and Hwang 2005; Jones et al. 2002). As a result, the PRI legislators were not usually buffeted by dual agents (Carey 2009) because the governors communicated their needs to the party's leaders in congress, which was normally receptive.

Several scholars have commented on potential collective-action problems within a legislature: if members of Congress vote their personal ideology or what they consider best for voters in their district, this could lead to splits within the party's legislative fraction and dilute the value of the party label with voters, thereby harming all of the party's politicians (Aldrich 1995; Cox and McCubbins 1993; Kiewiet and McCubbins 1991). Individual representatives delegate some of their authority over policy to their caucus leaders and allow party leaders to control the Chamber's agenda to mitigate problems of collective action. In a second-order delegation, the full floor of the Chamber allows its committees to specialize and gain knowledge and expertise to better resolve the business of the legislature (Maltzman 1998). However, the solutions that have been identified in the US case are not strictly applicable to Mexico because of the profound differences in institutional incentives and their effects on individual deputies (Carey 2009; Nacif 2000; Rosas and Langston 2011; Weldon 2005).

Voters in Mexico do not possess much authority over the representatives in the Chamber because deputies cannot return to their constituents to request their support to win another term and so continue their legislative careers. Rather, extramural and caucus leaders delegate their authority over deputies to committee leaders to produce desired legislative outcomes. Instead of examining the goals of committee members and how these affect committee assignments (Katz and Sala 1996; Shepsle 1976), this chapter illustrates the goals of caucus leaders when they choose committee leaders.

One should expect during the hegemonic period that PRI politicians with a closer relation to the federal government were more likely to win committee chairs than others who were not as close to the president, such as affiliated corporatist leaders or those allied to the party's governors. The presidential administrations had to assure that these lower level leaders within the PRI did not "ruin" government policy by using their committee-based power to write or modify policy favoring their specific interests within the revolutionary coalition against those of the president. It is also worth noting that the Secretary of Governance could monitor and sanction the activities of the PRI's legislative leaders to assure their compliance with the wishes of the president.

The backgrounds of almost 600 hegemonic PRI deputies from two legislatures, 1982–1985 and 1985–1988, are used in a logistic regression to pinpoint which "type" of hegemonic deputy was more likely selected by regime leaders to run committees and, as expected, those with prior political careers in the federal bureaucracy had a higher probability than those with either state careers or prior posts in a corporatist union of winning a panel leadership post.

THE HEGEMONIC CHAMBER OF DEPUTIES

During the authoritarian era, successive PRI presidents of Mexico controlled their legislatures through a variety of institutional and informal means, and one of the most important of these was the PRI majorities in both houses (Nacif 1995; Weldon 1997). However, presidents during the authoritarian period still had to invest time and energy to keep the legislative branch subordinate, as representatives to both houses were directly elected by voters and the legislature was a long-lived political institution that held some rule-based influence over public policy. The PRI coalition held within its ranks almost every major producer group, union, social class, religion, and region. The president and his trusted agents were careful to maintain strict controls over which party politician reached the Chamber, who became caucus leader, and the identity of committee chairs and secretaries.

The hegemonic Chamber was a weak institution that was unable to monitor the actions of the executive or provide oversight for the administrations' budgets (de la Garza 1972; Lujambio 1995; Ugalde 2000). The executive did not initiate all legislation, but it did have far higher success rates than the deputies (Rivera Sánchez 2004). PRI deputies did not debate legislation on the floor as that would have signaled dissention within the ranks, but the few opposition deputies that sprinkled the halls of the Chamber were happy to fill this role (Bejar 2003; de la Garza 1972; Martínez 1998). As de la Garza (1972) describes it, PRI leaders of the hegemonic Chamber were responsible for assuring the success of executive-backed legislation through the use of the internal chamber regulations, contained in the constitution, the Organic Law, and the Internal Code. Through its control over seats, the majority party placed the leader of the Leadership Committee (*Gran Comisión*)—the formal leader of the Chamber—as well as every committee leader from its own ranks. The president of Mexico controlled the Chamber through his control over the Lead Committee.[1] The head of the Leadership Committee had rule-based prerogatives to place both members and leaders of the committees (although he had to

---

1. During the hegemonic period, the Legislative Code ruled that the Leadership Committee decided the leaders of all committees only if there were a majority in the Chamber. The Leadership Committee was formed only by members of the majority party; informally, the president of Mexico decided who among his top politicians would run "his" congress before the election took place. The leaders of the PRI's state delegations were also members, which allowed the governors a direct line to the Chamber leadership that the corporatist unions did not enjoy.

propose them to the full house), decide congressional administrators, allocate the annual budget, and determine the agenda of floor votes, through its coordination with the Directive Group(*Mesa Directiva*, the body that coordinates the debates on the floor) and the committees.[2] This control over leadership roles assured the presidency that its bills would be taken care of by its party's legislators. The Leadership Committee was made up of leaders of the PRI's state delegations, allowing the governors (who placed the leaders of state delegations) to communicate better with Chamber leadership than the corporatist sectors could.

Because so few opposition deputies held office and because single-term limits made seniority in committees impossible, the PRI's leadership was able to bypass the opposition representatives in committee. For example, panels often did not meet and the signatures needed to remand a bill to the floor could be collected from the PRI deputies on the committee without the participation (or even knowledge) of opposition members. Members of non-PRI parties could not win committee leadership posts until 1988 because the internal rules allowed the majority party to control all of them. However, most of the PRI deputies in the Chamber were not treated much better by the overly powerful executive and his trusted caucus leaders in congress. During the first several decades of the PRI's seventy-year rule (until the Chamber's new building was inaugurated in 1981) deputies did not have fixed offices in the Chamber building; nor did they have reserved seats on the floor. Congress was in session for only four months of the year (de la Garza 1972). There was no record keeping of roll-call voting until the late 1990s. Deputies received a good deal of discretionary benefits from their leaders; but the trips, drivers, and staff were allocated depending on one's standing with the leader. Most committees did little work during the twice-yearly sessions; for example, Nacif (2000, 38) reports that in the first year of the 1988–1991 legislature, only thirteen of the thirty-nine standing committees reported bills to the floor.

From the time the PNR was created in 1929, through the first electoral reform designed to augment plurality of the Chamber in 1963, deputies modified only 18 percent of the legislative bills (Nava and Yáñez 2003, 46). Bill amendment rates later rose, which is partially explained by the rising numbers of opposition deputies: a slight increase in the mid-1960s that increased to 100 deputies after the 1977 electoral reform, and continued through the 1990s. Members of congress found it difficult to amend executive-sponsored legislation because the committee system provided an information-poor environment: deputies had little built-up knowledge or expertise, and while committee chairs could request information from an executive agency, the bureaucrats could simply ignore those requests.

2. According to Article 20 of the Organic Law, the Directive Group runs the floor sessions, making sure that the debates and votes go forward as planned.

Once the opposition was able to win more seats in the mid-1960s, the amendment rate rose in the period from 1964 through 1979, as the opposition, *not* PRI representatives, began to modify the president's bills, although most of these were to correct style, not content. From the 1977 reforms (that introduced a proportional representation element, and therefore, far more opposition deputies in the Chamber) through 2000, almost 50 percent of bills were changed before passing to a full-floor vote (Nava and Yáñez 2003).

Following Shaw's categorization (1979), the Mexican legislature was a nondecisional congress that deliberated, represented, legitimized, recruited, and socialized many of its members, so that, although it was weak, it did have a role to play.[3] The functions of the legislature were to open a communication channel between groups within the PRI regime to the executive; provide a weak check on each administration's policies, act as a channel for the demands of constituents, and press the federal bureaucracy for selective goods for their districts' voters (de la Garza 1972, xi).

De la Garza (1972, 54) explains that most of the executive's policy changes were debated and negotiated with relevant interest group leaders in the federal bureaucracy in the planning stage, *before* the bill reached the Chamber, rendering the legislature a weak policy-making partner. The hegemonic presidents made sure—via both the head of the Lead Committee and the committee presidents—that when the bills entered committee, they were examined and remanded to a floor vote in a timely manner without major modifications from PRI or opposition deputies.

One might assume that all members, leaders, presidents, and deputies of the PRI had similar interests but, given the nature of the hegemonic coalition, this was next to impossible. While the multiclass, multiregional nature of the PRI gave the party a wide support base, it caused problems as all groups pushed their policy preferences. Each president of Mexico had to make decisions over government priorities, which at times meant confronting the interests of different PRI factions (Grindle 1977; Mackinlay 2002; Maxfield 1990; Teichman 1995). Chapter 7 demonstrated that representatives from all areas of the political elite, from both the national and the local political arenas, were able to place their representatives in the Chamber. And because of the desire of the different party wings and factions to use numerous arenas of political action (including the legislature) to protect or advance their interests, the executive had to carefully place trusted allies into committee leadership posts, where they could block actions to modify or replace executive initiatives.

---

3. The PRI lost a single SMD race in the 1982 congressional elections that were concurrent with the presidential race. It lost eleven of 300 SMD races in the 1985 midterm elections, during one of the worst economic downturns of the postrevolutionary era.

If the committees had no policy-making influence whatsoever, then one would not expect to find any congruence between the deputy's group identity (or professional background) and the committee of which he was a member. That is, committee membership would be completely random. If committees had some policy relevance, then a deputy from an agricultural district should be a member of the Agricultural Committee. To strengthen the argument that the president and his trusted agents in the Chamber needed compliant committee chairs, one must first show that PRI deputies were assigned to panels that were connected to their state, industry, or sector.

In fact, the data on committee membership from the 1980s show that 73 percent of all PRI deputies from these two legislatures were placed on at least one relevant committee[4] (in the two hegemonic legislatures studied in this chapter, the average number of committees for which each deputy served was almost three). Bejar (2006, 210) and Nacif (2000) both argue that the leader of the caucus chose PRI deputies for specific committees to maintain the corporatist alliances and state interests that supported the hegemonic regime. And in effect, CTM deputies were members of the Labor and Social Security Committees (the latter oversaw the workers' pension schemes), as well as the Price Control Committees (*Bienes de Consumo*).[5] Agrarian-identified PRI legislators were found on both the Agriculture and Agrarian Reform panels, as one would expect. In general, those deputies who came from the federal government agencies were placed on the committee that controlled their issue area (bureaucrats from the Secretary of Communication and Transportation were on the Transport and Communication Committee, for example). PRI deputies with prior professional experience in the financial sector of the federal bureaucracy could be found on either the Budget or Treasury Committees (or both). Those who had worked in the Governance Ministry found themselves on Governance or Justice Committees. For the territorially based deputies, many gubernatorial allies were on the Governance Committee or on panels that represented their states' or districts' economic interests, such as deputies from the coastal states of Veracruz and Sinaloa who were members of the Fisheries and Marine Committees.

So, if almost three-quarters of all individual PRI legislators were placed on policy-relevant committees, and those party deputies did not necessarily share the same policy interests as their extramural regime leaders, how

4. The data on backgrounds from the 1982–1985 and 1985–1988 legislatures show that 426 of the 583 PRI deputies were placed on at least one committee that was relevant to their group.

5. This data point was determined in the following way: if labor leaders were on the Labor, Social Security Committee (which deals with pensions) or Consumer Price Control Committee, then it was considered a relevant placement, as were the peasant representatives found on either Agriculture or Agrarian Reform panels. Deputies who represented the federal government agencies were often placed on the committee that controlled their issue area. I thank Ignacio Marván for his help with this coding.

did the hegemonic presidents manage legislative outcomes without relying solely on the threat of ex post sanctioning? Precisely because relevant players could be found on the committees of their interest, successive executives under hegemony placed PRI legislators who were closer to the president and the executive bureaucracy to *preside* over the committees.

The committee chairs (also called committee presidents) had several prerogatives that allowed them to control the behavior of the other PRI deputies on their panels, as well as the opposition representatives. The chairs called sessions to order; but because there were no rules of quorum on committees, they could move a bill out of committee by gathering an absolute majority of signatures of their committee's members. This meant that the committee report could advance without a panel meeting to discuss its contents, and any member who did not agree with the proposal could be excluded from the committee's proceedings. This rule permitted the chairs to block unwanted bills and push through those of the president.

Lujambio (1995, 191–192) notes that committee chairs had the deciding vote in case of a tie; they could distribute intrapanel resources, and, most importantly, they could negotiate the agenda for their committee's bills with the head of the Leadership Committee. The committee secretaries supported the committee chairs, especially in rounding up a sufficient number of signatures to move the bill out of committee (during this period, only one secretary served per panel). The committee leaders had little opportunity to avoid large-scale mistakes on the part of the executive bureaucrats who wrote the bills and, as a result, many initiatives were badly written or had problems of coherence (Bejar 2006).

If, as Nacif (2000, 41) argued, the committee chairs were perfect agents of the leader of the party caucus, then we should expect to find a stronger connection between the professional-political background of PRI committee leaders and the principals who helped push their candidacy within the party—the president, the Secretary of Governance, or the relevant cabinet minister. Leaders of the corporatist unions came from very different educational and political backgrounds than the federal bureaucrats, especially those in financial areas of the federal bureaucracy, so one should not expect to find PRI politicians with union leadership backgrounds chairing committees, although they were often members of policy-relevant panels, as shown above.[6]

Well-matched agents can be defined as those who are "closer" to the interests of their principals. "Political closeness" between the president and the PRI deputies is measured by career backgrounds: those with a prior background

6. A former leader of the Gran Comisión in the 1980s states that the leader of the PRI delegation did not impose committee chairs. Instead, members of the PRI's caucus who belonged to that issue area decided on a leader and then negotiated with caucus and party leaders. However, interested deputies would not choose a committee leader who was not acceptable to regime leaders because they would not be able to promote their bills (interview subject 96).

in the federal bureaucracy had both greater expertise in the issue area and proven loyalty than those deputies who came from other parts of the hegemonic coalition. That is, federal bureaucrats came from party groups whose success depended more directly on the president and his closest allies. So, if the president and his cabinet ministers wanted better control over the legislative process, then a high proportion of committee leaders should have come from the executive bureaucracy, not from unions or state politics.

Table 9.1 contains the results from a logistic regression whose dependent variable is whether the individual deputy was a committee leader or not (a 1 was assigned to those who were chairs or secretaries and a 0 for those who were not). Information on both the career backgrounds and the committee posts are from two hegemonic legislatures from the early and mid-1980s. This

Table 9.1 LOGIT REGRESSION
FOR PRI COMMITTEE LEADERSHIP
UNDER HEGEMONY (1982–1985 AND
1985–1988 LEGISLATURES)

	Chair or Secretary
Age	0.023*
	[.013]
Prior legislative experience	0.354
	[.259]
Education level	.449***
	[.139]
Prior municipal background	omitted
Prior business	0.213
	[.814]
Prior state government	0.334
	[.537]
Prior state union	–1.98
	[.776]
Prior national union	0.388
	[.575]
Prior fed govt or party	1.42***
	[.235]
Year 1982	0.295
	[.235]
Constant	–4.72
	[.988]
Number of cases	581
Pseudo R2	0.214

information comes from the *Diccionario biográfico del gobierno mexicano*.[7] The deputies' prior political connections have been measured as a set of indicator variables, including a set of mutually exclusive variables denoting prior political paths. Those deputies who came from a union or union federation (one of the party's sectors) were assigned a 1 for the prior union variable and a 0 if they did not come from that background. Those whose careers were made in the federal government were assigned a 1 in the prior federal government variable; while those who came from the municipal arena were assigned a 1 in the other category and a 0 for all others. The background indicator variables are mutually exclusive so that deputies are assigned to only one of the seven background variables, and the prior municipal arena category is excluded in the model to provide a base-line for comparison.[8]

This model also includes control variables: older deputies would have greater experience, and so might be more likely to win committee presidencies and secretaries. Even with the constitutional prohibition against consecutive reelection, one can run for congress again after a term out of office; therefore, deputies with prior legislative experience (as senators, federal deputies, or local deputies) could have a higher probability of winning a committee chair. In the 1980s, Mexico was still not a highly educated nation; the average years of schooling of a child of fifteen years of age rose from 3.4 years in 1970, to 4.6 in 1980, to 6.5 in 1990 (Aguilar Morales, 2002). Education in this model is measured by assigning a 1 to those who completed primary and secondary school, 2 to high school, 3 to teachers' college, 4 to college studies, 5 for a master's, and 6 for a doctorate. In the sample of 587, the average educational attainment of the hegemonic PRI deputies was slightly less than a college degree, far higher than the population at large, but still, many PRI deputies had only a primary or high school education.[9] One might expect that

7. This indispensable source contains a short curriculum vitae of all deputies, both PRI and opposition, including prior political, business, and professional posts.

8. Municipal posts include city council, mayor, municipal government and local party posts. The state category includes experience in the state party or government or as well as local deputy. A state corporatist union leader is someone who came from a local or regional union, while the national union leaders came from either the national corporatist leadership or a national federation. Finally, those included in the federal category have a strong predominance of background posts in the federal administration or in the national party.

9. The average of the 587 PRI deputies was 3.5, between a teacher's two-year degree and college studies, far higher than the population at large. The author did not use a simple count of how many years of education first, because teachers' college implies a different type of political grooming than studying law; second, because many of the deputies did not finish their college education, so it is impossible to know exactly how many years they did study at university. However, 157 out of the sample of 587 deputies (27 percent) had only an elementary or high school education, while 356 (or almost 61 percent) had either a teacher's certificate or some college studies. Finally, sixty-nine (8.5 percent) had either a master's degree or doctorate.

those with more education would be more likely to become committee leaders because they had greater technical ability. This model does not include a variable controlling for whether the PRI deputy entered through a plurality or PR slot because the PRI did not win PR seats until a rule change in 1988. Both committee chairs and secretaries are considered leaders, because only one secretary was placed per committee (although the chair clearly had more power). Summary statistics are in Appendix 1.

As expected, these results show that both prior federal government experience and a background in a union are significant when compared to the base category of prior municipal experience, although their signs run in opposite directions. If a deputy were a leader of a state corporatist sector, then it was unlikely he would be assigned a committee leadership post (as compared to a municipal politician), even one in a relevant issue area, as shown by the significant and negative coefficient. Prior federal government experience, however, is both significant and positive; those who came from the federal government were more likely to win a leadership post, as compared to the base category of prior municipal background.

Age predicts success in winning a committee leadership post as shown by the positive, but small, coefficient. The older a deputy was, the more likely it was that he would win a leadership post. Also, the more educated deputies were more likely to win a committee chair; this is highly correlated with politicians with prior experience in federal government, who had much higher education attainment. In a counterintuitive finding, the prior legislative experience dummy variable does *not* come out significant, although the sign is in the expected direction, so political closeness and education was more important than prior legislative experience.

These empirical data help demonstrate that while committees under the hegemonic system were full of issue-area representatives from unions and state factions (legislators from the CNC on the Agriculture Committee, etc.), they were less likely to win leadership posts than their federal bureaucrats. The executive bureaucracy, led by each president in turn, did not trust the allies of the state governors or union leaders to be committee presidents. The federal bureaucrats were both closer to the president's allies and better educated.

The delegation of authority began with the president, passed to the Secretary of Governance, who dealt with the congressional leaders and the head of the Lead Committee (placed either by the president or the Secretary of Governance), who held very strong agenda and resource control over the Chamber's activities. The leader of the Chamber was ultimately responsible to the president for producing the administration's preferred legislation, but worked closely with the Secretary of Governance. The leader of the Chamber also delegated some authority to committee leaders so they could keep opposition and deputy-sponsored bills off the floor. Sanctioning was possible, but it was better to avoid problems by choosing close allies as the committee chairs.

DEMOCRACY AND THE CHANGING PRI
CONGRESSIONAL DELEGATION

As we saw in chapter 4, the late 1980s and 1990s proved to be very difficult years for the PRI at the ballot box. Anger against the economic disasters of the 1980s led to opposition victories, which fomented greater party pluralism in the Chamber after 1988. The growing number of seats controlled by the PAN and PRD allowed them to demand more leadership posts in the Chamber, both on the Lead Committee and regular panels. The internal rules governing the distribution of these posts were reformed during the 1990s, and gave opposition caucus leaders more power within the Chamber, even before the PRI lost Los Pinos. Individual deputies, however, continue to be agents of their party leaders, not their voters.

As partisan pluralism grew during the 1990s, so did the role of the Chamber and the Senate in policy making. The numbers show the sea-change that took place in the Chamber during the decade of the 1990s and after the defeat of the PRI. After the PRI's loss of the majority in the lower house in 1997, the number of bills passed by the Chamber began to rise: from 559 bills in 1985, to 673 in the 1997 legislature, to 2,800 bills in the 2003 legislature. A higher percentage of them were initiated by deputies, as opposed to the executive branch. Rivera Sánchez (2004, 286) reports that the percentage of all bills presented by the executive fell from 44 percent (155 of 352) in the 1982–1985 legislature, with a success rate of 97 percent, to 29 percent (85 of 294) in 1988–1991, with a success rate of 96 percent, to 7 percent (40 of 574) in 1997–2000, with a success rate of 82 percent. Casar (2008, 231, 240), using slightly different data, reports that in the period 2000–2003, the executive had a success rate of 78 percent, which dropped to 53 percent in the 2003–2006 legislature, and that in both of these plural legislatures, the percentage of executive-promoted bills was tiny as compared to parties in congress.

This pattern of principal-agent relations between the president and the different representatives of the party's interest groups changed as electoral competition grew in the late 1980s and through the 1990s. With the arrival of larger numbers of opposition deputies to the Chamber after 1988, the PRI leaders of the lower house were obligated to reform the internal rules of operation so that opposition deputies could become leaders of a few committees, even though the hegemonic party still held the majority of seats. During the 1990s, the internal regulations of the Chamber were reformed twice to reflect the multiparty legislature by dividing up the leadership posts on the panels proportionally among the registered parties (those that held at least five seats in the Chamber).

The second half of the chapter deals with the question of how the PRI's leadership organized its legislative delegation in a democratic system before the party's return to the presidency in 2012. In effect, the legislative branch has become more active in the policy-making process and is now at least an equal partner with the executive, but individual office holders are not significantly more autonomous than their hegemonic counterparts (this is true of the three major parties). Within this far more active legislature, committees take greater initiative in discussing and modifying bills, but their members are subservient to their committee chair, who continues to be a loyal agent to the caucus leader, or leaders outside the walls of the Chamber.[10]

The PRI leadership and governors continue to control candidate selection in a world with single-term limits, which affords party leaders great authority over the deputy, even though politicians now have the option of jumping parties (Kerevel 2013). Furthermore, the new Chamber rules (which were negotiated among the three major parties during the 1990s) have centralized certain aspects of the internal workings of the committee system even more than was the case under hegemony (Bejar 2003, 2006). PRI leaders—both within and outside the Chamber—are still able to use their rule-based authority to allocate panel leadership posts, even while committees have become more important participants in the legislative process (Rivera Sánchez 2004). The difference is of course, that they do not control all the Chamber's committees. The reform to the legislative rules closely mirrors the electoral reforms of the 1990s—regime leaders negotiated with opposition leaders in congress to make the Chamber organs more open to plural participation, but party leaders continued to maintain the office holders weak vis-à-vis caucus leaders.

The data on political trajectories of committee members and chairs elected in 2000 and 2003 are used to demonstrate that the national party headquarters and PRI governors are both Chamber principals. While the number of union leaders has fallen as a percentage of PRI deputies, the number of politicians whose home base is the municipality has grown considerably (see chapter 3). However, while these localist-type politicians win SMD races, they do not win committee leadership posts, in part because of their lack of expertise and in part because they are not politically close to the leaders who decide committee chair assignments within the PRI.

After 2000, two presidents from the PAN won office without a corresponding party majority in either house of congress, which forced them to negotiate legislative outcomes with the three legislative groups. Casar (2008, 236) shows that the leaders of the three major parties continue to negotiate the content of important bills before they reach the floor. Of the total number of the votes on the floor, 42 percent were approved with a coalition of all parties in 1997–2000, a figure that rose to 69 percent in the 2003–2006 period.

---

10. Article 27 of the current Organic Law states that each party's caucus leader expresses the will of the parliamentary group; she promotes the election of the members of the Mesa Directiva; and participates in the Joint Committee of Political Coordination, Chamber and Senate (JUCOPO), the new name for the Leadership Committee.

While the Chamber has become a far more important political actor and party leaders from all major parties now participate fully in policy making, party discipline in the Chamber has not fallen dramatically (Casar 2008; Weldon 2005). PRI leaders managed to keep their caucus members unified to negotiate successfully with the PAN government from 2000 to 2012. If the president of Mexico (a member of the PAN) had been able to "pick off" individuals or groups of PRI deputies to back his most important bills,[11] the PRI would not have been a serious veto player against presidential power. It was not in the interests of the PRI (out of power) to allow the PAN executive too many victories in the Chamber.

Both the delegation of authority and the identity of the principals have changed thanks to the arrival of large opposition delegations to the Chamber. Once the PRI no longer had the hegemonic president as its leader, its legislative strategies were negotiated among many internal groups. The CEN, the caucus leader, and the governors worked together to decide which bills to support and when to block the PAN executive. The new principals of PRI deputies between 2000 and 2012 were the leader of the CEN, the party's governors (of those deputies with a copartisan governor), and, to a lesser extent, the leader of the party in the Chamber of Deputies.

Between 2000 and 2012, the PRI had two main legislative strategies: first, to block most of the important structural reforms from the executive to protect their rent-seeking allies; and second, to protect the interests of their governors. Profound reforms on the economic front might have helped the nation at large, but would have had potential costs for the PRI. The PAN executive would have won most of the credit for positive reforms, while the PRI might pay the costs of betraying the interests of its long-term economic allies. Individual deputies, on the other hand, may or may not have policy preferences over a range of issues, but they are far more interested in their personal political survival after the single three-year term expires than they are in the fate of the party overall. But, to survive politically, they must obey their caucus leader and, if they are from a PRI-governed state, their governor as well.

The caucus leader still enjoys enormous power over the legislative agenda, committee appointments both for members and leaders, and internal chamber resources for staff, travel, and office space. The PRI's caucus leader relation with her deputies depends on whether the deputy in question has a copartisan governor. If the opposition controls the governorship of a state, then the caucus leader places the state coordinator from among the deputies of that state; each PRI governor places her own coordinator of the deputies from her state. The same is true for resources: the PRI's caucus leader channels money to deputies without a copartisan governor for political work, but

---

11. This was attempted at least once in the 2003 fiscal reform bill.

not for deputies with a governor. The state executives try hard to negotiate with the party's leader to place their deputies as presidents of the committees that matter most to their political or economic interests.[12] The caucus leader normally decides the leaders of the sectors in the congress. The leader of the PRI caucus is no longer a "perfect agent" of outside party leaders, although the national party headquarters does have some rule-based power over who becomes a caucus leader (Bejar 2006).[13] The caucus leaders tend to have a long and broad political career before becoming leader of the party's legislative fraction, which gives them greater political space in which to maneuver. It is now an empirical question whether the caucus coordinator owes allegiance to an outside power.[14] Many of these politicians were actively seeking to augment their power within the party, using the caucus coordination to do so, and so did not take cues exclusively from the leader of the CEN. They could also negotiate with the PAN executive, business groups, union leaders, and the governors.

The leader of the party delegation controls the flow of initiatives into and out of committee. The JUCOPO replaced the Lead Committee in the reforms of the 1990s and is now a collegial legislative organ in which much of the interparty negotiations take place. The JUCOPO determines which legislative bill will make it out of committee and which will remain in the "freezer."[15] Much legislation is stuck in committee and is not reviewed (accepted or rejected), so that every three years the committees' new members are confronted with a large backlog of bills (Rivera Sánchez 2004).

Committees under democratic conditions have more influence over policy outcomes than their authoritarian predecessors: deputies are far more likely to initiate legislation, and much of this work is done in committee.[16] One former Chamber staffer reports that the most important bills—those that imply either political or economic distributive effects—are negotiated among party leaders in the Chamber, and only the details are worked out in committee. But

---

12. Interview subject 87, a former PRI federal deputy, 2000–2003.

13. At the beginning of each legislative term, it sends the PRI deputies a list of possible candidates from which the caucus leader is chosen.

14. The following politicians were leaders of the PRI *bancada* since the onset of the democratic period: from 1997, Arturo Núñez; from 2000, first Beatriz Paredes and then Rafael Rodríguez Barrera; from 2003, first Elba Esther Gordillo and then Emilio Chuayffet; from 2006, Emilio Gamboa Patrón; and finally, from 2009, Francisco Rojas. Perhaps only Rodríguez and Rojas can be considered agents of the extramural party leader. Manlio Fabio Beltrones, leader of the 2012–2015 PRI caucus, was not a close ally of President Peña Nieto.

15. The JUCOPO includes all the parliamentary groups in the Chamber and is designed to promote negotiations among the different legislative parties; see Articles 33 and 34 of the Ley Orgánica. The president of the JUCOPO controls the agenda of the floor sessions (Art. 36 and Art. 38).

16. Interview subject 93.

the less contentious pieces of legislation, which cover roughly 70 to 80 percent of all bills, are worked on, discussed, and negotiated in committee, with less interference from caucus leaders.[17] But these types of bills can be difficult to move to a floor vote. If a report does make it to the floor, it will most likely be approved, albeit with amendments (Heller and Weldon 2003), because it already has the support of most or all parties.

The number of committees and leaders on those committees has grown dramatically since the early 1990s because the legislative leaders of the PRI had to allow opposition deputies to chair a few panels, but not at the expense of their copartisan representatives (Lujambio 1995). The number of opposition-chaired panels rose from zero in 1985 to 18 percent (eight out of forty-five) in 1991, to 33.3 percent (sixteen of forty-eight) in 1994, to 53.3 percent (thirty-two of sixty) in 1997, when the PRI lost the simple majority in the congress for the first time since its creation (Rivera Sánchez 2004, 267). As of 2009, there are sixty-four committees in the Mexican Chamber, a 45 percent increase over 1988. The number of secretaries grew from *one* per panel in the early and mid-1980s (or roughly forty-five), to ninety in the 1988 legislature, to 205 in the 1994 congress, before leveling off at 198 in 1997.

But as the number of committees grew, the amount of time each deputy could spend working on policy issues did not, so the quality of committee output has not improved greatly. The Organic Law of 1999 recognized the problems of shoddy committee work and included several provisions to obligate the members of each committee to perform their duties more fully.[18] However, these measures have little effect because the organizational incentives run strongly against a sustained work ethic: the deputies cannot translate their committee work to their next post; instead, they must obey their caucus leader (and governor) to continue their political career. Deputies belong to several committees, but do not have the staff or time to dedicate much effort to any but the most important.

The only rule covering the selection of committee members mentions that posts must be in proportion to the number of deputies each party holds (Art. 44 of the Organic Law). The committees are called by their chairs to session (Art. 93); to remand a bill to a floor vote, it must be signed by a majority of the members on the committee; any dissenter can write a minority report, which will be presented on the floor (Art. 88).

---

17. Interview subject 94A, a PAN congressional staffer.

18. The Organic Law of 1999 states that members must attend committee sessions and can be absent only with an excuse that has been communicated the president of the committee (Art. 44). If the committees do not have a quorum, they cannot meet.

The chair cannot relieve a copartisan of her committee slot—that must be done by the caucus leader (Art. 44, Organic Law). The chair calls the sessions to meet (the committees are obligated to meet at least once a week and report on their activities twice a year).[19] The chairs can call federal bureaucrats to inform the panel in their issue areas; they can channel selective goods to their panel's members (though not as much as the caucus leader or a copartisan governor). Regular members are not paid extra for their panel work; and even though the same rules apply for committee chairs and secretaries, these leaders do receive extra money and resources.[20] Committee chairs decide when the report will come up for a committee vote and make sure the signatures needed to remand the new measure for a floor vote are gathered (with the okay of the caucus leader, of course).

Thus, the leader of the PRI's parliamentary group delegates her authority to the party's committee leaders, but with a great deal of input from other principals who matter in today's democratic political arena: the governors, large business interests, and wealthy unions that are at least informally and/or partially linked to the PRI, such as the Oil Workers' Union and the Teachers' Union. Committee presidents—still without a seniority advantage—must answer to caucus leaders (not to their floor members), and they can still be "fired" at the will of the caucus leader.

What kind of PRI deputy should win a committee chair once the PRI lost control of the executive as well as congressional majorities? Under democratic conditions, one should continue to see politicians with national-level careers named as committee presidents both because national politicians (those who are members of the CEN or former members of the federal bureaucracy) have the expertise that many local politicians lack and because they are well connected (there were still plenty circulating during the period covered by this database, 2000–2006).

One should also expect to find deputies who are from states with a PRI governor to win chairmanships. PRI governors help many copartisan deputy candidates win their SMD races, give them resources during the course of their three-year term in San Lázaro, and help them find posts after the end of the term in office (Langston 2010).[21] Therefore, governors constitute principals of federal deputies and lobby hard to place their allies on panels

19. When Congress is not in session, only the chair can call a committee to order (Art. 93).

20. Article 86 of the Organic Law. This rule is ignored for the secretaries and presidents.

21. Interview subject 89, a former undersecretary of Hacienda and a federal deputy, stated simply, "The governors can influence their deputies because [the deputies] owe their posts to the governors."

that matter to their states.[22] And in fact, PRI deputies who do not come from copartisan-governed states have complained publicly of their inability to win legislative leadership posts. Furthermore, governors, as this book has shown, are crucial support bases for national party headquarters, and so are able to pressure the caucus leader to place state allies in as committee chairs.[23]

One might also expect national union leaders to win committee chairs on those panels that most directly affect their interests. Corporatism is far less important to the PRI's structure than it was under hegemony, but the large unions with resources have survived, such as the Teachers', Miners, or the Oil Workers' Union. It could be that because the party needs their resources, the caucus leaders allow the union leadership to place their representatives as committee leaders of their issue-relevant panels, such as education, energy, or social security.

One should not expect PRI politicians who come from the municipal political arena to win committee presidencies because they lack the administrative or bureaucratic knowhow and the required political networks with caucus leaders to win a chair. One would expect the same outcome for deputies with a prior background in business, as most of these are local business people, not heads of major corporations.

Using very similar variables as those from the hegemonic period (to facilitate comparison across periods), the logistic regression model in Table 9.2 measures the probability of any given deputy in two plural legislatures (2000–2003 and 2003–2006) has of being assigned as a committee chair for any of the sixty plus congressional panels. Because of the inflated numbers of committee secretaries, the model does not include secretaries as the hegemonic model did. The only two differences in the variables across the two periods are: first, whether the deputy entered the Chamber via an SMD race or the PR lists (because one might expect that SMD deputies are less expert than PR representatives because of their localist nature); and second, whether she came from a state governed by a member of the PRI (all governors were members of the PRI in the first data set).

As with the hegemonic logistic regression, this model uses indicator variables for the 424 PRI deputies' professional backgrounds before winning the Chamber election. All deputies can be classified in a mutually exclusive fashion in one of seven background variables, beginning with municipal party or

22. Perhaps the most relevant example was the chair of the Budget Committee between 2009 and 2012, Luis Videgaray, who had been the State of Mexico's Secretary of Finance under Governor Peña Nieto. As a former leader of the Treasury Committee explains, Peña Nieto placed his close ally as head of the Budget Committee to augment his state's budget going into 2012 and to help other PRI governors (interview subject 89).

23. Interview subject 92, a PRI deputy from the Estado de México.

Table 9.2 LOGISTIC MODELS
OF COMMITTEE LEADERSHIP
UNDER DEMOCRACY

Plurality deputy	−0.51
	[.442]
Age	0.052**
	[.023]
Prior legislative experience	0.48
	[.408]
Education level	0.24
	[.228]
PRI governor	0.867**
	[.452]
Prior municipal background	omitted
Prior business	−1.22
	[1.18]
Prior state govt	0.33
	[.369]
Prior State Union	−0.22
	[.961]
Prior national union	1.00
	[.841]
Prior fed govt or party	1.43**
	[.759]
Dummy 2000	−0.36
	[.369]
Constant	−6.80
	[1.8]
Number of cases	424
Pseudo R2	0.14

government, state party or government, state union, business owner, national union leader, or federal bureaucracy. The model uses prior municipal career as the base category, so the effects of the background variables can be compared to the prior municipal career. Also, like the first model, the deputies' educational level is a single continuous variable from 1 to 6. Standard robust errors are applied.

In the model in Table 9.2, the age variable comes out positive and significant, so that as age increases, the deputy has a greater likelihood of winning a committee chair, a reasonable finding if one believes that age is a rough proxy for both policy expertise and the ability to build a political network. A prior career in federal government and the national party also helped PRI politicians win committee chairs more than having come from a municipal background during this period, as expected. And as has been posited by this book, PRI governors appear to be influential in lobbying so that their allies win committee leadership posts, as one sees from the positive sign on the coefficient of "same party governor." Union membership has no discernable effect. Our expectations have largely been met: experts still run the committees, and the PRI governors are able to win leadership positions as well. This is the difference with the hegemonic congresses, where state interests were not well represented in committee leadership posts.

CONCLUSIONS

This chapter has helped demonstrate the importance of both the hegemonic and the democratic legislatures for the PRI leadership. Under hegemony, the authoritarian regime's leaders carefully chose among the thousands of PRI politicians, who would arrive at the Chamber of Deputies. In this first round of selection, the task was to benefit as many internal regime factions as possible, an important goal of elite management. The second round of selection decided who among the deputies would guide the executive's bills through congress without serious modifications on the part of the opposition deputies or, more worrisomely, on the part of the different factions within the regime. In this leadership round, those with ties to the federal government were placed as leaders of the committees.

Of course, the role of the Chamber of Deputies changed decisively with the onset of democratic, competitive elections, and it became an equal partner in policy making and negotiations with the executive between 2000 and 2012. However, the PRI did not wish to allow its legislative caucus the opportunity to vote against the policy preferences of the party leadership. As such, while one sees more decentralized recruitment to the Chamber as more local candidates win the right to compete under the banner of the PRI in SMDs, but leaders won entry to the legislature with high (and therefore, safe) slots on one of the five multimember district PR lists. With the party's governors playing more important roles in vote winning under democratic conditions, they have been granted not only greater influence in candidate selection and recruitment, but also a greater ability to place their allies into committee chairs. Of course, deputies with prior experience in the federal government and other leadership positions were also awarded panel chairs.

APPENDIX 1

DESCRIPTIVE STATISTICS FOR TABLES 9.1 AND 9.2

Hegemonic Era, Table 9.1

	Observations	Mean	S.D.	Min	Max
Age	584	45.7	9.95	24	85
President/secretary of commission	584	0.2	0.405	0	1
Prior legislative experience	584	0.339	0.47	0	1
Level of education	581	3.46	1.21	1	6
Co-partisan governor	587	1	0	1	1
Federal govt experience	587	0.21	0.4	0	1
Leader of a national union	587	0.13	0.34	0	1
State govt experience	587	0.247	0.43	0	1
Leader local union	587	0.31	0.46	0	1
Municipal govt experience	587	0.058	0.23	0	1
Business person	587	0.03	0.177	0	1

Democratic Era, Table 9.2

	Observations	Mean	S.D.	Min	Max
Age	432	47.4	8.52	25	71
Plurality candidate	433	0.67	0.47	0	1
President of committee	433	0.085	0.279	0	1
Committee secretary	433	0.37	0.48	0	1
Prior legislative experience	433	0.54	0.499	0	1
Level of education	427	4.04	0.91	0	6
Copartisan governor	430	0.686	0.46	0	1
Federal govt experience	433	0.13	0.33	0	1
National union leader	433	0.07	0.464	0	1
State govt experience	433	0.385	0.48	0	1
Local union leader	433	0.106	0.308	0	1
Municipal govt leader	433	0.147	0.355	0	1
Businessperson	433	0.145	0.353	0	1

CHAPTER 10

Comparing the PRI Experience to Kenya and Taiwan

This book has examined why the hegemonic PRI was able to survive the transition to democracy and twelve years out of national executive office and how it changed during this period. It finds that successful authoritarian parties must learn how to garner electoral victories under democratic circumstances while avoiding the pressures to fragment. However, this process is full of conflict because some internal party factions are better able to adjust to the new demands of competitive politics, while others are not. Political institutions set the context in which party factions battle over the resources as its leaders and ambitious office seekers seek to better their personal and factional positions; and in doing so, they transform the party into a successful electoral organization without the third-party enforcer. Federalism, the mixed-member majoritarian system, and generous public financing for party activities all played a role in determining how rising competition created winners and losers within the party organization. These institutions were also crucial in reducing the impact of the electoral opening on the party's tendency to fragment.

The substantive chapters of the book demonstrate how the party's most important tasks, selecting and recruiting its candidates, campaigning for elected office, and managing the legislative delegation, have changed due to the pressures of competitive elections. These chapters also illustrate how the different party factions were able to take advantage of the electoral challenges to strengthen their position within the organization, and how their actions transformed the party into a more competitive, decentralized party, without obligating it to become a more programmatic organization.

The inherited resources that mattered as the former authoritarian party struggled through the transition were those related to vote winning, as this is the single most important difference between party-based authoritarian regimes and democracies. Those groups that held or could develop electoral skills and campaign resources had a greater likelihood of taking over the party, while the factions or groups that "simulated" their strength among voters or were responsible for other activities, such as security or economic development, were routed when votes were actually counted.

Almost all authoritarian parties are better positioned than their upstart opposition party rivals when the transition to democracy begins and ends: they labels are better known among the population for having been in power for decades and they have larger territorial organizations. Party labels help voters reduce their costs of information search and so are extremely useful, especially in the early days of a transition to democracy, when new electoral options are often formed and dissolved quickly and it is difficult to establish which party organization (or, better said, groups of political leaders) represents different societal interests. The PRI was the most recognizable party by far, as it governed the nation for seventy years. Despite this, when voters were given a reasonable party alternative, they were willing to take it, as shown in chapter 6.

In addition to party identification, authoritarian parties almost always establish some sort of organizational presence "on the ground" in the different regions of the nation, and because of this territorial structure, they enjoy another advantage not held by newer, weaker, and poorer opposition parties. The empirical question for all authoritarian parties heading toward a transition to democracy, is how strong this territorial organization actually is. In the case of the PRI, the federal government and most governors refused to pay for the permanent work of party staffers, as opposed to work only during campaigns. Instead, the party relied on a semipermanent network of local leaders as well as the unending stream of copartisan elected officials to support copartisan candidates in their campaign efforts. These networks of local residents or brokers were specialists in winning resources from local governments and many survived the transition, and with certain exceptions, such as the Federal District, remained with the PRI. Because the PRI continued to win elections at the municipal and state levels, its leaders continued to benefit from the campaign work of their local officials and operators.

Finally, the present work emphasizes an underresearched issue: the tendency of authoritarian parties to fragment once they lose the resources of the national government and its bureaucracy. Growing electoral competition gives its ambitious politicians a viable exit option (which was not possible when the hegemon won all elections with huge margins). This problem worsens when the party finds itself in the opposition, and its leaders no longer control the instruments or government resources to sanction or benefit its own politicians or voters.

The PRI did not fragment after 2000 because its two groups of leaders—the national party headquarters and its governors—found ways to cooperate that were based on shared interests, autonomous resources, and some ability to sanction the other group. Thanks to federal institutions, when federal elections became more competitive, the PRI governors continued to win municipal, state, and even federal elections in their respective entities, giving their party an important presence in the Chamber of Deputies. Even though party leaders lost the federal government's resources, their copartisan governors became resource-rich, and so continued to be crucial bases of electoral support, as were the local leaders and vote brokers tied to them. The national party headquarters benefitted from the electoral reform of 1996 that allocated millions of pesos of public party resources to the organization, so even when it lost the presidency, it still remained an important actor.

Finally, the two-tiered mixed-member majoritarian system played an important role in how the PRI survived and changed. Under competitive conditions, the SMD tier meant that candidate recruitment and selection were more decentralized than they had been under hegemony because experienced candidates from the local political arena were more popular with voters than those sent down from the national bureaucracy or representatives of unions affiliated with the party. This local advantage gave the PRI's governors more power over politicians' political careers because they controlled candidate selection to most of the posts in their respective states. The PR tier, on the other hand, kept the national party leaders politically powerful because they controlled many of the assured places in the five regional multimember lists. These PR slots also gave the PRI's policy experts, its union chiefs, and party leaders the ability to win legislative seats without the risk of losing a SMD or a state race (for the Senate).

The PRI became a more decentralized electoral force focused primarily on vote winning and legislative negotiations; it did not become more open in its candidate selection methods or legislative delegation, again thanks to the institutional context in which it operates. With single-term limits, the party's bosses, both those within the national headquarters and the governors, were able to continue to control candidate selection, especially for legislative posts. Campaign finances for legislative candidates are controlled formally by the national party organization and, more informally, by the party's governors. And because both federal and state legislators were and continue to be dependent on these leaders for future political posts, legislative discipline continues to be quite high. One can expect that with the introduction of limited consecutive reelection in 2021, the individual legislative office seekers will grow stronger as compared to both the party's governors and the national party.

Legislative office seekers have not made great strides in winning control over campaign resources or candidate selection. One might think that those politicians who compete in the Chamber's 300 SMD races would gain control over campaign resources and pork spending in congress because of their importance in winning elections. But the constitutional prohibition against consecutive reelection dampens their power. However, after 2021, it is doubtful the national party office and governors will keep their informal lock over deputy nominations intact.[1] With this change, one should expect deputies to begin to represent their constituents by insisting on more spending for their districts while strengthening their committee work in the Chamber. Executive office seekers, on the other hand, are stronger vis-à-vis party leaders because voters identify far more with their image and because they understand the office. This gives executive office seekers with popular personal images greater power to exit the party and run against it. Furthermore, once an executive is in office, she controls more money and resources than does the typical senator or legislator.

COMPARING MEXICO'S PRI

This work on the PRI allows one to better understand instances of authoritarian party survival during and after democratic transitions in other nations. To demonstrate how institutions and authoritarian party factions interact under electoral pressures, I compare the cases of Kenya's Kenya African National Union (KANU) and Taiwan's Kuomintang (KMT): the first fragmented and almost disappeared after it lost the presidency for the first time after forty years, and the second returned to power after two terms out of the national executive.

If the argument concerning institutions and the ability of party factions to take advantage of growing electoral competition is correct, then one should expect different patterns of party survival or demise in other authoritarian parties, depending on the differences in the main explanatory variables. In both Kenya's KANU and Taiwan's KMT, as electoral competition rose, one should expect their ambitious politicians to attempt to break the autocrat's stranglehold over candidate selection in general and executive succession in particular, and with this, the possibility of elite splits should grow. Political

---

1. The deputies elected in 2018 will be eligible for reelection in 2021 provided that the same party that nominated them in 2018 nominates them again. This is yet another instance of the parties trying to control the behavior of their ambitious office seekers.

institutions have a central role to play in the ability of the authoritarian party to avoid massive defections: more permissive electoral laws—those that allow new parties to arise, compete, and survive—should lead to party fragmentation, while those that demand greater coordination, organization, and party identification should lead to a lower probability of party fissures that end in dissolution. Political institutions also play an important role in determining which internal factions are able to rise to the electoral challenges to take over the resources of the organization during the transition and beyond.

KANU was formed in 1960 by leaders of the nation's independence movement and quickly managed to become the nation's single party, whose presidents Jomo Kenyatta and Daniel Moi governed the presidential, unitary government with a formally single party system from the mid-1960s through 2002 (Elischer 2008; Kimathi 2010). Once it lost power in the 2002 presidential elections, however, it splintered and has largely become irrelevant in a party system in which many parties are short-lived electoral vehicles.

According to Cowen and Kanyinga (2002, 133), KANU had always been a coalition of tribal groupings, rather than a programmatic party, although Widner (1992) argues that in the 1960s, KANU had identifiable ideological currents. Ethnicity as an organizational tool in Kenya has existed since colonial rule, and as Kimathi (2010, 38) writes, "Kenya's post-independence history became that of personal rule riding on emasculated political institutions, and using ethnic mobilization as a basis for political legitimacy and survival." Once KANU became the only party capable of winning office, ideological platforms were not important voting cues in parliamentary elections that were held from the 1960s onward.

Under President Kenyatta's leadership, which lasted through his death in 1978, KANU's organization was kept weak as patronage was funneled through ethnic group leaders down to their own local vote brokers, a situation that changed under Daniel Moi's presidency, beginning in 1978 (Widner 1992). In 1982, four years after becoming president, Moi used a failed military coup to create a de jure one-party state (in practice, only KANU had participated in elections since the 1960s). Under Moi's leadership, KANU's party organization experienced a sharp increase in responsibilities and resources, to the extent that those who held party offices were able to take over certain responsibilities that had been under the purview of provincial administration during the Kenyatta years.

KANU became a major route to politically successful careers for ambitious party politicians as it was able to monopolize government media, and used public bureaucrats to carry out party tasks, especially during campaigns (Amiri 2007). Many party bosses were also bureaucratic leaders and they were able to channel selective benefits to their coethnic followers. Economic elites and party bosses (who were, at the same time, ethnic group leaders in their respective territories) were often one and the same (Cowen and Kanyinga

2002, 131; Widner 1994, 60). As a result, party and government leaders were able to parlay their political power into economic gain, and those who were excluded from government by the president were at risk of losing their economic privileges (Throup and Hornsby 1998). An exit from the KANU to compete for another party label was not a viable strategy because the president could punish those who did so, and benefit those who stayed.

The party depended on vote brokers at the local level for electoral mobilization. Voters were organized and mobilized along ethnic lines, so that their leaders (members of KANU) could garner resources and channel them to local coethnics. And even though one party controlled the political system, more than one KANU candidate per district competed in the parliamentary elections, and voters could (and did) vote against incumbents.[2] Campaigns were not run along programmatic lines and the exchange of votes for selective government goods was rampant in Kenya long before the onset of competitive multiparty elections in 1992 (Widner 1994, 55).

The SMD electoral rules made grassroot ties between voters and politicians more extensive, allowing some KANU elites to gain "broad regional constituencies and limited national followings" (Widner 1994, 68). This would be a crucial point once multiparty elections were reinstated in 1992: natural voting constituencies were captured by these regional ethnic elites, who—thanks to electoral rules that allowed the easy formation of new parties that could compete almost immediately in proximate elections—could switch from one party to another with relative ease, form new electoral vehicles, or pledge their voters to a coethnic leader.

The transition to democracy began in the late 1980s, as opposition to Moi's rule grew among church and civic leaders, and by 1990, international donors were also demanding a return to multiparty elections. Moi complied, and by 1992, several new parties had formed to run in multiparty elections, not with a serious ideological agenda, but with the goal of dethroning the president.

Much like the Mexican case, the regime's leader was able to dominate the lengthy transition process by doling out small legal concessions to opposition leaders, while retaining several unfair institutional advantages that made defeating the KANU difficult. First, the president could distribute patronage widely because of his control over government resources; second, the government was in charge of the newly created Electoral Commission of Kenya, allowing millions of voters to remain unregistered (Cowen and Kanyinga 2002, 128); and third, electoral districts were drawn to create disproportional units where Moi and KANU had more support (Lebas 2011, 231–232).

Permissive electoral laws which allow new parties to form and dissolve were written by President Moi in his attempts to hold onto power during the 1990s.

2. Cowen and Kanyinga (2002, 156) report over 40 percent of members of parliament were defeated by other candidates from the KANU during the authoritarian era.

The failure of the several opposition options to coalesce around a single candidate allowed Moi to win the presidential election of 1992 with only 36 percent of the vote. Further, KANU polled only 31 percent of the parliamentary vote, but thanks to less-proportional SMD electoral rules, the incumbent party won 52 percent of the seats. In the 1997 presidential elections, Moi did even better at 40 percent of the vote and won the presidency once again.

However, because his mandate was capped at two five-year terms, the party system began to show a greater tendency to fragment among many ethnic-based options, as top KANU leaders began to jostle over the 2002 presidential nomination. Several of the party's powerful ethno-factional leaders left KANU before 2002. In this period from 1997 to 2002, KANU split into two factions (A and B), one of which represented those KANU politicians without a strong regional voting base and another that was tied to tribal strongmen who represented a solid "ethno-regional" base (Cowen and Kanyinga 2002, 152). Outside of KANU, dozens of parties—many of them tied to single ethnic groups and their leaders—formed, coalesced, and then dissolved in the period 1991 to 2002. The effective number of parties in the parliament ranged from 4.1 to 4.5 between 1991 and 1997, and then dropped to 2.9 between 1997 and 2002 (Elischer, 2008, 6).

Despite the advantages held by KANU after the nation's return to multi-party elections, once it lost executive office in 2002, the party could not survive as a major electoral organization. KANU fragmented as its leaders left to either join or create other electoral vehicles, and they were able to do so for two central reasons. First, politicians in Kenya enjoyed other means to mobilize voters, and second, the electoral rules written by President Moi to stay in power made new party formation and survival relatively costless. In the authoritarian era, ethnic group leaders mobilized voters through their local brokers in favor of the overarching KANU coalition. Today, parties in Kenya continue to function as ethnic coalitions led by local and regional strongmen with the capacity to bring short-term benefits to coethnic voters in specific territorial regions of the nation (Cowen and Kanyinga 2002; Elischer 2008; Lebas 2011). The parties that circulate in the multiparty era have not been able to establish long-term cross-ethnic alliances, nor have they been able to root themselves in local constituencies (Lebas 2011, 213). Rather, party leaders mobilize their own ethnic voting blocks, using personal relations with vote brokers and patronage exchange.

After KANU's defeat in 2002 until the next elections in 2007, different KANU leaders left the party, formed new electoral organizations, and then either aligned with the government party or KANU during different crises. By the 2007 presidential election, KANU had become so weak that it did not run its own presidential candidate (although it did field some parliamentary candidates) and its parliamentary vote fell to 6 percent of the national vote.

On the other end of the demise-survival spectrum, the KMT of the Republic of China on Taiwan (or ROC) has enjoyed a successful trajectory since the transition to democracy, returning to executive power in 2008, after two terms out of office. The KMT was formed on the Chinese mainland in the early years of the twentieth century and took power in China at the end of the Second World War. It ruled China for four years before the Chinese Communist Party (CCP) defeated it in 1949. In 1945, the KMT government in China converted Taiwan to a province. When the CCP captured China's government, KMT's leader, Chiang Kai-shek, escaped to Taiwan, along with his government and over one million Mainlanders, and as a result, many native Taiwanese considered the KMT as an authoritarian regime imposed on "foreign" soil. For years, Chiang Kai-shek and the KMT ruled Taiwan as if it were a province of China, with the idea that one day it would return to govern all of China. But with the geopolitical changes of the 1970s, it became apparent that the KMT would have to govern Taiwan as if it were a nation.

Chiang Kai-shek redesigned the KMT as a quasi-Leninist party once he arrived on the island in the late 1940s (Cheng 1989). Party branches were established throughout the island, and at all levels of government—village, township, county, and city—and the provincial level (the entire island of Taiwan was known as the province of Taiwan, given the KMT argument that it ruled over all China). The party's officers controlled and supervised the administrative agencies of government and high-ranking party members held more power than their government counterparts (Cheng 1989, 475; Dickson 1996). The KMT's party branches were active outside of election time, and their paid employees were tasked with helping ordinary citizens in their dealings with local government (Dickson 1996; Fell 2011; Rigger 1999; Tan 2002).

The authoritarian party held enormous advantages over an incipient political opposition up through the mid-1980s: first, opposition parties were proscribed legally; second, the freedom to express political ideas, such as multiparty democracy (as well as freedom of assembly) was actively repressed by the government's security forces (Rigger 1999, 104–105); and finally, the KMT had resources with which it could pay vote brokers to win mobilize the electorate in local elections.

The Nationalist Party used government employees to help in campaign tasks. It allowed KMT candidates to use public television channels for their campaign advertisements, and sent party cadres to oversee the polling places on election day. The KMT bought large quantities of property, making it the wealthiest party in the world (while the PRI depended on government financing), and allocated the equivalent of millions of dollars to its favored candidates (Cheng 1989, 496). The KMT also held some corporatist elements similar to those of the PRI (Mattlin 2011) and was buttressed by strong ties to the army leadership and troops, civil servants, and farmers, who had benefitted from a large-scale land reform in the 1950s.

The ROC government was a semipresidentialist, unitary regime with a unicameral legislature, with local elections that were held regularly from the early 1950s. The single nontransferable vote (SNTV) was used until 2008 for provincial assembly and city council elections, while SMD rules were used for executive elections of city mayors and county magistrates, as well as the presidency beginning in 1996.

Under the SNTV system, voters have a single ballot to cast in multimember districts (magnitude 2–6), and votes for one candidate cannot be transferred to another candidate from the same party. The consequences of SNTV on Taiwanese politics and parties have been well studied (Fell 2011; Hsieh 1996, 199; Rigger 1994, 2002). If a major candidate in a multimember district wins most of the votes in a district, then he "wastes" many of those votes because copartisan candidates in the same district may lose a seat if they did not capture enough votes from those who were willing to support that party. If a party nominates too many candidates, they can divide the votes in such a way as to lose seats; and undernomination can also occur when the party underestimates the support that it could have divided up among more candidates.

Candidates cannot campaign on ideological platforms because they run against copartisans; rather, they must win support by offering services and clientelistic benefits to district residents. Local factions that were affiliated to the KMT—but not directly under the party's control—recruited vote brokers within each area to deliver gifts to residents and mobilize them to vote for the "correct candidate" (Rigger 1999, 51). These local factions predated the KMT's arrival on the island and were political machines responsible for vote mobilization. There was a great deal of competition among factions within the same area, and the KMT national leaders were careful not to allow the factions to grow outside the boundaries of their city or county (Bosco 1992). The party played one local faction against another, supporting some candidates over others, and in fact, the local factions needed the coordination supplied by the KMT.[3] As a result, even though the KMT was considered to be an immigrant elite different from and at times unconnected to the "Taiwanese local elite," it still won local elections (Bosco 1992, 176). Overall, the KMT's coordination of the SNTV system for local elections was highly successful as its candidates won 75–92 percent of the city council seats and 70–85 percent of the provincial assembly posts before the early 1990s.

Under KMT domination of the political system, the national legislature, or Legislative Yuan (as the unicameral legislature is called) was extremely weak: the regime used a strange fiction to simply freeze the original

---

3. Bosco (1992, 173) writes that the job of the party's secretary was to select which factional nominees won the KMT nomination. The candidates of the different local political machines then gave donations to the party in return for the nomination.

representatives of the first Legislative Yuan in place, so that those who had been elected on the Mainland in 1948 continued to hold office until 1992 (those who died or retired were replaced in supplementary elections beginning in 1969). Thus, the Legislative Yuan did not see an entirely new elected legislature for over forty years. The president of Taiwan was elected indirectly by the National Assembly (another national representative assembly that had last held elections at the end of the 1940s on the Mainland), and Chiang Kai-shek and later his son Chiang Ching-Kuo were elected repeatedly.

The transition to democracy began in the 1970s, as opposition groups demanded greater political freedoms and guarantees from the authoritarian regime. Taiwan had become far wealthier thanks to a successful land reform and an efficient export-led growth model that was developed from the late 1950s onward. The population had become better educated, had better communications, and several societal groups fought for greater political liberalization. In 1986, a new party formed illegally, named the Democratic Progressive Party (DPP). This organization stood for greater civil and political liberties, independence from China, and more government spending on social policies.

The negotiated liberalization consisted of ending martial law, revoking the temporary provisions, and allowing the formation of new parties, a freer press, new elections for the Legislative Yuan and the National Assembly (in charge of selecting the president), as well as the direct election of the president. The first new election of all the members of the National Assembly took place in 1991 and the election of a new Legislative Yuan in 1992. Each step required negotiations between regime moderates (led first by Chiang Ching-Kuo and then by his replacement, President Lee Teng-hui) and the DPP leadership, as well as academics and civil society leaders. Hardliners within the KMT were against opening the political sphere while moderates believed the KMT could continue to win in multiparty elections, much like Japan's Liberal Democratic Party.

The opposition DPP focused attention on new issue dimensions, most importantly the democratization of Taiwan, the island's relation with China, and expanding welfare policies. National identity, or the relation between Taiwan and China, has turned out to be one of the most enduring cleavages in Taiwanese politics (Fell 2005; Mattlin 2011; Niou and Hsieh 1996). The more pro-independence elements of the DPP swerved away from the status quo of the ruling KMT during these years and advocated an independent nation status, while the Nationalist Party under more moderate Lee (the first native Taiwanese to have ruled the nation under the KMT) insisted on continuing the careful nonaligned status, with the vague promise of one day returning to China. The hardliners within the regime balked at the negotiated reforms made by the moderates, which would finally contribute to a split within the

KMT and the creation of the New Party (NP) in 1993.[4] The NP remained small, however, and never represented a serious challenge to the KMT; in fact, for several years it has formed a part of the KMT-led Pan-Blue Coalition. The NP was ideologically more extreme than the status quo KMT and it was never able to convince or pay enough local brokers to work for its candidates. Another split from the KMT, called the Taiwan Solidarity Union (TSU), moved into a coalition (the Pan-Green) led by the DPP. It, too, has remained small.

During the transitional decade of the 1990s, the KMT continued to win local and the newly instituted national elections, including the first direct election for the presidency in 1996. When multiparty democracy was instituted for national as well as local elections in the early 1990s, the KMT's leadership worked closely with local factions in more rural areas to mobilize votes under competitive conditions (Chen 1996; Mattlin 2011). During this decade, the KMT began to adjust internally to the pressures of electoral competition. It attempted a short-lived experiment with closed-party primaries to nominate local candidates; it moderated its stance somewhat vis-à-vis the Chinese government; and it strengthened its ties to local factions as it continued to draw native Taiwanese into its leadership ranks. Despite this, in the 2000 presidential elections, the DPP defeated the KMT in large part because of a second large split within the KMT, when a popular politician, Peter Soong, was denied the KMT's presidential nomination. Soong ran against the KMT and the DPP as a presidential candidate and split the KMT vote, allowing the DPP to win the election. It is clear how dangerous internal divisions were to the KMT; again, however, the party created by Soong, the People First Party, has remained relatively insignificant as another element of the KMT coalition.

Some believed the KMT would collapse after its historic defeat: it no longer had control over the national bureaucracy and it suffered deep divisions within its ranks which caused electoral defeats. But the party survived, in part because the governing DPP was still so organizationally weak and in part because the local factions continued to work for the KMT (and because it enjoys great resources) (Choi 2014). Even though it controlled the government after 2000, the former opposition DPP did not have the local networks of the KMT and could not build up a huge party organization from the few hundred party workers it employed.[5] The DPP (much like Mexico's PAN) found it difficult to govern because the KMT was able to maintain a majority in the Legislative Yuan and blocked many of the policy initiatives of the new government.

4. Mattlin (2011, 92) argues that the 1993 split by the KMT's old guard was caused by a combination of factors, including constitutional design, electoral rules, and Taiwan's relation with China.

5. Personal communication with Mikael Mattlin, November 12, 2012.

Once the KMT lost power, its leaders continued to modify some of its internal processes.[6] For example, it actively recruited younger members and worked to institutionalize several important internal selection processes, both for elected and party posts. Most importantly, even with the enormous weight of the local factions both in campaigning and in fundraising, the national party leaders have been able to successfully maintain discipline in the Legislative Yuan, although there continue to be problems between legislators and party leaders.

Many politicians have advanced from grassroots politics to the Legislative Yuan, so that the local factions now have more influence in national politics. Campaigns are run with the grassroots work of family and local factional supporters, and are centered on mass rallies, door-to-door canvassing, and media coverage. The national party's campaign efforts in those areas where they have local factional support are not as strong, because candidates make use of local networks (Fell 20011; Mattlin 2011). However, several wealthier areas of the island no longer depend on local factions for voter mobilization. The KMT still does not have clear rules to choose their candidates for national office, and those who run under the label for national posts are mostly selected by the national party elite, despite periodic attempts to decentralize and democratize candidate selection (Hsieh 2010).

As one would expect, the three former authoritarian parties shared many characteristics. First and foremost, all three regimes studied above were authoritarian in that they limited opposition activity, controlled speech, employed selective repression, and used government resources to remain in power. Despite their authoritarian nature, the three regimes held elections continually during their stay in power; and in Kenya and Taiwan there was true competition, within the party in primaries in Kenya and in local races in Taiwan. An important part of vote winning in the three regimes was local-level distribution of patronage and clientelist benefits. All three had important origin movements: the revolution for Mexico, independence for Kenya, the loss of Mainland China for Taiwan (Levitsky and Wey 2010).

In terms of internal coalition control, the authoritarian executive was responsible for placing his successor (although Kenya and Taiwan had far fewer executive turnovers than Mexico because of the single six-year terms). The three parties had permanent party organization stretching across the nation, with the KMT being the most extensive, followed by the PRI, then KANU.

According to Grzymała-Busse (2002), the presence of reformist elites should play a central explanatory role in whether communist successor parties were able to survive their departure from power. These reformers were

---

6. Some, such as Wong (2008, 63), argue that despite electoral successes after its defeat in 2000, the KMT did not reinvent itself.

responsible for reducing the strength of the traditionalist rank-and-file members; centralizing authority to the national leadership; and finally, moderating the parties' ideological platforms. However, all the three parties discussed in this chapter had reformist factions before losing power, and yet, only two survived. As discussed above, during the transition period, Mexico's PRI held two different types of reformist groups: the first, a prodemocracy faction that left the party in 1987, and the second, the promarket (although not politically democratic) clique of President Salinas. Taiwan's KMT had both reform elites and more conservative factions circulating in the 1980s and into the transition period of the 1990s (Fell 2005). As mentioned above, the political sphere was split by two reinforcing cleavages early in the democratization process; the first concerned Taiwan's relation with China, which helped spur the creation of a more conservative, pro-unification faction, which eventually became the NP. The second centered on the pace and scope of democratization and constitutional change after 1986. The moderate, reformist faction prevailed and, within limits, allowed the KMT to moderate on the national identity question by bringing a significant number of native Taiwanese into the government and party (Fell 2005). This KMT faction also devised and implemented popular social welfare policies in the 1990s, in effect "stealing" this issue from the DPP in order to continue in power. In the KANU, Throup and Hornsby (1998) write of the hardliners in KANU, who did not believe the move to multiparty elections would benefit the party, versus those tied to Moi, who thought there was little choice and that, from the position of the presidency, Moi and KANU could continue to reign victorious. In terms of other inheritable resources, without a doubt, KANU, the KMT, and the PRI enjoyed greater name recognition, resources, and territorial extension than the fledgling opposition parties and coalitions in their respective nations. Yet, their organizations suffered serious divisions and exits by powerful politicians. Finally, Mexico, Kenya, and Taiwan all followed a long-form transition that took over ten years, giving all three ample time to adjust to growing competition. Because these characteristics are shared by the three parties, they cannot explain the differences in outcomes of Taiwan and Mexico on one hand and Kenya on the other.

Of course, the three authoritarian parties and their regimes were different as well, and one of these differences helped determine survival or fragmentation and demise. One of the sharpest differences is that Taiwan's authoritarian regime led a successful export-driven development model that dragged the nation out of poverty and transformed it into one of Asia's Five Tigers. While Mexico certainly developed and modernized during the PRI's seventy years in power, the regime's economic failings during its last twenty years in office helped keep millions of its citizens mired in poverty. Kenya under KANU was a case of stop-and-start economic growth and cycles of crisis. Second, the parties differed in terms of the importance of ideology: KANU never had a strong ideology to speak of, and did not change dramatically on the economic front before or after the subsequent transition (Widner 1994). In Mexico, economic crisis and reform helped split the party in 1987 between those opposed to economic liberalization and the technocratic reformers, leading to a near defeat for the PRI in the 1988 presidential elections, twelve years before it was finally ousted. So, in Mexico's case, ideological change and policy transformation actually harmed the electoral success of the hegemonic party in the short term. The KMT's refusal to modify its stance on Mainland China is popular with voters. It appears that ideology cannot explain the KANU's fragmentation.

Finally, one can look to differences in electoral rules that vary the costs of forming new parties and those that encourage strong parties. President Moi outlawed opposition parties between 1982 and 1991, but once they were legalized, he encouraged the creation of new labels through permissive electoral rules designed to fragment the opposition, so that KANU would continue to govern with small vote percentages. This strategy worked well in both 1992 and 1997 as the opposition (many of whose leaders were from defectors from KANU) split into several different electoral options, and KANU remained united. However, once Moi could no longer run for president and KANU lost the presidency (and access to government largesse) it suffered from the same incentives to fragment that had plagued the nation's other parties for a decade. Also, campaign finance in Kenya is not funneled through the parties' organizations: rather, the money required for electioneering is provided by the ethnic leader. Even rules that are meant to strengthen the parties, such as that which stipulates that party switchers in parliament must legally stand for a by-election, are in practice rule rarely enforced, encouraging further party weakness. In the case of Kenya, the role played by the party's territorial organization in campaigning has not been as important as in Taiwan or Mexico because local political machines, which are tied to ethnic leaders via clientelistic links, have access to government largesse and do not need a well-known party label to compete successfully for votes in their regions.

Taiwan, on the other hand, did not see the growth of their smaller breakaway parties, in part because they could not connect with the local factions that were crucial for voter mobilization. This allowed the KMT to retain its majority in the Legislative Yuan in the eight years out of power, effectively hamstringing the two terms of the DPP president. Campaigning in an SNTV system demanded great coordination skills on the part of party leaders and resources for clientelistic exchange that often come from local party or factional leaders.[7] In Mexico, several institutional rules strengthen the party leadership and force office seekers to rely on them for resources to continue their political careers. The bar is purposely set high to register new parties; and party switching in the Chamber is dangerous because intramural resources are given to the

7. Taiwan's electoral system was changed from SNTV to mixed-member majoritarian (MMM) in 2008.

party caucus, not the individual deputy. Independent candidates were barred until 2015; multiple terms in office are constitutionally banned until 2021. The single-round, single-district plurality elections for the presidency of Taiwan also promoted divisions in the party as the exit of a single popular KMT politician could divide the KMT vote. But as shown above, these splits did not turn into a fragmentation scenario because of the difficulty winning parliamentary seats for smaller parties that did not have access to local vote brokers. Thus, one of the central factors that help explain party survival under growing electoral competition is the presence of party-protecting electoral rules, including those that allow different factions within the party to cooperate once the autocrat has been voted out of power (Tsang 1999; Wu 2001).

THE PEÑA NIETO PRESIDENTIAL VICTORY AND ITS AFTERMATH

A last question is how the PRI has changed since it has retaken Los Pinos in the presidential elections of 2012. As pointed out by Samuels and Shugart (2010), presidential parties are different than their parliamentary counterparts because it is more difficult for them to sanction wayward presidents. One could have expected a stronger control of the PRI president over his party than was seen from the two PAN presidents over the PAN because of the traditions of PRI hierarchical control.

Even after the disastrous presidential elections of 2000 and 2006, the PRI managed to deny the PAN a majority in the two federal houses of Congress, and continued to win more governorships than the other two major parties combined. And when a popular PRI governor of the largest state in Mexico (the State of Mexico) became the party's frontrunner for the presidency soon after the 2006 elections, most expected the PRI to defeat the incumbent PAN and the PRD. Because of Enrique Peña Nieto's popularity with voters, disparate groups within the party had strong incentives to support his drive toward Los Pinos, which helped unify the party, rather than divide it, as Madrazo had done in 2005 and 2006. The PRI governors had done very well under the two PAN presidents, as shown in the spending figures presented in chapter 5. The peso equivalent of tens of millions of dollars was sent yearly to the thirty-two governors and head of the Federal District, allowing them to support the electoral efforts of their copartisans, and win influence in the federal congress. But with a PRI president of Mexico, not only would the governors continue to do relatively well, but all other types of PRI party politicians would as well: the popular presidential candidate would lift many copartisans policians into public office on his coattails; he could open up the doors of the federal government bureaucracy to party members; and he could spend on public works and social welfare projects that make the party label more popular.

Since the run-up to the 2012 electoral campaign, the CEN presidents have been placed by candidate Peña Nieto and then President Peña Nieto. The national party leadership under a strong presidency did not have much influence in the policy-making agenda of the new administration, whose key actors were firmly installed in the federal government. During the 2012 presidential campaign, the leader of the CEN—Pedro Joaquin Coldwell —played an active public role in defending the candidate and attacking the opposition (for which he was rewarded with a cabinet post). Once the new president took office, his hand-selected CEN leader became a less visible political figure than the CEN leader had been under the two PAN presidents. It appeared that the PRI's organization would once again remain weak against the power and resources of a copartisan president, and the governors would be obliged to lower their political profiles.

While the legislative bills dealing with the second generation of structural reforms (designed to weaken or destroy oligopolies and monopolies within the Mexican economic and educational sectors) originated in the executive, negotiations were carried out among the party leaders in the two houses of congress. After two years of successful negotiating with opposition party leaders over structural reforms, however, several scandals exploded, which weakened the Peña Nieto presidency while they strengthened the PRI's governors. These scandals included forty-three kidnapped (and presumed murdered) college students, several cases of conflict of interest in public infrastructural contracts, massacres involving the army, among many others. In the 2015 legislative midterms, the party did not perform as badly as many believed it would (thanks once again to a divided opposition and the party's governors), but it was clear that Peña Nieto was losing popularity with voters and support within his coalition. As a result, the president's strongest rival within the party, Manlio Fabio Beltrones, was able to take over the CEN leadership post in 2015, strengthening the party once again as it became a platform to win dozens of state and local elections in the run-up to the next presidential elections.

The PRI came out of the transition period and the twelve years out of office changed in many ways: it is more decentralized than it was under authoritarianism; its leaders are far more focused on vote winning and negotiations with their rivals in the legislature than they are on intra-elite management; and its national leadership has successfully modernized campaign appeals, while still relying on traditional mobilization tactics, such as vote buying. Yet, popular candidates, effective campaigns in media and on the ground, as well as clientelist vote-buying practices have meant it does not yet need to rely on only programmatic promises (although during the 2012 campaign, Peña Nieto did rely on the promise of ushering forth a second generation of structural reforms to free the economy of its oligopolistic binds).

Thus, the Institutional Revolutionary Party—the famous oxymoron of the twentieth century—has continued its old practices. Its leaders are ideological shape-shifters that propose, on one hand, to speak for peasants and workers and, on the other, protect rent-seeking activities of their business sector allies. President Peña Nieto has not understood how the perception of corruption could stymie his government, and he was famously accused by *The Economist* that the "president doesn't get that he doesn't get it"[8] on the fundamental issues of governmental conflict of interest and corruption.

Finally, because the president depended heavily on his co-partisan governors both for resources and manpower during his election and the mid-term races, he seemed unable to control their worst abuses while in office. This led to a string of PRI governors who are charged with stealing the peso equivalent of hundreds of millions of dollars from their state's coffers and in some cases, close ties to organized crime.[9] Again, this has tarnished both the party's reputation and the presidency.

These activities have not been prosecuted by the PRI government. The president of Mexico still needs his copartisan governors because he requires the support of their deputies in the Chamber and their campaign support to win votes.[10] In 2016, the PRI leaders in congress refused to sign a strong anticorruption bill; and finally, the federal government was called to task publicly for stonewalling an independent investigation into the disappearance and presumed murders of forty-three students by police working with criminal organizations.[11]

Because of the nation's electoral rules and pragmatic nature of many voters, the PRI has modernized its electoral strategies and found ways to manage its fractious candidate selection processes. But it has not been able to leave its clientelist and corrupt past behind.

8. Bello, "The Mexican Morass: A President Who Doesn't Get that He Doesn't Get It." *The Economist*, January 22, 2015.

9. These PRI governors include César Duarte of Chihuahua, Humberto Moreira, a former governor of Coahuila, Jorge Herrera of Durango, Jesús Reyna of Michoacán, Arturo Montiel of the State of Mexico, Rodrigo Medina de Nuevo Léon, Ulises Ruiz of Oaxaca, Enrique Borges of Quintana Roo, Eugenio Hernández and Tomás Yarrington, both former governors of Tamaulipas, Fidel Herrera, a former governor of Veracruz who has been formally accused by not charged, and Javier Duarte of Veracruz. Of course, governors from the PAN and the PRD have been accused as well, for example Guillermo Padrés of Sonora (PAN) and Marcelo Ebrard of Mexico City (PRD). Many of these former governors have not faced any judicial process.

10. One of the few instances of a PRI leader rebuking a PRI governor was quickly watered down. In February 2016, the leader of the CEN of the PRI, Manlio Fabio Beltrones, stated publicly that the PRI governor of a large state, Veracruz, should be held accountable for the manner in which he has spent public funds during his administration. The next day, Beltrones backtracked and argued that Duarte is a PRI governor and so can count on the party's support and that the rumors about Duarte are electorally instigated. See Andrea Becerril, Víctor Ballinas, and Alma Muñoz, "Recula Beltrones y ofrece apoyo a Duarte de Ochoa," *La Jornada*, February 25, 2016.

11. Grupo Interdisciplinario de Expertos Independientes, Ayotzinapa. The reports are available at http://prensagieiayotzi.wix.com/giei-ayotzinapa#!informe-/c1exv.

LIST OF INTERVIEW SUBJECTS

For various reasons I have decided not to reveal the identities of my inter-view subjects. Instead, I have identified each with a number, beginning with interview subject 1. The subjects are assigned numbers in the order in which I interviewed them, and the date of the interview is provided. In addition, the subjects are given a short biography, so the reader knows why this person's opinion is a valuable contribution to the theme at hand. Interview sources with a letter after their number simply means they were added after the origi-nal list was made.

1. Political analyst and former government bureaucrat. July 10, 1995.
1A. Former political strategist for a high-ranking politician in the Salinas term. December 7, 1995.
2. Former president of the CEN under President López Portillo and President de la Madrid. March 19, 1996.
3. Former governor and a former leader of the CEN under President de la Madrid. March 7, 1996.
4. Former Secretary of Education under President de la Madrid and former member of the CEN. May 31, 1996.
5. Former Director General of Governance under President Zedillo. July 1, 1996.
6. Political analyst. July 2, 1996.
7. Former representative of Baja California Sur to the federal government during the sexenio of President Zedillo. July 9, 1996.
8. Former federal deputy and former General Director of the Governance Ministry under President Salinas. July 11, 1996.
9. Former leader of the CEN during the sexenio of President Zedillo. July 23, 1996.
10. Former governor under de la Madrid; former Secretary General of the CEN under President Zedillo, 1996. February 15, 1997.

11. A former secretary of the CEN under President López Portillo. August 2, 1996.

11A. Former member of the CEN under President Salinas, September 10, 1996.

11B. Former Under-Secretary of Governance under Zedillo, December 10, 1996.

12. Former leader of the Jalisco state party leader. February 21, 1997.

13. Former leader of the CDE Jalisco, former spokesperson of the PRI in the IFE, 1990s. February 27, 1997.

13A. Former Governor under de la Madrid. March 6, 1997.

13B. Former federal deputy and former party delegate (delegado) to the state of Jalisco. March 14, 1997.

14. Former Secretary of Organization of the state PRI in Jalisco and member of the General Council of the Universidad de Guadalajara. March 17, 1997.

15. Former journalist of the newspaper *Siglo XXI*. March 18, 1997.

16. Former secretary of the Jalisco PRI. March 19, 1997.

17. Former president of a municipal committee of the PRI in Tlaquepaque. March 20, 1997.

18. Former federal deputy and then secretary of finances of the CEN, and later secretary in the CEN during the 1990s. February 25, 1997.

19. Campaign coordinator of the PAN's 1990 gubernatorial campaign in Queretaro. April 1, 1997. (With Scott Morgenstern).

20. Political reporter for the newspaper *Siglo XXI*. April 17, 1997.

20A. Former member of the state PRI in Jalisco. April 17, 1997.

21. Director of the newspaper *Siglo XXI*. April 17, 1997.

22. Former advisor to a councilor of the IFE, Joy Langston and Scott Morgenstern. June 9, 1997.

23. High-ranking political operator in the CNOP and SNTE. August 28, 1997.

23A. Former Director General of Governance. July 1, 1996.

24. Former PRI mayor of Chihuahua, federal deputy. February 2, 1998.

25. Former leader of Chihuahua's CDE of the PRI. February 2, 1998.

26. Former PRI governor of Chihuahua. February 3, 1998.

27. Former PRI mayor of Chihuahua, 1995–1998. February 4, 1998.

28. Former PRI leader of the state congress in the 1990s. February 4, 1998.

29. Former PRI local deputy and federal deputy from Chihuahua. February 4, 1998.

30. Former PRI mayor of Tecate during the 1980s, former second in command of the state government in the 1980s. He was also head of the CDE three times during the 1980s and 1990s. June 16, 1998.

31. Former staffer for the PRI in the State Assembly. June 15, 1998.

32. Former leader of the PRI in Baja California. June 15, 1998.
33. Former delegate from Bancomext in Baja California. June 15, 1998.
34. Former governor of Baja California. June 15, 1998.
35. Former leader of the State PRI in Baja California and former leader of the Municipal Party in Mexicali. June 16, 1998,
36. Former rector of the state university of Baja California and former federal deputy. June 17, 1998,
37. Former leader of the CDE of Baja California. June 17, 1998,
38. Former leader of the state Peasant Sector in Baja California. June 17, 1998.
39. Businessperson who had worked a great deal with the state of Baja California's affiliate to the National Chamber of Industry (CANACINTRA). June 18, 1998.
40. Former mayor of Tijuana and former governor of Baja California. June 18, 1998.
41. Former senator from Guanajuato. February 23, 1999.
42. Academic in Guanajuato. April 12, 1999.
43. Former leader of the PRI in Guanajuato. April 12, 1999.
44. Former director of *El Nacional*, a PRI newspaper and then director of the newspaper *El Correo*, Guanajuato. April 13, 1999.
45. Former president of the PRI CDE in the early 1990s. April 13, 1999.
46. Former member of the PRI CDE of Guanajuato in the 1990s. April 14, 1999.
47. Former city councilmen for the PRI, Leon, and former general secretary of the PRI in Guanajuato. April 14, 1999.
48. Local deputy and the general secretary of Guanajuato's state government in the early 1990s. April 15, 1999.
49. Former local deputy of the PRI fraction in Guanajuato's State Assembly, and then federal deputy. April 21, 1999.
50. PRI's 1995 candidate for the governorship of Guanajuato. May 10, 1999.
51. Delegate from Sedsol in the state of Jalisco starting in the 1990s. June 8, 1999.
52. Former federal deputy for the PRI. February 2, 2000.
53. Former member of the CEN in the 1980s and late 1990s. February 24, 2000.
54. Former federal deputy and senator and member of Presidencia. April 11, 2000.
54A. Former federal deputy for the PAN. Part of one of the traditional PAN families. June 12, 2000.
54B. Former member of the CEN in the 1980s and late 1990s. June 15, 2000.
54C. Former senator for the PAN. A long-time member of the PAN. June 19, 2000.

54D. Former coordinator of the PRI's presidential campaign. September 11, 2000.

55. Former federal deputy; he lost a second election for federal deputy, and former member of the CEN of the PRI. September 26, 2001.

56. Former pollster for the federal government. October 29, 2001.

57. Former pollster for the PRI. November 22, 2001.

58. Former Undersecretary of Elections in the CEN in 1991, and he was a member of the CPN in the 2000 elections, and worked in Presidencia. December 10, 2001,

59. Member of the Workers' Sector. Ran successfully for federal deputy in the 1990s, but then lost her election under democratic conditions. April 29, 2002.

60. Former senator, federal deputy, gubernatorial precandidate, Undersecretary of Governance and secretary of the CEN of the PRI. April 23, 2002

61. Former federal deputy during the early 1990s from Tamaulipas. April 29, 2002.

62. Former PRI president of Mexico. May 13, 2002.

63. Leader of the CNC and former governor. May 16, 2002.

64. Former federal deputy from the PRI in a mixed district Dip Fed, 2000–2003. Represented the CNC. He was elected in 1988, and again in 2000. May 22, 2002.

65. Former federal deputy for the PRI representing the Peasant Sector. May 23, 2002.

66. Former governor, former president of the CEN, former senator. June 18, 2003.

67. Former president of the CEN, former federal deputy, and former governor. September 10, 2003.

68. Former senator, leader of the CEN, secretary of the CEN, and federal deputy in the 1980s. November 21, 2003.

69. Former director of the Fundación Rafael Preciado, a PAN think tank. March 9, 2004.

70. Former federal deputy for the PRI. April 26, 2004.

71. Former federal deputy for the PRI from a rural district. April 29, 2004.

72. Former federal deputy for the PRI, from Jalisco, representing the Peasant Sector. May 6, 2004.

73. Former federal deputy for the PRI from a mixed district. May 25, 2004.

73A. Former federal deputy for the PRI from an urban district. May 13, 2004.

74. Former federal deputy for the PRI from an urban district. May 10, 2004.

75. Former federal deputy for the PRI from a rural district. May 26, 2004.

76. Former federal deputy for the PRI from a mixed district. June 1, 2004.

76A. Former federal deputy for the PRI. May 27, 2004.

77. Former federal deputy for the PRI from a rural district. May 31, 2004.

78. Former federal deputy for the PRI from an urban district. June 15, 2004.
79. Former federal deputy for the PRI from a rural district. February 16, 2005.
80. PAN candidate for federal deputy in the 1970s and 1980s. February 18, 2005.
81. Former federal deputy for the PAN from an urban district. February 23, 2005.
82. Former PAN federal deputy. February 24, 2005.
83. Pollster for the PAN. February 24, 2005.
84. Former PAN federal deputy from an urban district. March 2, 2005.
85. Former governor, federal deputy, and senator. February 17, 2009.
86. Former senator, former federal deputy, had left the PRI. March 9, 2009.
87. Former Undersecretary of the Treasury under President Zedillo and former federal deputy. May 19, 2009.
88. Former senator, former Secretary of Governance, former governor. May 28, 2009.
89. Former Undersecretary of Treasury in the 1980s and former federal deputy for the PRI. July 10, 2009.
90. Former PRD federal deputy from a mixed district. June 10, 2010.
91. Former federal deputy, PRI from an urban district after the transition. July 26, 2010.
92. Former federal deputy from the PRI from a urban district, who had also worked several jobs in municipal government. July 28, 2010.
93. Former federal deputy and former member of her state's cabinet. October 2, 2010.
94. Former advisor of a cabinet secretary from President Zedillo's term. March 5, 2012.
94A. PAN congressional staffer in the mid to late 2000s. November 9, 2011.
95. Special assistant to a PRI presidential candidate. March 21, 2012,
96. Former governor, leader of the PRI, federal deputy, Undersecretary of Governance. September 10, 2012.
97. Former representative of the PRI to the IFE during the 1990s and former federal deputy. June 10, 2013.

REFERENCES

Adler Hellman, Judith. 1978. *Mexico in Crisis*. New York: Holmes & Meier.

Agranoff, Robert. 1976. *The Management of Election Campaigns*. Boston, MA: Holbrook.

Aguayo, Sergio. 2001. *La charola: Una historia de los servicios de inteligencia en México*. Mexico City: Grijalvo.

Aguayo, Sergio. 2010. *Vuelta en U. Guía para entender y reactivar la democracia estancada*. Mexico City: Taurus.

Aguilar Morales, Mario. 2002. "La educación en México (1970–2000): De una estrategia Nacional a una estrategia Regional." *La Tarea* 16–17. http://www.latarea.com.mx/articu/articu16/maguila16.htm.

Alarcón, Víctor. 2006. "El Poder Legislativo en México: Evolución y tendencias en el contexto de la democratización." In *Treinta años de cambios políticos en México*, edited by Antonella Attili, 187–220. Mexico City: Porrúa/UAM-Iztapalapa.

Alcalde Justiniano, Arturo. 2006. "Balance sindical del gobierno de transición." In *Los sindicatos en la encrucijada del siglo XXI*, edited by Inés González Nicolás, 39–60. Mexico City: Fundación Friedrich Ebert.

Aldrich, John. 1995. *Why Parties? The Origin and Transformation of Political Parties in America*. Chicago: University of Chicago Press.

Almond, Gabriel, and Sidney Verba. 1963. *The Civic Culture: Political Attitudes and Democracy in Five Nations*. Princeton, NJ: Princeton University Press.

Alonso, Jorge. 1987. *Elecciones en tiempos de crisis*. Guadalajara: Universidad de Guadalajara.

Alvarado, Arturo. 1996. "Los gobernadores y el federalismo mexicano." *Revista mexicana de sociología* 3: 39–71.

Ames, Barry. 1970. "Bases of Support for Mexico's Dominant Party." *American Political Science Review* 64, no. 1: 153–167.

Amezcua, Adriana, and Juan Pardinas. 1997. *Todos los gobernadores del Presidente: Cuando el dedo de uno aplasta el voto popular*. Mexico City: Editorial Grijalbo.

Amiri, Jane. 2007. "Kenya." In *Parties and Democracy: The KAS Democracy Report, 2007*, 62–87. Berlin: Konrad-Adenauer-Stiftung.

Anderson, Roger. 1971. "The Functional Role of the Governors and Their States in the Political Development of Mexico, 1940–1964." PhD diss., Department of Political Science, University of Wisconsin.

Arnaut, Alberto. 1997. "The Partido Revolucionario Institucional (PRI)." In *Mexico: Assessing Neo-Liberal Reform*, edited by Mónica Serrano. London: Institute of Latin American Studies.

Ávila Ortiz, Raúl. 2012. "Vida interna, justicia electoral y pertinencia de una ley de partidos en México." In *¿Hacia una ley de partidos?*, edited by Raúl Ávila, Lorenzo Córdova, and Daniel Zovatto, 95–132. Mexico City: UNAM and IDEA.

Axelrod, Robert. 1984. *The Evolution of Cooperation*. New York: Basic Books.

Bailey, John. 1987. "Can the PRI be Reformed? Decentralizing Candidate Selection." In *Mexican Politics in Transition*, edited by Judith Gentleman, 63–92. Boulder, CO: Westview Press.

Bailey, John, and Leopoldo Solís. 1990. "The PRI and Political Liberalization." *Journal of International Affairs* 43, no. 2: 291–312.

Bartra, Roger. 1993. *Agrarian Structure and Political Power in Mexico*. Baltimore, MD: Johns Hopkins University Press.

Basurto, Jorge. 1984. *La clase obrera en la historia de México. Del avilacamachismo al alemanismo (1940–1952)*. Mexico City: Siglo XXI.

Becerra, Ricardo, Pedro Salazar, and José Woldenberg, eds. 1997. *La reforma electoral de 1996: Una descripción general*. Mexico City: Fondo de Cultura Económica.

Beer, Caroline. 2003. *Electoral Competition and Institutional Change in Mexico*. South Bend, IN: University of Notre Dame Press.

Bejar, Luisa. 2003. *El poder legislativo en México. Los diputados de partido: El primer eslabón del cambio*. Mexico City: UNAM and Gernika.

Bejar, Luisa. 2006. *Los partidos en el Congreso de la Unión. La representación parlamentaria después de la alternancia*. México: UNAM and Gernika.

Belloni, Frank P., and Dennis C. Beller. 1978. *Faction Politics: Political Parties and Factionalism in Comparative Perspective*. Santa Barbara, CA: ABC-Clio.

Beltrán, Ulises. 2007. "The Combined Effect of Advertising and News Coverage in the Mexican Presidential Campaign of 2000." *Political Communication* 24, no. 1: 37–63.

Bensusán, Graciela. 1995. "Entra la tradición y el cambio: El corporativismo sindical en México." In *Sindicalismo latinoamericano: Entra la renovación y la resignación*, edited by Maria Silvia Portella de Castro and Achim Wachendorfer, 67–82. Caracas, Venezuela: ILDES-FES, Editorial Nueva Sociedad.

Bensusán, Graciela. 2004. "A New Scenario for Mexican Trade Unions: Changes in the Structure of Political and Economic Opportunities." In *Dilemmas of Political Change in Mexico*, edited by Kevin Middlebrook, 237–285. London: Institute of Latin American Studies, University of London; La Jolla: Center for US-Mexican Studies, University of California, San Diego.

Bertaccini, Tiziana. 2009. *El regime priísta frente a las clases medias, 1943–1964*. Mexico City: Consejo Nacional para la Cultura y las Artes.

Blaydes, Lisa. 2011. *Elections and Distributive Politics in Mubarak's Egypt*. New York: Cambridge University Press.

Boix, Carles, and Milan Svolik. 2013. "The Foundations of Limited Authoritarian Government: Institutions, Commitment, and Power-Sharing in Dictatorships." *Journal of Politics* 75, no. 2: 300–316.

Booth, John A., and Mitchell A. Seligson. 1984. "The Political Culture of Authoritarianism in Mexico: A Reexamination." *Latin American Research Review* 19, no. 1: 106–125.

Bosco, Joseph. 1992. "Taiwan Factions: Gaunxi Patronage and the State in Local Politics." *Ethnology* 31: 157–183.

Brandenburg, Frank. 1964. *The Making of Modern Mexico*. Englewood Cliffs, NJ: Prentice-Hall.

Brinegar, Adam, Scott Morgenstern, and Daniel Nielson. 2006. "The PRI's Choice: Balancing Democratic Reform and Its Own Salvation." *Party Politics* 12: 77–97.

Brownlee, Jason. 2007. *Authoritarianism in an Age of Democratization*. New York: Cambridge University Press.

Bruhn, Kathleen. 1997. *Taking on Goliath: The Emergence of a New Left Party and the Struggle for Democracy in Mexico*. University Park: Pennsylvania State University Press.

Bruhn, Kathleen. 1999. "PRD Local Governments in Michoacán: Implications for Mexico's Democratization Process." In *Subnational Politics and Democratization in Mexico*, edited by Wayne A. Cornelius, Todd Eisenstadt, and Jane Hindley, 19–44. La Jolla: Center for US-Mexican Studies, University of California, San Diego.

Bruhn, Kathleen. 2014. "Choosing How to Choose: From Democratic Primaries to Unholy Alliances in Mexico's Gubernatorial Elections." *Mexican Studies/Estudios Mexicanos* 30, no. 1: 212–240.

Bruhn, Kathleen, and Kenneth Greene. 2007. "Elite Polarization Meets Mass Moderation in Mexico's 2006 Elections." *PS: Political Science and Politics* 40: 33–38.

Burgess, Katrina. 2004. *Parties and Unions in the New Global Economy*. Pittsburgh, PA: Pittsburgh University Press.

Burgess, Katrina, and Steven Levitsky. 2003. "Explaining Populist Party Adaptation in Latin America: Environmental and Organizational Determinants of Party Change in Argentina, Mexico, Peru, and Venezuela." *Comparative Political Studies* 36: 859–880.

Cain, Bruce, John Ferejohn, Morris Fiorina. 1987. *The Personal Vote. Constituency Service and Electoral Independence*. Cambridge, MA: Harvard University Press.

Camacho Solís, Manuel. 1980. *La clase obrera en la historia de México*. Mexico City: Siglo XXI.

Camp, Roderic. 1980. *Mexico's Leaders: Their Education and Recruitment*. Tucson: University of Arizona Press.

Camp, Roderic. 1990. "Camarillas in Mexican Politics: The Case of the Salinas Cabinet." *Mexican Studies, Estudios Mexicanos* 6: 85–108.

Camp, Roderic. 1995. *Mexican Political Biographies 1935–1993*. Austin: University of Texas Press.

Camp, Roderic. 1999. *Politics in Mexico. The Decline of Authoritarianism*, 3rd ed. New York: Oxford University Press.

Camp, Roderic. 2010. *Metamorphosis of Leadership in Democratic Mexico*. New York and Oxford: Oxford University Press.

Campbell, Angus, Philip E. Converse, Warren E. Miller, and Donald E. Stokes, eds. 1966. *Elections and the Political Order*. New York: Wiley.

Campuzano Montoya, Irma. 1990. "El impacto de la crisis en la CTM." *Revista mexicana de sociología* 52: 161–190.

Carey, John. 2009. *Legislative Voting and Accountability*. New York. Cambridge University Press.

Carey John M., and Matthew S. Shugart. 1995. "Incentives to Cultivate a Personal Vote: A Rank Ordering of Electoral Formulas." *Electoral Studies* 14: 417–439.

Casar, María Amparo. 2008. "Los gobiernos sin mayoría en México: 1997–2000." *Política y gobierno* 15: 221–270.

Casillas Ortega, Carlos. 2000. "Las primarias en el PRI: recuento de un experimento." *El Cotidiano* 191: 12–22.

Castelazo, José. 1985. *Nuestra Clase Gobernante*. Mexico City: Facultad de Ciencias Políticas y Sociales y Centro de Investigaciones en Administración Pública.

Casteñeda, Jorge. 1991. "El fraude moderno." *Proceso*, no. 773-17, August 26.

Casteñeda, Jorge. 1999. *La herencia: Arqueología de la sucesión presidencial en México*. Mexico City: Alfaguara.

Ceasar, James. 1990. "Political Parties: Declining, Stabilizing, or Resurging?" In *The New American Political System*, edited by Anthony King, 87–138. Washington, DC: American Enterprise Institute Press.

Centeno, Miguel. 1994. *Democracy within Reason. Technocratic Revolution in Mexico*. University Park: Pennsylvania State University Press.

Centro de Estudios Espinosa Yglesias (CEEY) and Integralia. 2013. *Fortalezas y Debilidades del Sistema Electoral Mexicano (2000–2012)*. Mexico City: CEEY and Integralia.

Chen, Ming-tong. 1996. "Local Factions and Elections in Taiwan's Democratization." In *Taiwan's Electoral Policy and Democratic Transition*, edited by Hung-Mao Tien, 174–192. Armonk, NY: M. E. Sharpe.

Cheng, Tun-Jen. 1989. "Democratizing the Quasi-Leninist Regime in Taiwan." *World Politics* 41: 471–499.

Cheng, Tun-Jen. 2006. "Strategizing Party Adaptation. The Case of the Kuomintang." *Party Politics* 12: 367–394.

Cheng, Tun-Jen. 2008. "Embracing defeat: The KMT and the PRI after 2000." In *Political Transitions in Dominant Party Systems: Learning to Lose*, edited by Edward Friedman and Joseph Wong, 127–147. London and New York: Routledge.

Cheng, Tun-Jen, and Yung-ming Hsu. 2009. "Long in the Making: Taiwan's Institutionalized Party System." In *Party System Institutionalization in Asia: Democracies, Autocracies, and the Shadows of the Past*, edited by Allen Hicken and Erik Martinez Kuhonta, 108–135. New York: Cambridge University Press.

Choi, Eunjung. 2014. "The Decline and Resurgence of the Kuomingtang in Taiwan." Paper presented for the Dominant Party Systems Conference, May 9–10, 2014, University of Michigan, Ann Arbor, Michigan.

Collier, Ruth Berins, and David Collier. 1991. *Shaping the Political Arena: Critical Junctures, the Labor Movement, and Regime Dynamics in Latin America*. Princeton, NJ: Princeton University Press.

Comparative Study of Electoral Systems (CSES), Public Opinion Polls. Various years. Mexican data available at Laboratorio Nacional de Políticas Públicas at CIDE, http://lnpp.cide.edu/.

Converse, Philip E. 1966. "The Concept of a Normal Vote." In *Elections and the Political Order*, edited by Angus Campbell, Philip E. Converse, Warren E. Miller, and Donald E. Stokes. New York: Wiley.

Coppedge, Michael. 1993. "Parties and Society in Mexico and Venezuela: Why Competition Matters." *Comparative Politics* 25: 253–274.

Coppedge, Michael. 2001. "Political Darwinism in Latin America's Lost Decade," in *Political Parties and Democracy*, edited by Larry Diamond and Richard Gunther, 173–205. Baltimore and London: Johns Hopkins University Press.

Córdova Vianello, Lorenzo. 2008. "La reforma electoral y el cambio político en México." In Reforma Política y Electoral en América Latina, 1978–2007, edited by Daniel Zovatto and J. Jesús Orozco Henríquez, 653–703. Mexico: Instituto de Investigaciones Jurídicas, Universidad Nacional Autónoma de México.

Cornelius, Wayne. 1975. *Politics and the Migrant Poor in Mexico City*. Palo Alto, CA: Stanford University Press.

Cornelius, Wayne, Anne Craig, and Jonathan Fox, eds. 1994. *Transforming State-Society Relations in Mexico: The National Solidarity Strategy*. La Jolla: Center for US-Mexican Studies, University of California, San Diego.

Cornelius, Wayne, Todd Eisenstadt, and Jane Hindley, eds. 1999. *Subnational Politics and Democratization in Mexico*. La Jolla: Center for US-Mexican Studies, University of California, San Diego.

Cosío Villegas, Daniel. 1975. *La sucesión presidencial*. Mexico City: Cuadernos de Joaquín Mortiz.

Cowen, Michael, and Karuti Kanyinga. 2002. "The 1997 Elections in Kenya." In *Multi-Party Elections in Africa*, edited by Michael Cowen and Liisa Laakso, 128–171. New York: Palgrave.

Cowen, Michael, and Liisa Laakso, eds. 2002. *Multi-Party Elections in Africa*. New York: Palgrave.

Cox, Gary, and Mathew McCubbins. 1993. *Legislative Leviathan: Party Government in the House*. Berkeley and Los Angeles: University of California Press.

Craig, Anne, and Wayne Cornelius. 1995. "Houses Divided: Parties and Political Reform in Mexico." In *Building Democratic Institutions: Party Systems in Latin America*, edited by Scott Mainwaring and Timothy Scully, 249–297. Palo Alto, CA: Stanford University Press.

Craske, Nikki. 1994. *Corporatism Revisited: Salinas and the Reform of the Popular Sector*. London: Institute of Latin American Studies.

Crespo, José Antonio. 1998. *¿Tiene futuro el PRI? Entre la supervivencia democrática y la desintegración total*. Mexico City: Grijalbo.

Crotty, William. 1968. "The Party Organization and Its Activities." In *Approaches to the Study of Party Organization*, edited by William Crotty, 247–306. Boston: Allyn and Bacon.

De Ita, Ana. 2003. *México: Impactos del Procede en los conflictos agrarios y la concentración de la tierra*." Mexico City: Centro de Estudios para el Cambio en el Campo Mexicano.

De la Garza, Rudolf. 1972. "The Mexican Chamber of Deputies." PhD diss., University of Arizona, Tucson.

Diáz Gómez, Everardo Rodrigo. 2006. "Desempeño legislativo y disciplina partidista en México: la Cámara de Diputados, 2000–2003." *CONfines* 2–3: 45–64.

Diaz-Cayeros, Alberto. 2006. *Federalism, Fiscal Authority, and Centralization in Latin America*. Cambridge: Cambridge University Press.

Diccionario biográfico del gobierno mexicano. 1984 and 1987. Mexico City: Presidencia de la República, Dirección General de Comunicación Social, Unidad de la Crónica Presidencial.

Dickson, Bruce. 1996. "The Kuomintang before Democratization: Organizational Change and the Role of Elections." In *Taiwan's Electoral Policy and Democratic Transition*, edited by Hung-Mao Tien, 42–78. Armonk, NY: M. E. Sharpe.

Dion, Michelle. 2010. *Workers and Welfare: Comparative Institutional Change in Twentieth-Century Mexico*. Pittsburgh, PA: University of Pittsburgh Press.

Domínguez, Alejandro. 2014. "Bases sociales del voto." In *El comportamiento electoral mexicano en las elecciones de 2012*, edited by Gustavo Meixuiero and Alejandro Moreno, 41–62. Mexico City: Centro de Estudios Sociales y de Opinión Publica y ITAM.

Domínguez, Juan, and James McCann. 1996. *Democratizing Mexico*. Baltimore, MD: Johns Hopkins University Press.

Downs, Anthony. 1957. *An Economic Theory of Democracy*. New York: Harper and Row.

Dresser, Denise. 1994. "Embellishment, Empowerment, or Euthanasia of the PRI? Neoliberalism and Party Reform in Mexico." In *The Politics of Economic Restructuring*, edited by Maria Lorena Cook, Kevin J. Middlebrook, and Juan

Molinar Horcasitas, 125–148. La Jolla: Center for US-Mexican Studies, University of California, San Diego.

Drijanski, Patricia. 1997. "La remoción de gobernadores y el federalismo mexicano, 1934–1994." BA thesis, Instituto Tecnológico Autónomo de México.

Duverger, Maurice. 1954. *Political Parties: Their Organization and Activity in the Modern State*. New York: John Wiley.

Eckstein, Susan. 1977. *The Poverty of Revolution: The State and the Urban Poor in Mexico*. Princeton, NJ: Princeton University Press.

Eisenstadt, Todd. 1999. "Electoral Federalism or Abdication of Presidential Authority? Gubernatorial Elections in Tabasco." In *Subnational Politics and Democratization in Mexico.*, edited by Wayne Cornelius, Todd Eisenstadt, and Jane Hindley, 269–293. La Jolla: Center for US-Mexican Studies, University of California, San Diego.

Eisenstadt, Todd. 2004. *Courting Democracy in Mexico*. New York: Cambridge University Press.

Eisenstadt, Todd. 2006. "Catching the State off Guard: Electoral Courts, Campaign Finance, and Mexico's Separation of State and Ruling Party." *Party Politics* 10: 723–745.

Elazar, Daniel, ed. 1994. *Federal Systems of the World: A Handbook of Federal, Confederal, and Autonomy Arrangements*. 2nd ed. Harlow, UK: Longman.

Elischer, Sebastian. 2008. "Ethnic Coalitions of Convenience and Commitment: Political Parties and Party Systems in Kenya." Hamburg: GIGA Working paper.

Epstein, Leon D. 1967. *Political Parties in Western Democracies*. New York: Praeger.

Espinoza Toledo, Ricardo. 2004. "El PRI. Relaciones internas de autoridad y falta de cohesión de la coalición dirigente." In *Partidos Políticos. Nuevos liderazgos y relaciones internas de autoridad*, edited by Rosa María Mirón Lince and Ricardo Espinoza Toledo. Mexico City: UNAM-AMEP.

Estévez, Federico, Alberto Diaz-Cayeros, and Beatriz Magaloni. 2008. "A House Divided against Itself. The PRI's Survival Strategy after Hegemony." In *Political Transitions in Dominant Party Systems. Learning to Lose*, edited by Edward Friedman and Joseph Wong, 42–56. London and New York: Routledge.

Estévez, Federico, Eric Magar, and Guillermo Rosas. 2008. "No Delegation Without Representation: An Examination of Mexico's Federal Electoral Institute." *Electoral Studies* 27: 257–271.

Fagen, Richard, and William Tuohy. 1972. *Politics and Privilege in a Mexican City*. Palo Alto, CA: Stanford University Press.

Fairris, David, and Edward Levine. 2004. "Declining Union Density in Mexico, 1984–2000." *Monthly Labor Review*, September 1, 10–17.

Fell, Dafydd. 2005. "Measuring and Explaining Party Change in Taiwan, 1991–2004." *Journal of East Asian Studies* 5: 105–133.

Fell, Dafydd. 2011. *Government and Politics in Taiwan*. London: Routledge.

Fiorina, Morris. 1981. *Retrospective Voting in American National Elections*. New Haven, CT: Yale University Press.

Flamand, Laura. 2006. "El juego de la distribución de recursos en un sistema federal: La influencia del gobierno dividido verticalmente en la asignación de fondos federales a los estados mexicanos." *Política y gobierno* 13: 315–361.

Flores Macías, Francisco. 2009. "Electoral Volatility in 2006." In *Consolidating Mexico's Democracy: The 2006 Presidential Campaign in Comparative Perspective*, edited by Jorge I. Domínguez, Chappell Lawson, and Alejandro Moreno, 191–208. Baltimore, MD: Johns Hopkins University Press.

Foweraker, Joe, and Ann L. Craig, eds. 1990. *Popular Movements and Political Change in Mexico*. Boulder, CO, and London: Lynne Rienner.

Fox, Jonathan. 1994. "The Difficult Transition from Clientelism to Citizenship: Lessons from Mexico." *World Politics* 46: 151–184.

Friedman, Edward and Joseph Wong, eds. 2008. *Political Transitions in Dominant Party Systems. Learning to Lose*. London and New York: Routledge.

Friedrich, Paul. 1965. "A Mexican Cacicazgo." *Ethnology* 4: 190–209.

Gallagher, Michael, and Michael Marsh, eds. 1988. *Candidate Selection in Comparative Perspective: The Secret Garden of Politics*. London: Sage.

Gandhi, Jennifer. 2008. *Political Institutions under Dictatorship*. New York: Cambridge University Press.

Gandhi, Jennifer, and Adam Przeworski. 2007. "Authoritarian Institutions and the Survival of Autocrats." *Comparative Political Studies* 40: 1279–1301.

Gandhi, Jennifer, and Or John Reuter. 2007. "Economic Performance and the Unraveling of Hegemonic Parties." *British Journal of Political Science* 41, no. 1: 83–110.

Garrido, Luis Javier. 1982. *El Partido de la Revolución Institucionalizada*. Mexico City: Siglo XXI.

Garrido, Luis Javier. 1987. "Un partido sin militantes." In *La vida política Mexicana en la crisis*, edited by Soledad Loaeza and Rafael Segovia, 61–76. Mexico City: Colegio de México.

Garrido, Luis Javier. 1990. "El Partido del Estado ante la sucesión presidencial en México (1929–1987)." *Revista mexicana de sociología* 49: 59–82.

Garrido, Luis Javier. 1993. *La ruptura*. Mexico City: Grijalbo.

Garrido, Luis Javier. 1994. "Reform of the PRI: Rhetoric and Reality." In *Party Politics in "An Uncommon Democracy": Political Parties and Elections in Mexico*, edited by Neil Harvey and Mónica Serrano, 25–40. London: Institute of Latin American Studies.

Garrido de Sierra, Sebastián. 2014. "The Definitive Reform. How the 1996 Electoral Reform Triggered the Demise of the PRI's Dominant-Party Regime." PhD diss., University of California, Los Angeles.

Geddes, Barbara. 1999. "What Do We Know about Democratization after Twenty Years?" *Annual Review of Political Science* 2: 115–144.

Geddes, Barbara. 2006. "Why Parties and Elections in Authoritarian Regimes?" Paper prepared for presentation in the annual meeting of the American Political Science Association, Washington, DC.

Gibson, Edward. 2005. "Boundary Control: Subnational Authoritarianism in Democratic Countries." *World Politics* 58: 101–132.

Gillingham, Paul. 2014. "We Don't Have Arms, but We Do Have Balls: Fraud, Violence, and Popular Agency in Elections." In *Dictablanda: Politics, Work, and Culture in Mexico, 1938–1968*, edited by Paul Gillingham and Benjamin T. Smith, 149–172. Durham, NC: Duke University Press.

Gillingham, Paul, and Benjamin T. Smith, eds. 2014. *Dictablanda: Politics, Work, and Culture in Mexico, 1938–1968*. Durham, NC: Duke University Press.

Golosov, Grigorii. 1998. "Party Organization, Ideological Change, and Electoral Success. A Comparative Study of Postauthoritarian Parties." Kellogg Institute for International Studies. Working Paper #258.

Gómez, Leopoldo, and John Bailey. 1990. "La transición política y los dilemas del PRI." *Foro Internacional* 31: 57–87.

González Casanova, Pablo. 1965. *La democracia en México*. Mexico City: Era.

González Oropeza, Manuel. 1987. *La intervención federal en la desaparición de poderes*, 2nd ed. Mexico City: Universidad Autónoma de México.

González Tule, Luis. 2007. "Cohesión partidista en la Cámara de Diputados: El caso del PRI, PAN y PRD (1997–2006)." *Revista de Investigaciones Políticas y Sociológicas* 6, no. 2: 177–198.

Graham, Lawrence. 1971. *Mexican State Government: A Prefectural System in Action*. Austin: LBJ School of Public Affairs, University of Texas at Austin.

Greene, Kenneth. 2007. *Why Dominant Parties Lose: Mexico's Democratization in Comparative Perspective*. New York and Cambridge: Cambridge University Press.

Greene, Kenneth. 2011. "Campaign Persuasion and Nascent Partisanship in Mexico's New Democracy." *American Journal of Political Science* 55, no. 2: 398–416.

Grindle, Marilee. 1977. *Bureaucrats, Politicians, and Peasants in Mexico*. Berkeley: University of California Press.

Grzymala-Busse, Anna. 2001. "The Organizational Strategies of Communist Parties In East Central Europe, 1945–1989." *East European Politics and Societies* 15, no. 2: 421–453.

Grzymała-Busse, Anna M. 2002. *Redeeming the Communist Past: The Regeneration of Communist Parties in East Central Europe*. Cambridge and New York: Cambridge University Press.

Grzymała-Busse, Anna M. 2008. "The Communist Exit in East Central Europe and Its Consequences." In *Political Transitions in Dominant Party Systems: Learning to Lose*, edited by Edward Friedman and Joseph Wong, 91–105. London and New York: Routledge.

Grzymała-Busse, Anna M. 2015. "The Revolution Eats Its Own Children? The Paradoxical Fate of the Communist Successor Parties." Paper prepared for "Life after Dictatorship: Authoritarian Successor Parties Worldwide," Conference, University of Notre Dame, April 17–18, 2015.

Gutiérrez, Jorge. 1975. "Comunidad agraria y estructura de poder." In *Caciquismo y poder político en el México rural*, edited by Roger Bartra, 62–87. Mexico City: Siglo XXI.

Haber, Steven, Herbert Klein, Noel Maurer, and Kevin Middlebrook. 2008. *Mexico since 1980*. Cambridge and New York: Cambridge University Press.

Hamilton, Nora. 1982. *The Limits of State Autonomy: Post-Revolutionary Mexico*. Princeton, NJ: Princeton University Press.

Hansen, Roger. 1971. *The Politics of Mexican Development*. Baltimore, MD: Johns Hopkins University Press.

Hale, Henry. 2006. *Why Not Parties in Russia? Democracy, Federalism, and the State*. New York: Cambridge University Press.

Harbers, Imke. 2010. "Decentralization and the Development of Nationalized Party Systems in New Democracies: Evidence from Latin America." Unpublished PhD diss., University of Leiden.

Hardin, Russell. 1982. *Collective Action*. Baltimore, MD: Johns Hopkins University Press.

Hardy, Clarisa. 1984. *El Estado y los campesinos. La Confederación Nacional Campesina (CNC)*. Mexico: Editorial Nueva Imagen.

Harmel, Robert, and Kenneth Janda. 1994. "An Integrated Theory of Party Goals and Party Change." *Journal of Theoretical Politics* 6: 259–287.

Hazan, Reuven Y. 1996. "Candidate Selection." In *Comparing Democracies: Elections and Voting in Global Perspective*, edited by Lawrence LeDuc, Richard G. Niemi, and Pippa Norris, 108–126. Thousand Oaks, CA: Sage.

Heller, William, and Jeffrey Weldon. 2003. "Reglas de votación y la estabilidad en la Cámara de Diputados." In *El Congreso Mexicano después de la alternancia*, edited by

Rosa María Mirón Lince and Luisa Béjar Algazi, 85–120. Mexico City: Asociación Mexicana de Estudios Parlamentarios.

Hernández, Fausto, and Brenda Jarillo. 2008. "Is Local Beautiful? Fiscal Decentralization in Mexico." *World Development* 36: 1547–1558.

Hernández Rodríguez, Rogelio. 1991. "La reforma interna y los conflictos en el PRI." *Foro Internacional* 32: 222–249.

Hernández Rodríguez, Rogelio. 1998. "The Partido Revolucionario Institucional." In *Governing Mexico: Political Parties and Elections*, edited by Mónica Serrano, 71–113. London: Institute of Latin American Studies.

Hernández Rodríguez, Rogelio. 2008. *El centro dividido: La nueva autonomía de los gobernadores*. Mexico City: Colegio de México Press.

Hernández Rodríguez, Rogelio. 2014. "Strongmen and State Weakness." In *Dictablanda: Politics, Work, and Culture in Mexico, 1938–1968*, edited by Paul Gillingham and Benjamin Smith, 108–125. Durham, NC: Duke University Press.

Hsieh, John. 1996. "The SNTV System and Its Political Implications." In *Taiwan's Electoral Policy and Democratic Transition*, edited by Hung-Mao Tien, 193–212. Armonk, NY: M. E. Sharpe.

Hsieh, John. 2010. "Is the Kuomintang Invincible?" In *Taiwan's Politics in the 21st Century: Changes and Challenges*, edited by Wei-Chin Lee, 25–40. Hackensack, NJ: World Scientific.

Hughes, Sallie. 2006. *Newsrooms in Conflict: Journalism and the Democratization of Mexico*. Pittsburgh, PA: University of Pittsburgh Press.

Hufbauer, Gary Clyde, and Jeffrey J. Schott. 2005. *NAFTA Revisited: Achievements and Challenges*. Washington, DC: Institute for International Economics.

Hunter, Wendy. 2010. *The Transformation of the Workers' Party in Brazil, 1989–2009*. New York and Cambridge: Cambridge University Press.

Huntington, Samuel. 1968. *Political Order in Changing Societies*. New Haven, CT: Yale University Press.

Hurtado, Javier. 1993. *Familias, política y parentesco: Jalisco, 1919–1991*. Mexico City: Fondo de Cultura Económica-Universidad de Guadalajara.

Ishiyama, John, ed. 1999. *Communist Successor Parties in Post-Communist Politics*. Commack, NY: Nova Science.

Jones, Mark P., and Wonjae Hwang. 2005. "Party Government in Presidential Democracies: Extending Cartel Theory beyond the U.S. Congress." *American Journal of Political Science* 49: 267–282.

Jones, Mark, Sebastian Saiegh, Pablo Spiller, and Mariano Tommasi. 2002. "Amateur Legislators—Professional Politicians: The Consequences of Party-Centered Electoral Rules in a Federal System." *American Journal of Political Science* 46: 656–669.

Katz, Jonathan, and Brian Sala. 1996. "Careerism, Committee Assignments, and the Electoral Connection." *American Political Science Review* 90: 21–33.

Kaufman, Robert R., and Guillermo Trejo. 1997. "Regionalism, Regime Transformation and Pronasol: The Politics of the National Solidarity Programme in Four Mexican States." *Journal of Latin American Studies* 29: 717–745.

Kerevel, Yann P. 2013. "Party Loyalty and Disloyalty in the Mexican Party System." Paper prepared for delivery at the 2013 Congress of the Latin American Studies Association, Washington, DC, May 29–June 1.

Key, V. O. (1942) 1958. *Politics, Parties, and Pressure Groups*. Fourth Ed. New York: Crowell.

Kiewiet, D. Roderick, and Mathew McCubbins. 1991. *The Logic of Delegation. Congressional Parties and the Appropriations Process.* Chicago: University of Chicago Press.

Kimathi, Leah. 2010. "Toward Democratic Consolidation in Kenya: The Role of Political Parties." In *Political Parties and Democracy*, edited by Luc Kindjoun, Marian Simms, and Kay Lawson, 37–52. Santa Barbara, CA: Praeger.

Kitschelt, Herbert. 1989. *The Logics of Party Formation. Ecological Parties in Belgium and West Germany.* Ithaca, NY: Cornell University Press.

Kitschelt, Herbert, Zdenka Mansfeldova, Radoslaw Markowski, and Gábor Tóka. 1999. *Post-Communist Party Systems: Competition, Representation, and Inter-Party Cooperation.* Cambridge and New York: Cambridge University Press.

Klesner, Joseph. 1997. "The Mexican Midterm Congressional and Gubernatorial Elections of 1997: End of the Hegemonic Party System." *Electoral Studies* 16: 567–575.

Klesner, Joseph. 2001. "The End of Mexico's One-Party Regime." *PS: Political Science and Politics* 34, no. 1: 107–114.

Klesner, Joseph. 2005. "Electoral Competition and the New Party System in Mexico." *Latin American Politics and Society* 47:103–142.

Klesner, Joseph. 2007. "The 2006 Mexican Elections: Manifestation of a Divided Society?" *PS: Politics and Political Science* 40, no. 1: 27–32.

Koelble, Thomas. 1992. "Recasting Social Democracy in Europe: A Nested Games Explanation of Strategic Adjustment in Political Parties." *Politics and Society* 20: 51–70.

Lajous, Alejandra. 1979. *Los orígenes del partido único en México.* Mexico City: Universidad Nacional Autónoma de México, Instituto de Investigaciones Históricas.

Landry, Pierre. 2008. *Decentralized Authoritarianism in China: The Communist Party's Control in the Post-Mao Era.* Cambridge and New York: Cambridge University Press.

Langston, Joy. 2001. "Why Rules Matter: Changes in Candidate Selection in Mexico's PRI, 1988–2000." *Journal of Latin American Studies* 22: 485–511.

Langston, Joy. 2002. "Breaking Out is Hard to Do: Exit, Voice, and Loyalty in Mexico's One-Party Hegemonic Regime." *Latin American Politics and Society* 44: 61–88.

Langston, Joy. 2003. "Rising from the Ashes? Reorganizing the PRI's State Party after Electoral Defeat." *Comparative Political Studies* 36: 293–318.

Langston, Joy. 2006. "The Birth and Transformation of the *Dedazo* in Mexico." In *Informal Institutions and Democracy in Latin America*, edited by Gretchen Helmke and Steven Levitsky, 143–159. Baltimore, MD: Johns Hopkins University Press.

Langston, Joy. 2009. "The PRI's 2006 Presidential Campaign." In *Consolidating Mexico's Democracy: The 2006 Presidential Elections in Comparative Perspective*, edited by Jorge I. Domínguez, Chappell Lawson, and Alejandro Moreno, 152–168. Baltimore, MD: Johns Hopkins University Press.

Langston, Joy. 2010. "Governors and "Their" Deputies. New Legislative Principals in Mexico." *Legislative Studies Quarterly* 36: 235–258.

Langston, Joy. 2013. "Candidate-Centered Campaigning in a Party-Centered Electoral Context: The Case of Mexico." Paper presented at conference Elecciones en México: Cambios, permanencias y retos, Colegio de México, November 11.

Langston, Joy, and Javier Aparicio. 2012. "Gender Quotas are Not Enough." Working Paper. Mexico City: Centro de Investigación y Docencia Económicas.

Langston, Joy, and Scott Morgenstern. 2009. "Campaigning in an Electoral Authoritarian Regime: The Case of Mexico." *Comparative Politics* 41: 165–181.

Lawson, Chappell. 2000. "Mexico's Unfinished Transition: Democratization and Authoritarian Enclaves in Mexico." *Mexican Studies* 16, no. 2: 267–287.

Lawson, Chappell. 2003. *Building the Fourth Estate. Democratization and the Rise of a Free Press in Mexico*. Palo Alto, CA: Stanford University Press.

Lebas, Adrienne. 2011. *From Protest to Parties: Party-Building and Democratization in Africa*. Oxford: Oxford University Press.

Levitsky, Steven. 2003. *Transforming Labor-Based Parties in Latin America: Argentine Peronism in Comparative Perspective*. Cambridge: Cambridge University Press.

Levitsky, Steven, and Maxwell Cameron. 2003. "Democracy without Parties? Political Parties and Regime Change in Fu jimori's Peru." *Latin American Politics and Society* 45, no. 3: 1–33.

Levitsky, Steven, and Lucan A. Way. 2010. *Competitive Authoritarianism: Hybrid Regimes after the Cold War*. New York and Cambridge: Cambridge University Press.

Loaeza, Soledad. 1999. *El Partido Acción Nacional: la larga marcha: 1939–1994. Oposición leal y partido de protesta*. Mexico City, Fonda de Cultura Económica.

Loret de Mola, Carlos. 1978. *Confesiones de un gobernador*. Mexico City: Grijalbo.

Loxton, James. 2016. "Authoritarian Successor Parties Worldwide: A Framework for Analysis." Working Paper, University of Sydney.

Loyola Díaz, Rafael. 1990. "1938: El despliegue del corporativismo partidario." In *El partido en el poder: Seis Ensayos*, 129–182. Mexico City: Instituto de Estudios Políticos, Económicos, y Sociales/Partido Revolucionario Institucional.

Lujambio, Alonso. 1995. *Federalismo y congreso en el cambio político de México*. Mexico: Universidad Nacional Autónoma de México.

Lupu, Noam. 2014. "Brand Dilution and the Breakdown of Political Parties in Latin America." *World Politics* 66, no. 4: 561–602.

Lustig, Nora. 1998. *Mexico: The Remaking of an Economy*. 2nd ed. Washington, DC: Brookings Institution Press.

Lust-Okar, Eleanor. 2006. "Elections under Authoritarianism: Preliminary Lessons from Jordan." *Democratization* 13, no. 3: 456–471.

Mackinlay, Horacio. 2002. "La CNC y el 'Nuevo movimiento campesino' (1989–1994)." In *Neoliberalismo y organización social en el campo mexicano*, edited by Hubert C. de Grammont, 165–238. Mexico City: Universidad Nacional Autónoma de México and Plaza y Valdes.

Madrazo, Roberto. 2006. *La traición: Conversación con Manuel S. Garrido*. Mexico City: Planeta.

Magaloni, Beatriz. 2006. *Voting for Autocracy: Hegemonic Party Survival and its Demise in Mexico*. New York: Cambridge University Press.

Magaloni, Beatriz. 2008. "Credible Power-Sharing and the Longevity of Authoritarian Rulers." *Comparative Political Studies* 41, no. 4–5: 715–741.

Magar, Eric. 2012. "Gubernatorial Coattails in Mexican Congressional Elections." *Journal of Politics* 74, no. 2: 383–399.

Mainwaring, Scott, and Timothy Scully. 1995. "Introduction: Party Systems in Latin America." In *Building Democratic Institutions. Party Systems in Latin America*, edited by Scott Mainwaring and Timothy Scully, 1–36. Palo Alto, CA: Stanford University Press.

Maltzman, Forrest. 1998. *Competing Principals: Committees, Parties, and the Organization of Congress*. Ann Arbor: University of Michigan Press.

Manuel, Víctor and Muñoz Patraca, eds. 2006. *Partido Revolucionario Institucional, 1946–2000: Ascenso y caída del partido hegemónico*. Mexico City: Siglo XXI and UNAM.

March, Luke. 2006. "Power and Opposition in the Former Soviet Union." *Party Politics* 12, no. 3: 341–365.

Martínez Assad, Carlos, and Álvaro Arreola Ayala. 1987. "El poder de los goberna-dores." In *La vida política mexicana en la crisis*, edited by Soledad Loaeza and Rafael Segovia, 107–130. Mexico City: El Colegio de México.

Martínez, Cecilia. 1998. "Las legislaturas pequeñas; La evolución del sistema de comis-iones en la Cámara de Diputados de México, 1824–2000." BA thesis, Instituto Tecnológico Autónomo de México.

Marván, Ignacio. 1990. "La dificultad del cambio (1968–1980)." In *El partido en el poder: Seis Ensayos*, 255–290. Mexico City: Instituto de Estudios Políticos, Económicos, y Sociales/Partido Revolucionario Institucional.

Mattlin, Mikael. 2011. *Politicized Society: The Long Shadow of Taiwan's One-Party Legacy*. Copenhagen: NIAS.

Maxfield, Sylvia. 1990. *Governing Capital. International Finance and Mexican Politics*. Ithaca, NY: Cornell University Press.

Medina Peña, Luis. 1993. *Hacia el nuevo Estado, México, 1920–1993*. Mexico City: Fondo de Cultura Económico.

Mena, Marco. 2010. "¿Cuestan demasiado las elecciones en México?" Mexico City: Centro de Investigación y Docencia Económicas, Working Paper.

Merino, Mauricio. 2003. *La transición votada. Crítica a la interpretación del cambio político en México*. Mexico City: Fondo de Cultura Económica.

Meyer, Jean. 1973. *La guerra de los cristeros*. Mexico City: Siglo XXI.

Meyer, Lorenzo. 1986. "Un tema añejo siempre actual: El centro y las regiones en la historia mexicana." In *Descentralización y democracia en México*, edited by Blanca Torres, 23–33. Mexico City: El Colegio de México.

Middlebrook, Kevin. 1985. *Political Liberalization in an Authoritarian Regime: The Case of Mexico*. La Jolla: Center for US-Mexican Studies, University of California, San Diego.

Middlebrook, Kevin. 1989. "The Sounds of Silence: Organised Labour's Response to Economic Crisis in Mexico." *Journal of Latin American Studies* 21: 195–220.

Middlebrook, Kevin. 1991. "State/Labor Relations in Mexico: The Changing Economic and Political Context." In *Unions, Workers, and the State in Mexico*, edited by Kevin Middlebrook, 1–25. La Jolla: Center for US-Mexican Studies, University of California, San Diego.

Middlebrook, Kevin. 1995. *The Paradox of Revolution: Labor, the State, and Authoritarianism in Mexico*. Baltimore, MD: Johns Hopkins University Press.

Mirón Lince, Rosa María. 2011. *El PRI y la transición política en México*. Mexico City: UNAM/Facultad de Ciencias Políticas y Sociales/Ediciones Gernika,

Mizrahi, Yemile. 2003. *From Martyrdom to Power: The PAN*. South Bend, IN: University of Notre Dame Press.

Modoux, Magali. 2006. "Geografía de la gobernanza: ¿La alternancia partidaria como factor de consolidación del poder de los gobernadores en el escenario nacional mexicano?" *Foro Internacional* 46: 513–533.

Molinar, Juan. 1991. *El tiempo de la legitimidad: Elecciones, autoritarismo y democracia en México*. Mexico City: Cal y Arena.

Montero, Alfred. 2007. "The Limits of Decentralisation: Legislative Careers and Territorial Representation in Spain." *West European Politics* 30, no. 3: 573–594.

Moreno Sánchez, Manuel. 1970. *Crisis política de México*. Mexico City: Editorial Extemporáneos.

Moreno, Alejandro. 2009a. *El votante mexicano: Democracia, actitudes políticas y con-ducta electoral*. 2nd ed. Mexico City: Fondo de Cultura Económica.

Moreno, Alejandro. 2009b. "The Activation of Economic Voting in the 2006 Campaign." In *Consolidating Mexico's Democracy: The 2006 Presidential Campaign in Comparative Perspective*, edited by Jorge I. Domínguez, Chappell Lawson, and Alejandro Moreno, 209–228. Baltimore, MD: Johns Hopkins University Press.

Moreno, Alejandro. 2012. "Who is the Mexican Voter?" In *The Oxford Handbook of Mexican Politics*, edited by Roderic Ai Camp, 571–595. Oxford and New York: Oxford University Press.

Morris, Stephen. 1993. "Political Reformism in Mexico: Past and Present." *Latin American Research Review* 28: 191–205.

Murillo, Maria Victoria. 2002. *Labor Unions, Partisan Coalitions, and Market Reforms in Latin America*. New York: Cambridge University Press.

Nacif, Benito. 1995. "The Mexican Chamber of Deputies: The Political Significance of Non-consecutive Reelection." PhD diss., University of Oxford.

Nacif, Benito. 2000. "El sistema de comisiones permanentes en la Cámara de Diputados." In *La Cámara de Diputados en México*, edited by Germán Pérez and Antonio Martínez, 33–59. Mexico City: Cámara de Diputados del H. Congreso de la Unión and Facultad Latioamericana de Ciencias Sociales.

National Archives Project-Mexico. 2006. "Draft Report Documents 18 Years of 'Dirty War' in Mexico." National Security Archive. February 26. http://www.gwu.edu/~nsarchiv/NSAEBB/NSAEBB180/index.htm.

Nava, María del Carmen, and Jorge Yáñez. 2003. "The Effects of Pluralism in the Legislative Activity: The Mexican Chamber of Deputies, 1917–2000." Paper prepared for the International Research Workshop, Washington University in St. Louis, May 28–June 1.

Navarro, Aaron. 2010. *Political Intelligence and the Creation of Modern Mexico, 1938–1954*. University Park: Pennsylvania State University Press.

Newell, Roberto, and Luís Rubio. 1984. *Mexico's Dilemma: The Political Origins of Economic Crisis*. Boulder, CO: Westview.

Neumann, Sigmund. 1956. "Towards a Comparative Study of Political Parties." In *Modern Political Parties: Approaches to Comparative Politics*, edited by Sigmund Neumann, 395–421. Chicago: University of Chicago Press.

Niou, Emerson, and John Hsieh. 1996. "Issue Voting in the Republic of China on Taiwan's 1992 Legislative Yuan Election." *International Political Science Review* 17: 13–27.

Norris, Pippa, ed. 1997. *Passages to Power: Legislative Recruitment in Advanced Democracies*. Cambridge and New York: Cambridge University Press.

North, Douglass. 1990. *Institutions, Institutional Change and Economic Performance*. Cambridge and New York: Cambridge University Press.

Ortega, Jorge. 2004. *Diagnóstico jurídico y presupuestario del Ramo 33: Una Etapa del Federalismo en México*. Mexico City: CIDE.

Pacheco, Guadalupe. 1990. "Estructura y resultados electorales." *Examen* 15, August 15.

Pacheco, Guadalupe. 1991. "Los sectores del PRI en las elecciones de 1988." *Argumentos* 7: 253–282.

Pacheco, Guadalupe. 1997. "Un caleidoscopio electoral: ciudadades y elecciones en México, 1988–1994." *Estudios Sociológicos* 15, no. 44: 319–350.

Pacheco, Guadalupe. 2013. "Las elecciones presidenciales de México en 2012. Las bases regionales del regreso del PRI a la Presidencia." *Veredas* 26: 7–29.

Pacheco, Guadalupe, and Juan Reyes del Campillo. 1989. "La estructura sectorial del PRI y las elecciones federal de diputados, 1979–1988." *Sociológica* 4: 59–74.

Padgett, Vincent. 1966. *The Mexican Political System*. Boston: Houghton Mifflin.

Panebianco, Angelo. 1982. *Modelos de partido: Organización y poder en los partidos políticos*. Madrid: Alianza Universitaria.

Pansters, Wil. 1996. *Política y poder en Puebla: Formación del cacicazgo avilacamachista, 1937–1987*. Mexico City: Fondo de Cultura Económica.

Paoli Bolio, Francisco José. 1985. "Legislación electoral y proceso político, 1917–1982." In *Las elecciones en México: Evolución y perspectivas*, edited by Pablo González Casanova, 129–162. Mexico City: Siglo XXI.

Pardinas, Juan. 2008. "Decentralisation and Budget Accountability in the Twilight of Mexican Presidentialism." PhD diss., London School of Economics.

Paré, Luisa. 1975. "Caciquismo y estructura de poder en la sierra Norte de Puebla." In *Caciquismo y poder político en el México rural*, edited by Roger Bartra, 31–61. Mexico City: Siglo XXI Press.

Paré, Luisa. 1985. *El proletariado agrícola en México*. Mexico City: Siglo XXI.

Pérez Correa, Fernando. 2003. *Temas de federalismo: ¿De la centralización a la fragmentación?* Mexico City: Facultad de Ciencias Políticas y Sociales, Universidad Nacional Autónoma de México.

Pomper, Gerald. 1990. "Party Organization and Electoral Success." *Polity* 23, no. 2: 187–206.

Poiré, Alejandro. 2006. "In the Public Interest or Poisoned Subsidy?" Harvard University and MIT Working paper.

Purcell, Susan Kaufman. 1977. "The Future of the Mexican System." In *Authoritarianism in Mexico*, edited by José Luis Reyna y Richard S. Weinert, 173–191. Philadelphia: Institute for the Study of Human Issues.

Ranney, Austin. 1981. "Candidate Selection." In *Democracy at the Polls. A Comparative Study of Competitive National Elections*, edited by David Butler, Howard Rae Penniman, and Austin Ranney, 75–106. Washington, DC: American Enterprise Institute.

Ramírez de la O, Rogelio. 1996. "La crisis del peso mexicano y la recesión de 1994–1995." In *La crisis del peso mexicano*, edited by Riordan Roett, 26–57. Mexico City: Fondo de Cultura Económica.

Reuter, Ora John, and Rostislav Turovsky. 2014. "Dominant Party Rule and Legislative Leadership in Authoritarian Regimes." *Party Politics* 20, no. 5: 663–674.

Reveles Vázquez, Francisco. 2003a. "La estructura de un partido corporativo en transformación." In *Partido Revolucionario Institucional: Crisis y refundación*, 41–77. Mexico City: Universidad Nacional Autónoma de México and Gernika.

Reveles Vázquez, Francisco. 2003b. "La lucha entre fracciones priístas en la selección de candidatos presidenciales (1987–2000)." In *Partido Revolucionario Institucional: Crisis y refundación*, 79–151. Mexico City: Universidad Nacional Autónoma de México and Gernika.

Reveles Vázquez, Francisco. 2003c. "PRI: Crisis y refundación." In *Partido Revolucionario Institucional: Crisis y refundación*, 9–40. México: Universidad Nacional Autónoma de México and Gérnika.

Reyes del Campillo, Juan. 1990. "El movimiento obrero en la Cámara de Diputados (1979–1988)." *Revista mexicana de sociología* 52: 139–160.

Reyes del Campillo, Juan. 1992. "Candidatos y campañas en la elección federal de 1991." In *Las elecciones federales de 1991*, edited by Alberto Aziz and Jacqueline Peschard, 143–159. Mexico City: Centro de Investigaciones Interdisciplinarias en Humanidades, Universidad Nacional Autónoma de México.

Reyes García, Luis. 2005. "La coalición dominante del Partido Revolucionario Institucional: auge, auge crisis y recomposición." *El Cotidiano* 133: 60–73.

Reyna, José Luis. 1985. "Las elecciones en el México institucionalizado, 1946–1976." In *Las elecciones en México: Evolución y perspectivas*, edited by Pablo González Casanova, 101–118. Mexico City: Siglo Veintiuno.

Reyna, José Luis, and Richard Weinert. 1977. *Authoritarianism in Mexico*. Philadelphia: Institute for the Study of Human Issues.

Riedl, Rachel Beatty. 2014. *Authoritarian Origins of Democratic Party Systems in Africa*. New York: Cambridge University Press.

Rigger, Shelley. 1994. "Machine Politics in the New Taiwan: Institutional Reform and Electoral Strategy in the ROC on Taiwan." PhD diss., Harvard University.

Rigger, Shelley. 1999. *Politics in Taiwan: Voting for Democracy*. London and New York: Routledge.

Rigger, Shelley. 2002. "Weighing a Shadow: Toward a Technique for Estimating the Effects of Vote-Buying in Taiwan." Paper presented to conference Trading Political Rights, MIT, Cambridge.

Riker, William H. 1964. *Federalism: Origin, Operation, Significance*. Boston: Little, Brown.

Rivera Sanchez, José. 2004. "Democratización y sistema de comisiones en el congreso mexicano." *Política y gobierno* 11: 263–314.

Rizova, Tatiana. 2008. "The Party is Dead, Long Live the Party! Successor Party Adaptation to Democracy." PhD diss., University of California, Los Angeles.

Roberts, Kenneth M. 1998. *Deepening Democracy? The Modern Left and Social Movements in Chile and Peru*. Palo Alto, CA: Stanford University Press.

Rodríguez, Victoria, and Peter Ward. 1994. "Disentangling the PRI from the Government in Mexico." *Mexican Studies-Estudios Mexicanos* 10: 163–186.

Rodríguez Araujo, Octavio, and Volker Lehr. 1984. *Manual Biográfico del Congreso de la Unión*. Mexico City: UAEM, ENEP-Acatlán, Universidad Nacional Autónoma de México.

Rodríguez Kuri, Ariel. 2008. "Los años maravillosos. Adolfo Ruiz Cortines." In *Gobernantes mexicanos*, vol. 2, *1911–2000*, edited by Will Fowler, 263–286. Mexico City: Fondo de Cultura Económica.

Rodríguez Prats, Juan José. 1990. *Adolfo Ruiz Cortines*. Jalapa: Gobierno del Estado de Veracruz.

Rosas, Guillermo, and Joy Langston. 2011. "Gubernatorial Effects on the Voting Behavior of National Legislators." *Journal of Politics* 73, no. 2: 477–493.

Rousseau, Isabelle. 1998. "La SPP y la dinámica de la constitución de un equipo, 1982–1988." *Foro Internacional* 38: 302–339.

Rousseau, Isabelle. 2010. "Las nuevas élites y su proyecto modernizador." In *Del nacionalismo al neoliberalismo, 1940–1994*, edited by Elisa Servín, 242–294. Mexico City: CIDE, FCE.

Rubin, Jeffrey. 1990. "Popular Mobilization and the Myth of State Corporatism." In *Popular Movements and Political Change in Mexico*, edited by Joe Foweraker and Ann Craig, 247–267. Boulder, CO: Lynne Rienner.

Rustow, Danwart. 1970. "Transitions to Democracy: Towards a Dynamic Model." *Comparative Politics* 2, no. 3: 337–363.

Sanderson, Steven. 1986. *The Transformation of Mexican Agriculture*. Princeton, NJ: Princeton University Press.

Samstad, James G., and Ruth Berins Collier. 1995. "Mexican Labor and Structural Reform Under Salinas: New Unionism or Old Stalemate?" In *The Challenge of Institutional Reform in Mexico*, edited by Riordan Roett, 9–38. Boulder, CO, and London: Lynne Rienner.

Samuels, David. 2003. *Ambition, Federalism, and Legislative Politics in Brazil*. New York and Cambridge: Cambridge University.

Samuels, David, and Matthew Shugart. 2010. *Presidents, Parties, Prime Ministers: How the Separation of Powers Affects Party Organization and Behavior*. New York and Cambridge: Cambridge University Press.

Sartori, Giovanni. 1976. *Parties and Party Systems: A Framework for Analysis*. New York: Columbia University Press.

Schedler, Andreas, ed. 2006. *Electoral Authoritarianism. The Dynamics of Unfree Competition*. Boulder, CO: Lynne Rienner.

Schlesinger, Joseph. 1966. *Ambition and Politics: Political Careers in the United States*. Chicago: Rand McNally.

Schlesinger, Joseph. 1985. "The New American Party System." *American Political Science Review* 79: 1152–1169.

Schmitt, Karl. 1969. "Congressional Campaigning in Mexico: A View from the Provinces." *Journal of Inter-American Studies* 11: 93–110.

Scott, Robert. 1964. *Mexican Government in Transition*. Urbana: University of Illinois Press.

Shaw, Malcolm. 1979. "Committees in Legislatures." In *Committees in Legislatures*, edited by John Lees and Malcolm Shaw, 361–434. Oxford: Martin Robertson.

Shea, Daniel M., and Michael John Burton. 2001. *Campaign Craft: The Strategies, Tactics, and Art of Political Campaign Management*. Revised edition. Westport, CT: Praeger.

Shepsle, Kenneth. 1976. *The Giant Jigsaw Puzzle. Democratic Committee Assignment in Congress*. Boston: Little, Brown.

Shirk, David. 2005. *Mexico's New Politics. The PAN and Democratic Change*. Boulder, CO: Lynne Reinner.

Siavelis, Peter, and Scott Morgenstern, eds. 2008. *Pathways to Power: Political Recruitment and Candidate Selection in Latin America*. University Park: Pennsylvania State University Press.

Sirvent Gutiérrez, Carlos. 1975. "La burocracia en México: El caso de la FSTSE." *Estudios Políticos* 1, no. 1: 5–31.

Slater, Daniel, and Joseph Wong. 2013. "The Strength to Concede: Ruling Parties and Democratization in Developmental Asia." *Perspectives on Politics* 11, no. 3: 717–733.

Smith, Benjamin. 2005. "Life of the Party: The Origins of Regime Breakdown and Persistence under Single-Party Rule." *World Politics* 57, no. 3: 421–451.

Smith, Peter. 1979. *Labyrinths of Power: Political Recruitment in Twentieth-Century Mexico*. Princeton, NJ: Princeton University Press.

Smyth, Regina. 2006. *Candidate Strategies and Electoral Competition in the Russian Federation*. Cambridge and New York: Cambridge University Press.

Solís, Leopoldo. 1970. *La realidad económica mexicana: retrovisión y perspectivas*. Mexico City: Fondo de Cultura Económica.

Somuano, María Fernanda. 2014. "Las identidades partidistas de los mexicanos y la elección de 2012." In *El comportamiento electoral mexicano en las elecciones de 2012*, edited by Gustavo Meixuiero and Alejandro Moreno, 117–140. Mexico City: Centro de Estudios Sociales y de Opinión Publica and ITAM.

Stevens, Evelyn. 1977. "Mexico's PRI: The Institutionalization of Corporatism?" In *Authoritarianism and Corporatism in Latin America*, edited by James Malloy, 227–258. Pittsburgh, PA: University of Pittsburgh Press.

Stoner-Weiss, Kathleen. 2002. "Central Governing Incapacity and the Weakness of Political Parties: Russian Democracy in Disarray." *Publius* 32: 125–146.

Story, Dale. 1986. *The Mexican Ruling Party. Stability and Authority.* New York: Praeger.

Tan, Alexander. 2002. "The Transformation of the Kuomintang Party in Taiwan." *Democratization* 9: 149–164.

Tavits, Margit. 2012. "Organizing for Success: Party Organizational Strength and Electoral Performance in Postcommunist Europe." *Journal of Politics* 74, no. 1: 83–97.

Taylor, Phillip. 1960. "The Mexican Election of 1958: Affirmation of Authoritarianism?" *Western Political Quarterly* 13: 722–733.

Teichman, Judith. 1995. *Privatization and Political Change in Mexico.* Pittsburgh and London: University of Pittsburgh Press.

Tello, Carlos, and Rolando Cordera. 1981. *La disputa por la nación.* Mexico City: Siglo XXI.

Throup, David, and Charles Hornsby. 1998. *Multi-Party Politics in Kenya: The Kenyatta and Moi States and the Triumph of System in the 1992 Election.* Oxford: James Currey.

Torcal, Mariano. 2014. "Bases ideológicas y valorativas del votante mexicano y su efecto en el voto: Síntomas de una creciente institucionalización." In *El comportamiento electoral mexicano en las elecciones de 2012*, edited by Gustavo Meixuiero and Alejandro Moreno, 91–116. Mexico City: Centro de Estudios Sociales y de Opinión Publica and ITAM.

Torres, Jorge. 2009. *CISEN: Auge y decadencia de los servicios secretos en México.* Mexico City: Debate Editors.

Tsang, Steve. 1999. "Transforming a Party State into a Democracy." In *Democratization in Taiwan: Implications for China*, edited by Steve Tsang and Hung-Mao Tien, 1–22. Basingstoke: Macmillan.

Tucker, William. 1957. *The Mexican Government Today.* Minneapolis: University of Minnesota Press.

Ugalde, Antonio. 1970. *Power and Conflict in a Mexican Community.* Albuquerque: University of New Mexico Press.

Ugalde, Antonio. 1973. "Contemporary Mexico: From Hacienda to PRI, Political Leadership in a Zapotec Village." In *The Caciques: Oligarchical Politics and the System of Caciquismo in the Luso-Hispanic World*, edited by Robert Kern, 119–134. Albuquerque: University of New Mexico Press.

Ugalde, Luís Carlos. 2000. *The Mexican Congress: Old Player, New Power.* Washington, DC: Center for Strategic and International Studies Press.

van Biezen, Ingrid. 2000. "On the Internal Balance of Party Power: Party Organizations in New Democracies." *Party Politics* 6: 395–417.

Von Sauer, Franz. 1974. *The Alienated "Loyal" Opposition in Mexico.* Albuqurque, NM: University of New Mexico Press.

Ward, Peter, and Victoria Rodríguez. 1999. "New Federalism, Intra-Governmental Relations and Co-Governance in Mexico." *Journal of Latin American Studies* 31: 673–710.

Ward, Peter, Victoria Rodríguez, and Enrique Cabrero. 1999. *Bringing the States Back In: New Federalism and State Government in Mexico.* Austin: Lyndon B. Johnson School, University of Texas.

Wattenberg, Martin. 1991. *The Rise of Candidate Centered Politics. Presidential Elections of the 1980s.* Cambridge, MA: Harvard University Press.

Wattenberg, Martin, and Matthew Shugart. 2001. *Mixed-Member Electoral Systems: The Best of Both Worlds?.* New York: Oxford University Press.

Weldon, Jeffrey. 1997. "Political Sources of *Presidencialismo* in Mexico." In *Presidentialism and Democracy in Latin America*, edited by Scott Mainwaring and Matthew Shugart, 225–258. Cambridge: Cambridge University Press.

Weldon, Jeffrey. 2005. "Institutional and Political Factors for Party Discipline in the Mexican Congress since the End of PRI Hegemony." Unpublished manuscript, Instituto Autónomo Tecnológico de México.

Weldon, Jeffrey. 2006. "El Congreso, las maquinarias políticas y el Maximato: Las reformas antireleccionistas de 1933." In *El legislador a examen. El debate sobre la reelección legislativa en México: Una perspectiva histórica e institucional*, edited by Fernando F. Dworak, 33–53. Mexico City: Fondo de Cultura Económica and La Cámara de Diputados.

Widner, Jennifer. 1992. *The Rise of a Party-State in Kenya: From "Harambee!" to "Nyayo!"*. Berkeley: University of California Press.

Widner, Jennifer. 1994. "Political Reform in Anglophone and Francophone African Countries." In *Economic Change and Political Liberalization in Sub-Saharan Africa*, edited by Jennifer Widner, 49–79. Baltimore, MD: Johns Hopkins University Press.

Willis, Eliza, Christopher Garman, and Stephan Haggard. 1999. "The Politics of Decentralization in Latin America." *Latin American Research Review* 34: 7–56.

Wong, Joseph. 2008. "Maintaining KMT Dominance: Party Adaptation in Authoritarian and Democratic Taiwan." In *Political Transitions in Dominant Party Systems. Learning to Lose*, edited by Edward Friedman and Joseph Wong, 57–74. London and New York: Routledge.

Wu, Chung-li. 2001. "The Transformation of the Kuomintang's Candidate Selection System." *Party Politics* 7:103–118.

Wuhs, Steven T. 2007. *Savage Democracy: Institutional Change and Party Development in Mexico*. University Park: Pennsylvania State University Press.

Zapata, Francisco. 1995. *El sindicalismo mexicano frente a la restructuración*. Mexico City: El Colegio de Mexico.

Zazueta, César, and Ricardo de la Peña. 1984. *La estructura del Congreso del Trabajo: Estado, trabajo y capital en Mexico, un acercamiento al tema*. Mexico City: Fondo de Cultura Económica.

INDEX

Printed in the USA/Agawam, MA
June 21, 2017

654019.038